Unsettled

In the series *Asian American History and Culture*, edited by David Palumbo-Liu, K. Scott Wong, Linda Trinh Võ, and Cathy Schlund-Vials. Founding editor, Sucheng Chan; editor emeritus, Michael Omi.

Also in this series:

Audrey Wu Clark, *The Asian American Avant-Garde: Universalist Aspirations in Modernist Literature and Art*

Jeffrey Santa Ana, *Racial Feelings: Asian America in a Capitalist Culture of Emotion*

Jiemin Bao, *Creating a Buddhist Community: A Thai Temple in Silicon Valley*

Elda E. Tsou, *Unquiet Tropes: Form, Race, and Asian American Literature*

Tarry Hum, *Making a Global Immigrant Neighborhood: Brooklyn's Sunset Park*

Ruth Mayer, *Serial Fu Manchu: The Chinese Supervillain and the Spread of Yellow Peril Ideology*

Karen Kuo, *East Is West and West Is East: Gender, Culture, and Interwar Encounters between Asia and America*

Kieu-Linh Caroline Valverde, *Transnationalizing Viet Nam: Community, Culture, and Politics in the Diaspora*

Lan P. Duong, *Treacherous Subjects: Gender, Culture, and Trans-Vietnamese Feminism*

Kristi Brian, *Reframing Transracial Adoption: Adopted Koreans, White Parents, and the Politics of Kinship*

Belinda Kong, *Tiananmen Fictions Outside the Square: The Chinese Literary Diaspora and the Politics of Global Culture*

Bindi V. Shah, *Laotian Daughters: Working toward Community, Belonging, and Environmental Justice*

Cherstin M. Lyon, *Prisons and Patriots: Japanese American Wartime Citizenship, Civil Disobedience, and Historical Memory*

Shelley Sang-Hee Lee, *Claiming the Oriental Gateway: Prewar Seattle and Japanese America*

A list of additional titles in this series appears at the back of this book

Unsettled

*Cambodian Refugees in
the New York City Hyperghetto*

Eric Tang

 TEMPLE UNIVERSITY PRESS
Philadelphia • *Rome* • *Tokyo*

TEMPLE UNIVERSITY PRESS
Philadelphia, Pennsylvania 19122
www.temple.edu/tempress

Library of Congress Cataloging-in-Publication Data

Tang, Eric, 1974–
    Unsettled : Cambodian refugees in the New York City hyperghetto /
Eric Tang.
        pages cm. — (Asian American history and culture)
    Includes bibliographical references and index.
    ISBN 978-1-4399-1164-8 (cloth : alk. paper) — ISBN 978-1-4399-
1165-5 (pbk. : alk. paper) — ISBN 978-1-4399-1166-2 (e-book)
    1. Cambodians—New York (State)—New York. 2. Refugees—
Cambodia. 3. Refugees—New York (State)—New York. 4. Inner
cities—New York (State)—New York. 5. Immigrants—New York
(State)—New York—Social conditions. 6. Immigrants—Cultural
assimilation—New York (State)—New York. I. Title.
    F128.9.K45T36 2015
    305.9'069140747—dc23
                                                        2015008594

♾ The paper used in this publication meets the requirements of the
American National Standard for Information Sciences—Permanence
of Paper for Printed Library Materials, ANSI Z39.48-1992

Printed in the United States of America

9 8 7 6 5

Contents

List of Figures   *vii*

Acknowledgments   *ix*

Introduction: Refugee in the Hyperghetto   *1*

1   War/Time   *28*

2   Housed in the Hyperghetto   *52*

3   Welfare Resistance   *77*

4   Workfare Encampments   *95*

5   Sweatshops of the Neoplantation   *114*

6   Motherhood   *135*

Conclusion: "Unsettled"   *157*

Notes   *181*

Bibliography   *201*

Index   *213*

Photo gallery follows page 94.

Figures

Unnumbered figure: The Bronx   xiv

Photo gallery follows page 94.

1 Ra Pronh in 1980 at the Khao-I-Dang refugee camp, Thailand

2 Ra Pronh, her ex-husband, and their two oldest children
   at the Khao-I-Dang refugee camp ca. 1982

3 Ra in 1986 selling porridge at the U.S. Refugee Processing
   Center in the Philippines and visibly pregnant with her son
   Rith, her fifth child

4 ACVA Statement of Understanding

5 Broken Promises/Falsas Promesas, 1980

6 Cambodian residents of the Northwest Bronx protesting cuts
   in translation services at a local health clinic, 1998

7 Chhaya Chhoum and members of Mekong NYC in 2013

8 Ra Pronh and her granddaughter Jade in 2008

9 Ra with four of her children in 2014

Acknowledgments

There are no words to adequately express my gratitude to Ra Pronh for entrusting me with her story. Still, allow me to simply say that Ra's courage and generosity were matched only by her hospitality. She invited me into her home and gave our sessions care and attention that exceeded all of my expectations. Her son Rith Chy was the lynchpin of this project. Rith not only coordinated our sessions and served as interpreter but carefully organized and archived family documents and photos, allowing us to slowly piece together Ra's long and often jagged sojourn.

I owe an enormous debt to the Bronx community leaders who shaped many of the ideas found in this book. Chhaya Chhoum took time away from her busy schedule to share with me her thoughts on the intersection of organizing, healing, and redemption, and to reflect back on our time working together. Blanca Ramirez granted me multiple interviews that exposed the unsparing truth about the early days of Cambodian resettlement to the Bronx. Among the few resources possessed by the Southeast Asian refugee community of the Northwest Bronx none are more precious than Joyce Wong and Sara Phok, who have coordinated the Indochinese Mental Health Program on a shoestring budget for more than twenty years. They are my inspiration. During my years with the Youth Leadership Project of CAAAV: Organizing Asian Communities, I had the privilege of working alongside and learning from some very committed and skilled organizers. I am forever grateful to the board, staff, and youth organizers—far too many to individually name here—who granted me the opportunity to be part of that important moment and movement. Alongside Chhaya Chhoum, several of these organizers remain active with the Mekong Center: Ngô Thanh Nhàn, Thoul Tong, Daroth Kuch, Johnny Tan, Khamarin Nhann, and Khemara S. Nhann. Their ongoing work shaped many of the ideas that went into this book.

At New York University, Robin D. G. Kelley was that once-in-a-lifetime teacher and adviser. From my junior year in college to the filing of my dissertation, he remained a consistent intellectual and political guide. Along with committee members Andrew Ross, Arlene Dávila, Lisa Duggan, and Gary Okihiro, he was the first to encourage me to write about my experiences in the Northwest Bronx.

There are few things more ironic than starting a book project about your hometown just as you are packing to leave it. I had spent my entire life in New York City until fall 2007. Then, along with my partner and our three-year-old daughter, we left it behind. Over the next three years, our travels took us to Cambridge, Chicago, and finally Austin. To be sure, the book's title is an apt description of the time in which it was largely conceived and researched. Yet what appeared to be a stretch of bad timing was in fact a rewarding experience, one enriched by colleagues and friends who supported me along the way.

I am grateful to the Department of History at Harvard University, particularly to Walter Johnson, for granting me a year as a visiting faculty member. My time in Cambridge was instrumental in mapping out this project. At the University of Illinois at Chicago, I benefited from the wisdom and generosity of colleagues such as Beth Richie, Barbara Ransby, David Stovall, Michelle Boyd, Helen Jun, Mark Chiang, Anna Guevarra, Gayatri Reddy, Karen Su, and Kevin Kumashiro.

Since grounding myself at the University of Texas at Austin, I have had the privilege of becoming a member of the new Department of African and African Diaspora Studies. Edmund Gordon, founding chair, has been an invaluable mentor and friend. The department's staff, particularly Anna-Lisa Plant and Nia Crosley, have supported my teaching and research in immeasurable ways. I am also indebted to present and former directors of the Warfield Center for African and African American Studies—Omi Osun Joni Jones, Frank Guridy, Shirley Thompson, Lisa Thompson, and Cherise Smith—for granting me research funds during the first years of my appointment. This support allowed me to return to New York City to complete the book. The College of Liberal Arts granted me crucial support in the form of course releases and a book subvention award.

The University of Texas at Austin has been an exciting place to explore the contested terms "community-engaged" and "activist scholarship." My friends João Costa Vargas, Charles Hale, and Shannon Speed have advanced my thinking on this issue; the traces of our conversations are apparent from cover to cover. Meanwhile, the university's Division of Diversity and Community Engagement (DDCE) has afforded me the opportunity to put those ideas into action. I am grateful to Gregory Vincent, vice president, for supporting me all of these years as a DDCE faculty fellow.

At the Center for Asian American Studies, my colleagues Madeline Hsu, Julia Lee, Nhi Lieu, Madhavi Mallapragada, Naomi Paik, Sharmila Rudrappa, and Snehal Shingavi critically engaged my work while creating an opportunity for me to workshop my chapters. Through a workshop set up by the center, I also received invaluable feedback from Simone Brown, Ben Carrington, Kali Gross, Nicole Guidotti-Hernández, Minkah Makalani, and Sam Vong. These scholars, along with others I have the privilege of conversing with on a daily basis—Jossianna Arroyo-Martínez, Kevin Cokley, Kevin Foster, Lyndon Gill, Juliet Hooker, Steve Marshall, Deborah Paredez, Rich Reddick, Erica Saenz, Victor Saenz, Matt Richardson, Christen Smith, Omise'eke Tinsley, and Jennifer Wilks—were positive influences on the earliest part of my career. A special shout-out goes to Naomi Paik, who, along with her partner Henry Liu, kept me committed to my writing deadlines, weekend-long runs, and *food*—always the food.

Working with Janet Fracendese on this book has been one of the most rewarding professional experiences of my career. When I began reading ethnic studies texts as an undergraduate during the mid-1990s, the books published by Temple University Press were essential reading. Only later did I realize that Janet was the editor behind several of my favorite titles. Janet got into the weeds with this manuscript; she never let anything get by her while she kept me focused on the political stakes of my project. Meanwhile, Cathy Hannabach's superb editing kept Ra's story moving.

Series editor Linda Trinh Võ carefully read through multiple drafts of the book; her thoughtful criticism and encouragement helped me realize my original vision for this project. I am grateful to Cathy Schlund-Vials and George Lipsitz for reading a very early (and very raw) version of the manuscript. Cathy's groundbreaking ideas on Cambodian American politics, culture, and resistances are apparent throughout this book. George, whose generosity is legendary, was responsible for helping me "find what rhymes."

Some remarkable people helped me get to the finish line. They offered moral support and countless hours of child care, and read through draft chapters during crunch time: Ujju Aggarwal, Andrea Black, Nicole Burrowes, Lisa Byrd, Ricardo Contreras, Rosa Gonzalez, Josué Guillén, Martha Ramos, Ricardo Rojas, Ixchel Rosal, and Ximena Urrutia-Rojas. To say that I could not have done this without them is a vast understatement. Indeed, this team, along with my longtime friends Mario Lugay, Izumi Miyake, and Mercy Romero, supported me through a serious health crisis in 2012. (On that note, many thanks to the doctors and nurses at Seton Medical Center for putting me back together again.)

My family in New York City keeps me grounded. To my brothers Jack, Mark, and Nelson Tang: thank you for your loyalty, irreverence, and outrageous sense of humor. To my sister-in-law Eileen Kim: many thanks for keeping me housed and fed during my trips to New York. In many ways, my mother Susan put this book in motion when I was a child. She was the first to teach me what it means to love the Bronx (during the burnt-out 1980s, no less). Those childhood memories on Tremont Avenue stayed with me as I wrote this book.

At the heart of all things are my truest teachers, my children: Xue-li and Camino Rojas-Tang. They brought clarity and purpose to this project in ways that only they could. Moreover, they taught me how to write like a fugitive—in those stolen moments away from their laughter and brilliance.

Finally, I dedicate this book to Paula X. Rojas, whose infinite support and patience can never be repaid. Paula read every word, pushed back on every argument, and breathed life into this book when I held it in doubt. To Paula, who has made the journey worth it—thank you.

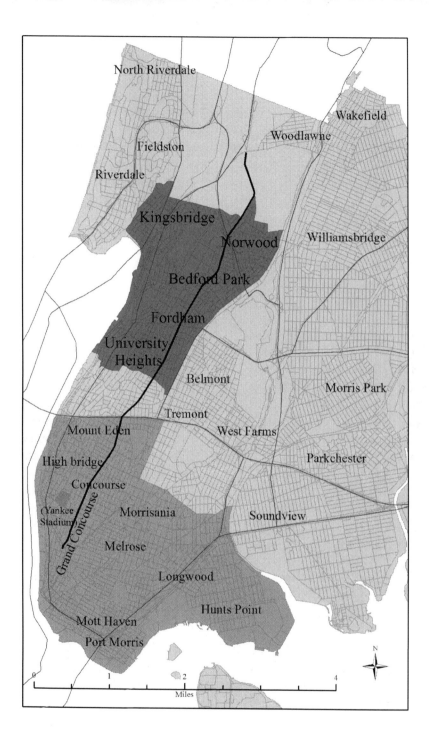

North Riverdale

Wakefield

Woodlawne

Fieldston

Riverdale

Kingsbridge

Norwood

Williamsbridge

Bedford Park

Fordham

University Heights

Belmont

Morris Park

Tremont

Mount Eden

West Farms

High bridge

Parkchester

Concourse

(Yankee Stadium)

Morrisania

Soundview

Grand Concourse

Melrose

Longwood

Hunts Point

Mott Haven

Port Morris

N

0   1   2   4
Miles

Introduction: Refugee in the Hyperghetto

The Refugee

Ra Pronh tells me that she wants to stay in this apartment for as long as she can, which strikes me as ironic because we have been discussing how often she has moved since her arrival in the Bronx two decades ago, in the spring of 1986. On this May 2009 afternoon, we are sitting in the living room of the apartment she has occupied for almost two years. We are creating a record of the many Bronx residences she and her Cambodian[1] family have occupied since their arrival. By our count, Ra has lived in twelve different homes across the Northwest Bronx—some she describes as mere stops. Ra's twenty-three-year-old son Rith concurs with our findings: Ra's length of stay in each Bronx residence has averaged slightly less than two years, and Rith seems taken aback by this figure. He is certainly cognizant of how difficult his mother's life has been over the past twenty-two years,

FACING PAGE. The Bronx. The darkly shaded areas are the Northwest Bronx neighborhoods where Cambodian refugees were resettled during the 1980s and early 1990s. The lightly shaded areas are South Bronx neighborhoods. The South Bronx was the site of a devastating arson epidemic during the 1970s and early 1980s. Map created by Loraine Ng.

and yet these numbers reveal to him a pattern of unsettledness that even he finds surprising.

Ra is a fifty-year-old survivor of the Cambodian genocide. From April 1975 to January 1979, Pol Pot's Democratic Kampuchea (DK) regime—run by the communist Khmer Rouge party—subjected Cambodians to execution, starvation, disease, and forced labor. One-fourth of the Cambodian population was killed.[2] During these years, the Khmer Rouge led a revolution that called for cleansing the country of those perceived to be "contaminated" by the West and for the creation of a national program of ultra-agrarian socialism.[3] Ra was only twenty years old when Khmer Rouge cadres took control of her farming village in the northwestern province of Battambang. It was January 1975, just a few months before they took the capital city of Phnom Penh on April 17, inaugurating the era of genocide. From that point forward, Ra became a captive, forced to work in a massive program of indentured servitude that the Khmer Rouge euphemistically described as a cooperative. She was also forced to marry a complete stranger, a man named Heng.

The Cambodian genocide—known to many as the "zero years" or the "killing fields" era—came to an end following the Vietnamese invasion of Cambodia on December 25, 1978. Within a few weeks—by January 7, 1979—Vietnamese forces had overpowered the Khmer Rouge fighters and taken control of Phnom Penh, installing a new government known as the People's Republic of Kampuchea (PRK). Vietnamese leaders claimed that its objectives were twofold: to stop Khmer Rouge offenses in Vietnamese border communities and to liberate Cambodians from a homicidal regime—one that it once considered an ally in the war against U.S. imperialism.

Not all Khmer Rouge captives were immediately released following the events of January 1979. Realizing that his armies did not stand a chance against the Vietnamese, Pol Pot ordered his cadres to retreat into the western border territories and take as many hostages with them as possible.[4] Ra and Heng were among the thousands of villagers taken into the forests of western Cambodia on the Thai border. Held at gunpoint, they remained under Khmer Rouge control for nearly a year before they were finally able to escape.

At our May 2009 meeting, Ra does not share with me how she and Heng ultimately freed themselves. She only tells me that as time wore on her Khmer Rouge captors, lacking provisions and worn down by illness, eventually lost control of their captives. By December 1979, Ra, her husband, and their newborn daughter Rann crossed into Thailand.

Ra and Heng spent nearly six years in refugee camps in Thailand and the Philippines before moving to the Northwest Bronx in May 1986 as part of a refugee resettlement program. Now divorced, the couple had seven children together—four sons and three daughters. Rann, their oldest child, was born in October 1979 just before the family crossed into Thailand. She is the only one of their children to have been born in Cambodia. While living in Khao-I-Dang, a United Nations refugee camp in Thailand, Ra gave birth to two sons, Rasmey in 1981 and Rom in 1982, as well as another daughter, Rorth, in 1984. In 1986, in preparation for their departure to the United States, the family was sent to a U.S. refugee processing center in the Philippines where Rith was born. After they arrived in the United States, Ra and Heng had two more children—daughter Sonya, born in 1990, and son Vanna, born in 1992.

Between 1975 and 1994, 150,000 Cambodian refugees were resettled in the United States (since then the Cambodian population in the country has nearly doubled owing to U.S. births and the regular immigration of approximately 1,000 Cambodians per year).[5] These were the years of a major Southeast Asian resettlement program—the largest such program in the nation's history—which granted asylum to nearly 1 million refugees from the wars in Vietnam, Cambodia, and Laos. During the 1980s, up to 10,000 Cambodian refugees arrived in the Bronx, according to local leaders and service providers, but the majority stayed in the area for only a short time, quickly leaving in search of better housing and opportunities in other northeastern cities. By the early 1990s, the Bronx Cambodian population had leveled off at approximately 4,000.[6] Virtually all of them were part of the "second wave" of Cambodian refugees who, having survived the genocide and the refugee camps, were granted asylum under the 1980 Refugee Act. By and large, these second-wave Cambodian refugees were poorer and less formally educated (most came from farming backgrounds) than those of the much smaller first wave that resettled in the United States before 1980.[7] The first-wave refugees had been evacuated from Cambodia immediately after Phnom Penh fell to the Khmer Rouge so they had been spared the horrors of the genocide.

Resettlement in the Bronx was supposed to mark a new chapter in Ra's life, but it merely continued her itinerancy. After four years of hard labor under the Khmer Rouge, followed by six years of carving out a meager existence in overcrowded camps where the rations were never enough to feed her family, Ra moved to a Bronx neighborhood beset by poverty, crime, and derelict housing. She survived on welfare and by piecing together odd jobs. This period of her life was also shaped by intertwined personal and structural upheavals: Ra divorced Heng, was convicted of a felony she committed in defense of her daughter Rann, battled multiple times with the city's child welfare agency, and was forced to stay for a time in a city homeless shelter with her youngest child Vanna. All of this instability can be traced back to her several housing displacements.

After reviewing her list of residences, Ra, Rith, and I determine that the family's longest period of continued residency in a single Bronx home—a house she rented in a relatively quiet section of the neighborhood—lasted three years and nine months. This interval was shorter than the four and a half years the family spent in the Khao-I-Dang refugee camp, where she spent more time than in any single place between 1975 and 2009, when we began our interviews for this book. Despite the camp's popular representation as temporary, it was the most permanent, settled home Ra has had since 1975. Looked at in this way, the camp seems slightly more stable than the Bronx.

Most sociological accounts of immigration depict a transition timeline from immigrant to permanent resident to citizen, with each phase supposedly bringing greater stability. Ra's journey tells a different story. For her, instability persisted as a result of woeful housing conditions, unabated working poverty, punitive welfare regulation, and a justice system that would sooner criminalize poor women than protect them from interpersonal violence. More than half of her displacements occurred between 2002 and 2007 alone. With each year in the United States, Ra's situation became more and more precarious.

As Ra's story demonstrates, the cycle of uprooting, displacement, and captivity that defines the refugee experience persists long after resettlement. *Unsettled* traces this cycle, documenting the latest stage of Ra's long history of displacement and captivity. In so doing, it demonstrates that the refugee's racialized and gendered fugitive status persists despite U.S. insistence that the refugee condition is temporary and provisional. *Unsettled* troubles political-juridical uses of the term "refugee" as well as the assumed inevitability of refugee crossing, transfiguration, and settlement. It joins "critical refugee studies," an emergent field that, as Yen Le Espiritu states, refuses to locate the refugee as an object to be studied, a problem to be solved, or a legal classification to be dissected.[8] Rather, critical refugee studies deconstruct the refugee concept as an ideological and discursive formation, tracing the forms of power that are reinforced and extended through the "refugee" label. In particular, Espiritu critiques the construction of the "good refugee" who represents the "solution" to the nation-state's failures.[9] She speaks specifically of Vietnamese refugees who were rescued from communism and then delivered into U.S. liberalism, or so it has been said since 1975. For forty years, this good refugee has served as the solution to America's troubled war in Southeast Asia, according to Espiritu—indeed, the only war the United States has ever lost. Throughout *Unsettled*, I argue that Cambodian refugees have also been hailed as a solution, not only to the bad war in Southeast Asia but also to the veritable war against the poorest residents in contemporary urban America.

Unsettled is not another portrait of refugee suffering highlighting the failures and hardships of resettlement that only ends in redemption. Rather, it argues that refuge is never found, that discourses on rescue mask a more profound urban reality characterized by racialized geographic enclosure, displacement from formal labor markets, unrelenting poverty, and the criminalization of daily life. I resist the terms of resettlement that require one to first acknowledge that a threshold has been crossed, that the displaced have entered entirely new conditions and matrices of power. If the refugee is never allowed to arrive, if refuge is a fiction, then to what extent is crossing itself a mere abstraction? How, instead, does the refugee experience the unclosed sojourn, the open interval? How, in other words, does she remain a captive in late-capitalist urban America?

When I first met Ra in 1999, she had been in the United States for twelve years and I was a community organizer in the Northwest Bronx. I directed the Southeast Asian Youth Leadership Project (YLP), a program that trained refugee teenagers to become community organizers around issues of housing and welfare discrimination. Because of their bilingual and bicultural skills, many young refugees were already advocating for their families. The goal of YLP was to support and enhance their work, to turn their individualized efforts into collective action. Three of Ra's children—Rom, Rorth, and Rith—were YLP members. The program was founded by the Committee Against Anti-Asian Violence (CAAAV), a Manhattan-based group formed in 1986 to address the growing number of racially motivated hate crimes against Asian Americans during the 1980s. By the mid-1990s, the organization had expanded its definition of violence to include the multiple forms of state, economic, and environmental violence that disproportionately affected the immigrant poor. In so doing, it shifted its work from anti–hate crimes advocacy to community and labor organizing. To signify this political shift, the organization changed its name during the late 1990s to CAAAV: Organizing Asian Communities.[10]

In the spring of 1995, after learning of the deplorable housing conditions that Southeast Asians in the Northwest Bronx were living in, CAAAV formed a team to learn more about these and other issues facing local refugees. The goal was to determine the viability of a refugee-focused organizing project in the borough. I was an undergraduate at the time, and I joined this team as a volunteer. A year later, in 1996, I was hired to direct YLP's first full-length summer program.

By the time CAAAV began this work, refugees from Cambodia and Vietnam had been living in the Northwest Bronx for well over a decade. The area was at that time home to the largest concentration of Cambodians in New York City (seconded only by a small enclave in Brooklyn),[11] but few New Yorkers outside of those in the immediate vicinity knew of the community's existence. The refugees seemed hidden. Save for two small Cambodian grocery stores, there were no visible signs typical of an immigrant enclave—restaurants, beauty salons, clothing shops, and the like. Even the local Cambodian Buddhist temple was merely a nondescript house. Most refugees lived in racially mixed buildings that offered no sign of their presence. One had to search for the public spaces where the refugees congregated: a particular stoop, a distinct corner of a local park, a pool hall. Indeed, the Northwest Bronx's Southeast Asian refugee community was one of the few Asian immigrant enclaves in New York that exhibited absolutely no characteristics of an "ethnic economy"—the term sociologists give to immigrant neighborhoods that produce economic activity through self-capitalization and coethnic employment.[12]

Instead, the overwhelming majority of Cambodians in the Northwest Bronx survived on public assistance, with approximately two-thirds receiving a monthly welfare check during the mid-1990s. Even after enactment of federal welfare policies that sought to drastically cut welfare, YLP found that approximately 80 percent continued to use some form of safety net program to survive—food stamps, Medicaid, or Social Security for the disabled and elderly.[13] To supplement these meager benefits, Cambodians found work in New Jersey factories; as home-based garment workers; or by selling food to fellow residents in the park. All of these supplemental streams of income went unreported because they feared losing their welfare benefits if the state determined that they were "overearning."

Our CAAAV team noticed that the Cambodian community consisted of a very large number of teenagers, most of them born in the refugee camps during the 1980s, a period in which many refugee adults were attempting to make up both for time and for the many children lost to the zero years. This observation led to the creation of YLP.

The youth I worked with spoke of the indignities of poverty, the anonymity of new immigrant life, and the street violence that kept many of them in a constant state of fear. They lived in apartments that were borderline uninhabitable, and their lives were marked by routine trips to local welfare offices, where they watched bureaucrats humiliate their parents. At home, they worked alongside their parents, completing orders for hair accessories, for which their families were paid only a few cents per piece. Some worked after-school and evening jobs in New Jersey factories, where they packed perfumes, candy, or pet food.

All of the Cambodian youth I worked with believed that society was indifferent to them and their families. "Cambodians walk around here invisible, like a bunch of ghosts," one said, and whatever attention they did receive was often unwelcome. During the early resettlement years, Black and Latino teenagers saw their Cambodian counterparts as easy marks, to be routinely disrespected and attacked. Some, particularly the young men, responded with their own propensity for violence. Not only did they fight back to earn the respect of their tormentors; they even joined the Black and Latino "sets" that robbed and sold drugs in the neighborhoods. Cambodian teens were not spared the intense monitoring and harassment of local police. Along with African Americans and Latinos, they were routinely "stopped and frisked" on their way to school or work. At times they were caught up in building drug sweeps and taken into custody on charges of possession and selling. During my years directing YLP, I spent countless hours in precincts and courtrooms. Before long, I became adept at writing letters to judges, probation officers, and parole boards, requesting leniency for neighborhood youths who had fallen into trouble. Cambodian youth were not spared the spasms of street violence that seriously injured and occasionally took the lives of their siblings and friends. I recall the deafening silence that routinely followed news that somebody close to our program had been a victim of a stabbing or a shooting.

All told, YLP members described a life that was anything but the peaceful future their parents had hoped for when they left the refugee camps. The repose and stability portended by the refugee resettlement program was a fantasy. Most were too young to have their own memories of the war their parents had lived through, but they now claimed to be living through a war of their own. Over my nine years of working in the refugee neighborhoods of the Northwest Bronx, I came to realize that this invocation of war was not metaphorical but real; although new immigrants from around the world had resettled in working-class and poor communities throughout New York City during the 1980s and 1990s, only Southeast Asian refugees had arrived en masse in the "hyperghetto."

The Hyperghetto

According to historian Sucheng Chan, approximately 55 percent of the 150,000 Cambodians resettled in the United States between 1975 and 1994 were sent to inner cities beset by extreme poverty, joblessness, and crime.[14] Along with the Hmong, Cambodians are among the poorest ethnic groups in the United States. According to 2000 census data, 42.8 percent of Bronx Cambodians were living in poverty, 23.9 percent were unemployed, and 62 percent had less than a high school education.[15]

These statistics were evident in the urban landscape. There were few if any immigrant communities in the urban United States that exhibited the economic homogeneity found in the Cambodian community of the Northwest Bronx. Bronx Cambodians were overwhelmingly impoverished; their welfare participation rates, as mentioned, were as high as 80 percent; and the community did not include capitalized entrepreneurs or professionals. These realities were rooted not just in decades of Southeast Asian warfare but also in the specific tragedy of the Cambodian genocide, in which the majority of the country's middle class—businesspeople, teachers, cultural workers, physicians, technicians, and other professionals—were destroyed. In this sense, to speak of "Southeast Asian refugees in the United States" as a common category is somewhat misleading (to say nothing of lumping Cambodians under the broader Asian American rubric). Indeed, the economic, political, and geographic trajectories of Cambodian refugees are distinct from those of Vietnamese refugees, whose ethnic economies and professional classes are prevalent. This is not to say that Vietnamese refugees do not share the hyperghetto status with Cambodians; on the contrary, the Northwest Bronx is home to a significant number of Vietnamese refugees whose struggles are almost identical to those of Cambodians—most are on welfare, and working poverty is still the rule. However, their economic heterogeneity remains far greater than that of their Cambodian counterparts.[16] The overwhelming presence of the Cambodian working poor and unemployed in the Bronx and other cities, and the concomitant *absence* of a Cambodian middle/entrepreneurial class elsewhere in these cities, is what makes the Cambodian experience in urban America unique. Few if any other immigrant and refugee groups resettled so exclusively and in such large numbers in the poorest urban areas during the era of post-1965 new immigration.

The two largest Cambodian communities in the United States are in Long Beach, California, and Lowell, Massachusetts, with populations of approximately 20,000 and 14,000, respectively. However, the majority of Cambodians are spread out among much smaller and homogenously poorer enclaves—some numbering only a thousand. In addition to the Northwest Bronx, enclaves can be found in the poorest sections of northeastern cities such as Providence, Danbury, Camden, and Philadelphia.[17] On the surface, these neighborhoods appear to conform to the common, troubling images of the twentieth-century inner city: blight, infrastructural decay, economic divestment, crime, and joblessness. Since the late 1960s, however, they have also been sites of a distinct form of low-intensity warfare that represents the conversion of the traditional ghetto into what sociologist Loïc Wacquant terms the "hyperghetto."

The hyperghetto names not only the intensification of intractable inner city problems but also the way in which the traditional ghetto has become what Wacquant refers to as a space of "naked relegation." It is reserved for the isolation and enclosure of the poorest urban residents who are no longer regarded as those to be recruited and disciplined into the lowest rungs of the workforce; rather, they are seen as subjects to be warehoused.[18] In particular, the hyperghetto has functioned as a site of captivity for a decidedly post-Civil Rights and, more significantly, *postinsurrectionist* Black subproletariat.[19]

The origins of the hyperghetto can be traced to the wave of urban unrest in the late 1960s, a period in which Black urban communities engaged in hundreds of insurrections protesting the failure of Civil Rights legislation to address segregation, poverty, and relentless police brutality. The U.S. state and private capital responded to urban unrest not with social, economic, or police reform but with strategies aimed at dispersing Black communities to prevent future rebellions and enclosing and criminalizing those who remained in the ghetto. These strategies were carried out in several ways: local and federal governments refused to rebuild and reinvest in destroyed areas and engaged in "planned shrinkage"—the removal of key public institutions and services such as firehouses, schools, and garbage collection—to drive residents away. Those who remained were isolated and monitored by an increasingly militarized police force that saw little difference between extreme poverty and criminal behavior. Throughout the 1970s and 1980s, these sites became hyperghettos, areas reserved for the "hard-core" urban poor, who, in the wake of urban unrest, were viewed as a population to be criminalized, detained, and punished. According to Wacquant, these punitive measures were carried out by the state's fusing of its social welfare and penal arms. Indeed, he calls attention to how "welfare and criminal justice are two modalities of public policy toward the poor [that] must imperatively be analyzed— and reformed—together."[20] He shows how this marriage of welfare and penality has been apotheosized by "workfare" programs: no-wage worksites that compel the labor of welfare recipients.[21]

In Wacquant's rendering, the hyperghetto is formed as a hybrid of the impoverished and racially segregated neighborhood and the hypertrophic expansion of the prison system, one that includes jails, juvenile facilities, probation, parole, and criminal databases. In this way, the neighborhood serves as a gateway (and then as a revolving door) for hyperincarceration, particularly Black incarceration. For more than four decades, it has steadily fed the prisons, contributing to the United States becoming home to the largest prison population on earth.[22] To say that African Americans are disproportionately incarcerated is a gross understatement. As legal scholar Michelle Alexander states, there were more Black adults under correctional control in 2010 than there were enslaved in 1850.[23] Alexander is one of a diverse group of contemporary scholars who have proven that mass incarceration is the primary mode through which white supremacist governance and the forms of captivity and punishment endemic to slavery and Jim Crow are revisited on the Black population during an age in which state and civil society avow statutory racial equality. The difference between the hyperghetto and the traditional ghetto is not a matter of varying "degrees" of racial oppression between two periods in U.S.

history; rather, it marks the celebration of the ongoing capture and punishment of Black bodies as an act of "colorblindness." In sum, the hyperghetto signifies the failures of racial liberalism to resolve white supremacist rule.

It follows that Wacquant conceives of the hyperghetto as slavery's fourth iteration, preceded by slavery itself, Jim Crow, and the segregated ghettos of the industrial North.[24] In this, he echoes Hortense Spillers, who has long maintained that the "time of slavery" is unending and always pervasive. According to Spillers, slavery did not end with abolition, but has carried forth as that irrevocable "American grammar" through which the U.S. citizenry continues to understand its value—both metaphorically and literally—against the captive and violated Black body.[25]

The challenge for the scholar in studying the hyperghetto is to recognize slavery's permutations without representing its residents as monolithically abject and isolated—as those who are unable to engage complex and meaningful political and economic practices. As anthropologist Steven Gregory reminds us, to the extent that terms such as "Black ghetto" and "inner city" have been useful in "heightening recognition of the ferocity of racial segregation and urban poverty," they can also "obscure far more than they reveal."[26] This is certainly true if such terms are deployed as tropes characterizing those who reside in these communities—that is, to mark their false autonomy or separation from the rest of society. Throughout *Unsettled*, I use the term *hyperghetto* to identify the workings of the regime, not of those who are subjected to that regime's violences. I demonstrate that Cambodian refugees who are held captive in the hyperghetto engage in complex forms of survival and resistance that evince their centrality to (as opposed to their separation from) the main currents and contradictions of the state and its economies.

The Convergence

Unsettled poses several overarching questions: What does it mean for the Cambodian refugee to resettle in this distinct time and space of slavery's continuance?[27] How do we understand her movement from one space of captivity to the next? And how does the racial and gendered project of the hyperghetto come together with the racial and gendered project of asylum and refugee resettlement, particularly for Cambodian refugees in the Northwest Bronx?

If we begin by viewing the Cambodian refugee as merely a subject of humanitarianism, we might conclude that her presence in the hyperghetto marks a major programmatic failure, as if something went terribly awry in the resettlement process. However, my first objective is to reveal the refugee as the subject of a long, unresolved colonial and imperial project carried out by the United States in Southeast Asia, a white supremacist project that wrought unprecedented death and destruction on Vietnam and turned Cambodia into the most heavily bombed country in history. Refugee resettlement in the hyperghetto, I argue, represented not the end of this project but its continuance. Specifically, I demonstrate that Northwest Bronx Cambodians were routinely enlisted as figures to be "saved" from a new theater of war: liberal warfare in the hyperghetto. And just as these refugees were once "incidentally" violated by the destruction wrought by their ostensible saviors, so they continue to function as collateral damage in the war against the hyperghetto's long-standing residents, specifically African Americans and Puerto Ricans.

In calling attention to the specific role that Cambodians have been enlisted to play in the hyperghetto, I argue against two overly simplified and diametrically opposed readings of the racialization and gendering of Southeast Asian refugees. First, I challenge the notion promulgated by the mainstream media and some policy makers that Southeast Asian refugees, following other Asian Americans, were "model-minority" figures who achieved economic success despite having arrived penniless in the United States. The model-minority argument is rather easy to dispense with because there is very little evidence to support it. Cambodians and other Southeast Asian refugees never achieved the levels of ostensible economic success associated with Chinese American, Japanese American, Korean American, and Indian American groups in the United States. Suffice it to say that model-minority tropes never effectively applied to most Southeast Asian refugees; indeed, Asian Americans who sought to challenge such stereotyping often invoked the economic and educational struggles of refugees as their first line of rebuttal.

Second, I challenge the opposite notion postulated by some scholars that impoverished Cambodians have been racialized and gendered as a new "underclass."[28] The term underclass is a pejorative one—coined by academics but wielded in a wide discursive field—that refers to those whose poverty is said to be the result of cultural and behavioral deviance and dysfunction, not structural inequality. As historian Michael Katz and others argue, underclass has been used as shorthand for "undeserving" Black urban poverty—poverty that should be either neglected or met with punitive public policy.[29]

In *Unsettled*, I demonstrate how Bronx Cambodians were discursively removed from underclass status by policy makers, landlords, social workers, and researchers. I show how these agents routinely cast refugees as those who would eventually achieve the successes portended by liberalism even as all empirical evidence pointed to the contrary. I term this discursive removal *refugee exceptionalism*—the ideologies and discursive practices that figure refugees as necessarily *in* the hyperghetto but never *of* it. It is the process whereby refugees are resettled into and then recurrently "saved" from the hyperghetto and its attendant modalities of captivity: uninhabitable housing stock, permanent exclusion from the labor market, and punitive social policy. However, refugee exceptionalism never actually removes the refugee from hyperghetto spaces and institutions (certainly not in any material sense); on the contrary, it requires that she be held in perpetual captivity so that she can be used over and over again.

The goals of refugee exceptionalism are twofold. First, it masks the systemic inequalities and violences of a refugee resettlement program that, as an extension of the U.S. colonial and imperial project in Southeast Asia, proclaimed Cambodians and other Southeast Asian refugees to be the beneficiaries of American liberal freedoms that the United States could not successfully deliver through its acts of warfare. By casting refugees as subsisting in an unending state of arrival at liberalism, whose struggles with poverty in the urban United States are deemed perpetually temporary and "adaptive," refugee exceptionalism preserves and extends the narrative of the Southeast Asian subject's salvation through U.S. intervention. Second, by insisting that refugees be saved from the grips of the underclass, it reinforces the terms that produce African Americans (and to varying degrees Latinos) as the undeserving poor, "domestic minorities" for whom the underclass concept was formulated. In other words, refugee exceptionalism preserves and extends the justification for punishment of certain populations in the hyperghetto. We might say that, taken together, the Cambodian refugee presence in the hyperghetto, mediated through refugee exceptionalism, represents the convergence of two distinct yet *relational* genealogies of white supremacist governance: colonialism and slavery. Ra's presence here elucidates the hyperghetto as slavery's afterlife. In turn, the hyperghetto reveals the contours of an unfinished colonialism.

In Chapter 1, I draw out the connections between the refugee's life as a subject of imperialist warfare and her life as a subject of the hyperghetto. I begin by reviewing the United States' role in enabling the rise of Pol Pot and the Khmer Rouge, drawing briefly on Ra's experiences under this genocidal regime. Despite this history, the United States publicly positioned itself as the champion of displaced Cambodians, passing the 1980 Refugee Act and casting it as a global freedom project and Cambodian refugees as needing rescue by U.S. liberalism. In this way, refugees were persistently called on to perform as rescued victims of an unending war—what some have termed "liberal warfare." I conclude the chapter by demonstrating how Ra understood the nature of ongoing warfare; that is, she read her movement from the Cambodian war zone to the Thai camps and eventually to the Bronx hyperghetto not as moments of transition and transfiguration but as one long and unbroken state of captivity.

This continuity between past and present warfares is elucidated in Chapter 2, where I discuss how the Bronx hyperghetto served as the new site of liberal warfare from which Cambodian refugees were to be saved. I begin by tracing the origins of the hyperghetto to the urban insurrections of the late 1960s and the Bronx arsons of the 1970s. I then demonstrate that this warfare continued to play out in the poor housing conditions and many housing displacements to which Ra and other Cambodian refugee tenants were subjected. I draw on the recollections of housing organizer Blanca Ramirez, who organized in refugee neighborhoods several years before Ra's arrival in 1986. I note the landlords and social workers in the hyperghetto who confined refugees to substandard housing units, simultaneously insisting that these newcomers did not belong among their stigmatized neighbors.

In Chapter 3, I turn to another front of hyperghetto warfare: the punitive U.S. welfare state. Since the 1980s, the Bronx welfare bureaucracy has thoroughly and arbitrarily governed the lives of Ra and other Cambodian refugees. This chapter explores how they understood the notion of welfare "rights" in relation to such arbitrary rule. Here I pay particular attention to how welfare regulation took a decidedly punitive turn in 1996, with the passage of the Personal Responsibility and Work Opportunity Reconciliation Act. Euphemistically described as "welfare reform," this law completely overhauled the modern welfare state by setting a time limit on cash assistance, requiring mandatory workfare, removing noncitizens from key programs, and tightening verification requirements. To community organizers, the new law epitomized U.S. social welfare policy's "neoliberal turn." By removing welfare recipients (or compelling their self-removal) from the rolls, welfare reform pushed the poorest of the poor into the precarious low-to-no wage work that defined late twentieth-century capitalism. However, Cambodian refugees in the Bronx experienced this not as something new but rather as a continuation of a previous form of arbitrary rule and entrapment. I discuss a distinct form of refugee knowledge about the welfare state and how it interrupts not only the dominant story of neoliberal capitalism but also the discourse of "rights" that was central to the community and labor organizing that sought to challenge welfare reform.

In Chapter 4, I discuss how workfare played out in the lives of Bronx Cambodian refugees. Workfare was a mandatory no-wage work program that welfare recipients were compelled to attend in exchange for their monthly welfare check. Departing from Ra's story, I describe the travails of another Cambodian single mother, Kun Thea, who was trapped between workfare and low-wage factory work. There were few organizing strategies that could free Kun Thea from her entrapment—that is, without reinscribing her captivity. From here, I turn to the work of Chhaya Chhoum, a young Cambodian community organizer, who proposed alternative ways of thinking about resistance beyond the narrow purview of community organizers' strategies and tactics.

Such alternative forms of resistance were grounded in the daily survival tactics of refugees. In Chapter 5, I turn to these practices by exploring Ra's labor as a low-wage home worker in the global garment industry. From one of her many Bronx apartments, she and her family were plugged into an assembly line that stretched from the free trade zones of the Third World to the hyperghettos of the United States. Here I discuss the fact that the hyperghetto is too often left out of globalization discussions, and I locate the "neoplantation," described as such by geographer and Black studies scholar Clyde Woods, as indelibly inscribed in the global economy.

The hyperghetto is a distinctly gendered space of captivity, and in Chapter 6 I analyze the unbroken line of gendered violence that held Ra captive from her days under the Khmer Rouge in the 1970s through her days in the Bronx in the mid-2000s. This gendered violence took many forms: forced marriage, a felony charge for defending her daughter, run-ins with the child welfare agency, and eviction from her home. Ra's experiences, though certainly tethered to her colonial past, also resonated powerfully with the gendered violence shaping poor Black women's lives in the hyperghetto. In the 1980s and 1990s, Cambodian refugee women were depicted in political, economic, and cultural discourses as maintaining relative privilege over refugee men—seemingly the same depiction that demonized Black women through the figure of the Black matriarch. However, I argue that Cambodian refugee women were not subjected to the matriarchal trope but rather to the discourse of refugee exceptionalism that cast them as foreign subjects to be saved by liberalism, specifically by liberal feminism. Here, again, refugee exceptionalism was mobilized to separate Cambodian refugee women from other women in the hyperghetto—a move that at once obscured the realities of the former while normalizing violence against the latter.

In the Conclusion, I argue that, through her constant spatial and temporal movements, Ra rejected stasis. Like many other Cambodian refugees in the hyperghetto, she used movement as a strategy to resist final captivity. In her escape to Thailand, her migration through the refugee camps, her many Bronx relocations, and her maneuverings within welfare and work confines, Ra's constant movement kept open the possibility of future redemption. Movement is how she sustained what Saidiya Hartman and Stephen Best describe as the "interval between 'the no longer and the not yet,' between the destruction of the old world and the awaited hour of deliverance."[30] Lastly, I discuss Ra's children's adoption of their mother's penchant for movement.

Methodology

As an ethnographic study, *Unsettled* draws on two main sources: notes from my years as a community organizer in the Northwest Bronx's refugee neighborhoods (1995–2004) and extensive interviews with Ra Pronh conducted from February 2009 through December 2012, with several follow-up interviews conducted in 2014.[31] The former, which include participant-observer reflections and unstructured interviews with refugee community members and community advocates, provide valuable information on the political and economic contradictions defining the hyperghetto as well as the responses of various activists and advocates to those conditions. The latter serve as the empirical evidence that allows me to conceptualize refugee temporality. In this sense, they critique my earlier notes. Ra's understandings and representations of her long captivity correct established political and economic analyses as well as my own and other activists' rendering of it.

As a participant-observer study, *Unsettled* is part of a rich tradition in Southeast Asian American refugee studies that have adopted ethnographic methods to study impoverished, urban-based refugees. Aihwa Ong's *Buddha Is Hiding: Refugees, Citizenship, the New America*, Sucheng Chan's *Not Just Victims: Conversations with Cambodian Community Leaders in the United States*, Nazli Kibria's *Family Tight Rope: The Changing Lives of Vietnamese Americans*, and Lynn Fujiwara's *Mothers without Citizenship: Asian Immigrant Families and the Consequences of Welfare Reform* are but a few works that draw on interviews (unstructured and structured), conversations, and, most significantly, shared experiences with the refugees being studied. Across each one, refugees' viewpoints come across with a breadth, complexity, and heterogeneity worthy of their struggles.

Unsettled departs from these ethnographic works in one crucial respect, however: it centers on the story of a single individual, Ra Pronh. My interviews with Ra began in the winter of 2009. At the time I was beginning the first phase of research on a book about refugee exceptionalism, which I envisioned as demonstrating how this concept played out in the U.S. settings in which Cambodian refugees found themselves: the housing market, the welfare state, the helping professions (including social work and counseling agencies), and community organizations. I wanted to analyze how the organizing work I was involved in during the late 1990s and early 2000s both challenged and contributed to refugee exceptionalism. For there were certainly moments when, in working to address the myriad ways in which the resettlement program had failed Bronx Cambodians, I was guided by the notion that something else should have awaited them on their arrival to the United States. In this way, I discussed refugee resettlement as a broken promise as opposed to an impossible one, contributing to the notion that refugees were somehow misplaced in the hyperghetto, that their resettlement in urban abjection represented the exceptional circumstance.

Among the first community residents I interviewed for this project was Ra. We first met in 1999 when I helped her and her family with their welfare troubles. At the time, her daughter Rorth and son Rom were members of YLP. Her son Rith joined the group two years later. Ra made an immediate impression on me. She was talkative and quick-witted and possessed a bold sense of humor. She held strong opinions on why the welfare state was mistreating her and other recipients, and she often challenged my framing of the state's actions. Ra's personality allowed us to develop a quick rapport; I found it challenging yet engaging to advocate for someone who not only excoriated those in power but also questioned the remedies proposed by those who sought to help her. At the same time, Ra brought levity to our relationship. She often joked about her predicament and occasionally ribbed me about my life choices: Why did I spend so much time working on welfare cases and hanging out with teenagers in the neighborhood? When was I going to start a family of my own?

I fell out of contact with Ra after I left community organizing and moved out of the Northwest Bronx in 2004. As I explain, Ra lived nomadically during the first half of the 2000s, moving from one friend's or family member's apartment to the next, and this made it difficult for me to locate her when I returned to the refugee neighborhoods for routine visits. For a time she even lived in a homeless shelter. Still, I remained in regular contact with her son Rith, with whom I often talked about his ongoing political commitments as he continued as a YLP youth organizer while branching out to citywide organizing efforts. We also talked of his decision to either stay in college or pursue a career as a hairstylist (he eventually chose the latter). In the summer of 2007, Rith told me that Ra had finally secured an apartment of her own.

I paid a visit to Ra approximately a year after she moved into her new apartment, and was quickly reminded of our dynamic. By then I was a sleep-deprived father of a three-year-old daughter. I marveled as Ra gave verbal instructions to her two-year-old granddaughter to take a nap. Without any assistance, the toddler climbed onto a bed in the corner of the living room, covered herself with a blanket, and fell asleep. Perhaps picking up on my disbelief, Ra asked me how I was enjoying fatherhood. I confessed to her that my daughter still did not sleep through the night, much less put herself to bed. It seemed like years since I had enjoyed a full night's rest. Ra feigned a lack of sympathy as she chided me for being a pushover: "Train them early."

Several months after our reunion, I asked Ra if she would allow me to interview her for my book project. I explained my objectives and why I believed she would be an important informant. I told her that my questions would focus on her perception of those who were responsible for her resettlement from the camps to the Bronx and the years that followed. Ra agreed, and we held our first session in February 2009. Because I do not speak Khmer, I asked Rith to interpret when needed, believing that he could also share his own perspective on his family's struggles with housing, welfare, and low-wage work. However, Ra was quick to point out that for the previous three years she had made a steady commitment to improving her English—she took classes and made sure to "go here and there, talk to new people." She would speak in English during the interviews as much as she could.

In light of our existing relationship, I anticipated that our first unstructured interview would be a free-flowing and relatively comfortable exchange. However, I did not expect Ra to be as open and engaged as she was. With very little prompting from me, she spoke about her arrival in the United States and her first days in the Bronx. She offered rich accounts of her dealings with landlords as she moved from one apartment to the next in her first few years of Bronx unsettlement. I was so riveted by her tales that I lost track of my questions. Beyond the objectives of my research, Ra was letting me know that she had a story to tell, and midway through our first interview she instructed me to tell it. "I've gone through a lot," she said. "I want people to know my story. Everything I did—I want people to know it."

By our second interview, in May 2009, it became clear to me that my book about refugee exceptionalism would be a story about Ra's sojourn. I saw a political project to be shared between my desire to explain refugee resettlement in the hyperghetto as a continuation of a long history of warfare and Ra's desire to tell her story of a life in the United States that defied dominant narratives of refugee resettlement as deliverance and redemption. I would write not an exhaustive biography but an analysis of her experiences over several distinct captivity sites in the urban United States. I would focus on how she understood what had happened to her over three decades of Bronx unsettlement. Although I did not know it at the time, Ra presented me with a theory complementary to that of refugee exceptionalism, one that spoke to how the refugee herself understood the long and unbroken time and space of her captivity. I term this understanding *refugee temporality*.

Refugee temporality names the refugee's knowledge that, with each crossing, resettlement, and displacement, an old and familiar form of power is being reinscribed. It is the knowledge that Ra drew on as she engaged in forms of survival that disavowed the state's insistence that she had been simultaneously saved and redeemed by its refugee resettlement program. Through refugee temporality, Ra resisted the ways in which various powers enlisted her in the service of the salvation narrative both abroad (imperial and colonial warfare) and at "home" (warfare in the hyperghetto).

From the outset, Ra had only one condition for me as an author. She wanted me to focus on how she survived, on how she got as far as she did. She was going to share the story of how she *maneuvered*—across the border, into the camps, and through the U.S. welfare state and low-wage economy. In this, Ra was implicitly setting a boundary. She would not go into detail about her traumatic experiences under the Khmer Rouge and other state and paramilitary forces; she would not recount the atrocities she had witnessed. I was more than accepting of these terms. My goal was to examine the complex forms of refugee survival and resistance over the course of nearly three decades of unsettlement in the U.S. hyperghetto. Such a project did not require that informants provide a detailed account of their past traumas. Moreover, conversations with (and published work by) Richard Mollica of the Harvard Program in Refugee Trauma convinced me that those who listen to and record a refugee's trauma story should do so with one goal: contributing to her long-term healing.[32] According to Mollica, the trauma story should be told as part of a process in which the survivor is invited to analyze and reinterpret what she shares. Anything short of this amounts to an unproductive "debriefing therapy"—a rehashing of brutal and ultimately unrepresentable events that runs the risk of retraumatizing the survivor.[33] Whether or not Ra would have found sharing her trauma story with me therapeutic, I cannot say. (That she ultimately chose not to seems a rather resounding answer to this question.) What is certain, however, is that I was not trained in the techniques of listening to and providing feedback to the trauma story and so did not solicit one.

My unstructured interview questions were typical of those used in most oral history projects. I began with the widest frame: "What do you remember most about the camp?" or "Describe your first days in the Bronx." Ra then elaborated, presenting a sequence of events, scenes, and impressions. This was the text from which we worked, and my follow-up questions hewed to it. I asked her to clarify dates and locations. I asked her to interpret what she had just described. For instance, after she explained to me that she was placed in derelict housing by a resettlement agency, I asked her why she believed the agency made this decision. I then offered my own interpretation of the agency's handling of refugees, and our dialogue ensued.

In following Ra's lead, I was making a distinct methodological choice, one that, in the words of Sandra Harding, seeks to "maximize objectivity . . . [by] 'starting off thought' from the lives of marginalized peoples."[34] According to Harding, "beginning in those determinate, objective locations in any social order will generate illuminating critical questions that do not arise in thought that begins from dominant groups' lives."[35] She argues that this is neither an ethnocentric nor relativist claim but rather one that recognizes how oppressed groups' worldviews tend to be less partial and distorted than those of more privileged subjects who often, avowing objectivity, leave uninterrogated their own social values, interests, and biases.

In a similar vein, Robin D. G. Kelley exposes the racial and gendered biases found in ethnographies of the twentieth-century U.S. ghetto and hyperghetto. He claims that many ethnographies on postwar Black urban life, particularly those conducted after the 1960s urban insurrections, are so steeped in the racist fantasies of white male ethnographers that they amount to "playing the dozens" on the Black urban poor.[36] That is, they reproduce essentialist, voyeuristic, and ultimately damaging portraits of Black survival, which anthropologist John Langston Gwaltney describes as "street corner exotica."[37] Kelley points to Gwaltney's *Drylongso: A Self Portrait of Black America* as one of the few exceptions to this otherwise troubling field of urban ethnography. What distinguishes Gwaltney's study is the way in which his informants frame their lives against various systems of oppression and challenge and redirect the researcher's questions to meet their own priorities, speaking openly about the racism of the social sciences while knowingly participating in his study.

Throughout *Unsettled*, I discuss how Ra challenged my presumptions, contradicted my claims, or simply demurred. However, in demonstrating how she took the lead in these instances, my intention is not say that I was somehow able to exert minimal influence over my informant's responses. To the contrary, grounding this study in Ra's epistemological standpoint meant locating my own positions of power in relation to her. Some specific terms of this power-laden position are middle-class professional, second-generation Chinese American, English speaker, cisgender male. Although Ra never used these terms to describe me, they represent coordinates of power that fundamentally determined what Ra would share with me and how she would share it. Two important aspects of our differences stood out during the interview sessions: language and gender.

My inability to speak Khmer delimited Ra's statements because she knew that whatever she said in Khmer would be mediated through her son. (Throughout, italics indicate where Ra is speaking through Rith's interpretation.) And although Ra clearly took pride in her English, her direct statements seemed at times carefully parsed. She spoke English not at length but in shorter clips when she wanted to emphasize a certain point or main idea. These statements were poignant yet very concise, especially when compared with the lengthier statements of fluent English speakers who are quoted in the book.

How might Ra's points of emphasis in English have come across differently (both qualitatively and quantitatively) had she spoken them in Khmer? That she spoke to me in English at key moments in our interview sessions was not a choice per se but a political negotiation with my positionality. Ra had no choice but to speak in English if she wanted to make an uninterpreted point.

Beyond the language constraint, my position and performance as a heterosexual male interviewer also determined what was possible for Ra to share. She spoke in detail about her struggles with housing, the welfare state, the home-based sweatshop economy, and factory work. In contrast, she spoke only in general terms about her interpersonal experiences with patriarchal power. Under the Khmer Rouge, sexual violence against women was epidemic; as I discuss in Chapter 6, Ra's Khmer Rouge–arranged marriage should be understood as part and parcel of such violence. During our second interview, Ra made sure to underscore the importance of this event: "I want to talk about when I was forced to marry Rith's father." We had been discussing her final days under the Khmer Rouge when she suddenly pivoted back to this defining moment in her life, suggesting that, if I was to fully understand her Khmer Rouge captivity, it was important for her to return to the day she was separated from her family of origin and forced to become a wife and mother.

As Ra spoke of this pivotal moment, however, she struck a careful balance: describing how she felt about what happened to her and how she was forever changed by the event, but not describing any specific acts of violence committed against her by the men who orchestrated it. So, too, beyond the forced marriage she never talked about any other instances of sexual violence that she might have suffered or witnessed under the Khmer Rouge, in the camps, or throughout her Bronx unsettlement. Perhaps this was in keeping with her decision not to share her trauma story, but it was clear to me that she was also making an explicitly gendered and sexualized negotiation in consideration of her interviewer. To say that she felt uncomfortable sharing such information with a man is to state the obvious. Underlying this discomfort, however, is a more complex rendering of how patriarchal power works: if Ra was a survivor of such crimes, then sharing this particular information with me—unlike sharing the details of her exploitation and abuse as a worker or welfare recipient—posed the potential threat of male judgment and misrepresentation complicit with the gendered and sexualized logics in which violence against women is rooted.

Rith's presence added a complex gendered dimension to the interview sessions. I am sure that having her son in the room influenced what Ra ultimately decided to share about her family life, particularly her relationship with Rith's father. At the same time, Rith seemed to put Ra at ease during our interviews because of their close and trusting relationship. During the interviews, the two often went back and forth, giving our sessions the feel of a family conversation. There were also times when one or more of Rith's siblings decided to join our sessions. Here I tried in vain to facilitate a group interview as Ra and her children volleyed over key facts and dates, laughed about the things they once said and did, and reminisced with one another about a childhood that was by turns tragic and tender. These exchanges granted me a fuller understanding of Ra's influence on her children: how she imparted to them her humility and her truculence as well as her belief that as refugees they had to keep things moving, that they could never settle. It goes without saying that the presence of Rith and of Ra's other children during our interview sessions fundamentally shaped my findings.

I offer these methodological reflections neither to qualify my findings nor to make axiomatic claims about the possibilities and limitations of ethnographic research.[38] Rather, my point is a political one: our interview sessions, like our advocacy sessions years earlier, were political negotiations. Ra and I certainly held a personal affinity for one another based on a mutual trust developed over several years.

However, feelings of friendship and trust should not be misconstrued as factors mitigating power differentials. Rather, I am persuaded by sociologist John Brown Childs, who asserts that trust is the precondition for engaging in shared practice across those differences.[39] In expounding the theory of "transcommunality," Childs proposes that autonomous political subjects should pursue trust not for the sake of leveling differences and arriving at political uniformity (what he describes as a politics of "conversion"); rather, trust should be the starting point from which subjects begin the process of determining "what kinds of relations are possible, but also . . . what kinds of relations are *not* possible."[40] Indeed, working through such impossibilities to arrive at an "ethics of respect" is one of the most important social justice projects one can undertake.[41] To this, I would add that it is also the very meaning of activist scholarship.

Because *Unsettled* emerged from my political commitment to the refugee community, it can be characterized as the work of an activist scholar. By this I mean a scholar whose research produces new knowledge through direct political engagement with the issues being analyzed. In this way—and within the field of Southeast Asian refugee studies in particular—it builds on activist-oriented works such as Bindi V. Shah's *Laotian Daughter: Working toward Community, Belonging, and Environmental Justice*, in which Shah, working closely with the Asian Pacific Environmental Network, studies the activism of Laotian teens resisting economic, racial, gendered, and environmental injustices.[42] *Unsettled* also owes a debt to the community-engaged scholarship of Peter Kiang, Shirley Tang, and their colleagues at the University of Massachusetts Boston, who for decades have set an example of politically engaged and collaborative research through their work with Southeast Asian refugee communities in the greater Boston area. In *Engaging Contradictions: Theory, Politics and Methods of Activist Research*, Kiang and Tang describe how they developed horizontal relationships between researchers and those being researched, how they welcomed refugee community residents to both shape and challenge their research, and how they viewed their scholarship as fundamentally committed to social equality and justice.[43]

These and other examples teach us that activist-oriented scholarship is not so much about chronicling and analyzing activism (either one's own or that of one's group) but more about developing processes whereby the knowledge of the researcher and the knowledge of those directly affected by injustice shape one another in a shared political project. George Lipsitz and Barbara Tomlinson describe this form of activist scholarship as "accompaniment": it allows differences and disagreements between the researcher and those he or she studies to "be seen as evidence of problems yet to be solved, discussions yet to be conducted, understandings yet to be developed."[44]

At various points throughout *Unsettled*, I show where my views and analyses—on organizing, neoliberalism, the notion of redemption, and the like—were challenged and ultimately transformed by my critical engagements with Ra and others. In this sense, the book is less concerned with highlighting what I accomplished as an organizer than with reflecting on what escaped me, on understanding my gaps. We might say that as a work of activist scholarship *Unsettled* exhibits three temporalities: the time of the refugee, the time of the community organizer doing his work, and the time of the researcher looking back to recover what he missed.

1
War/Time

In the wake of the Cambodian genocide, the majority of Cambodians seeking asylum and resettlement in another country fled to neighboring Thailand. By crossing into another country, they redefined themselves from "internally displaced people" to "refugees," according to the Office of the United Nations High Commissioner for Refugees (UNHCR).[1]

Crossing into Thailand in itself, however, did not guarantee entry into a refugee camp from which the refugees could make an asylum claim. Once across, the refugees had to gain entry into a camp that was jointly administered by UNHCR and the Thai government, whereupon they could submit their application to a third and final country of asylum, including the United States. Many Cambodians never made it that far. They were stopped by Thai soldiers who either pushed them back into Cambodia or into non-UNHCR camps run by exiled Cambodian factions (including the Khmer Rouge) who opposed the Vietnamese-backed People's Republic of Kampuchea (PRK) regime. Among those who crossed, the most unfortunate were the men, women, and children murdered by ruthless Thai soldiers.

Ra crossed over from Cambodia into Thailand in early December 1979, nearly one year after the Vietnamese invaded Cambodia. The invasion ended the four-and-a half-year Cambodian genocide carried out by the Khmer Rouge. If Ra, Heng, and Rann had crossed only six months earlier, they might have been driven back into Cambodia by Thai forces. Indeed, they might have been among the estimated thousands who were massacred at Mount Dangrek in June 1979, forced at gunpoint into a borderland ravine riddled with landmines.

On the other hand, if Ra and her family had crossed only two months later, after February 1980, they might have been among those deemed ineligible for entry into the UNHCR refugee camps, the only camps granting interviews for resettlement in another country. Fortuitously, they entered during that brief window of time—October 1979 through February 1980—in which Thai authorities, responding to the international outcry over their nation's treatment of Cambodian asylum seekers, instituted an "open-door" policy that allowed as many Cambodians as possible to enter UNHCR camps.[2] In December 1979, Ra and her family were granted entry to the UNHCR Sa Kaeo holding center before being transferred three months later to Khao-I-Dang, the largest UNHCR refugee camp in Thailand, where the family's application for resettlement in the United States was eventually approved.

According to Ra, her family's experience was entirely arbitrary. Nothing separated them from the thousands of other Cambodian genocide survivors who were denied asylum and resettlement because they missed the open-door period. In this sense, Ra affirmed what some political theorists have long maintained: the "refugee" designation is entirely mutable. The granting of refugee status has less to do with displaced subjects' ability to meet essential criteria than with how they meet or fail to meet the political needs of the sovereign nation-states that define the refugee category. These political needs can take the form of discrediting the governments and regimes from which displaced subjects are fleeing or bolstering the images of those nations granting asylum and resettlement. At times the refugee category serves as justification for warfare itself because extreme violence attends the delivery of "freedom" and "human rights" to those said to be stripped of such supposedly universal attributes.

In this chapter, I trace the multiple uses of the Cambodian refugee, beginning with how this subject was produced in the context of the U.S. war in Vietnam and the Khmer Rouge genocide. I then show how the 1980 Refugee Act cast Southeast Asian refugees as key protagonists in a grand fiction that not only cloaked ongoing U.S. imperial ambitions but, more significantly, granted the expansion of what some have termed "liberal warfare." From here, I propose that the Cambodian refugee experienced each of these enlistments as one long, unbroken interval—what I term "refugee temporality."

Cambodia and the Khmer Rouge

In 1965 the U.S. government was ten years into fighting what it called the Vietnam War. In October of that year, President Lyndon B. Johnson approved a relentless, covert bombing campaign target- ing countries bordering Vietnam: namely, Cambodia and Laos. The bombing campaign aimed to root out and destroy Vietnamese com- munist forces operating in eastern Cambodia and neutralize Cam- bodia's growing communist guerilla movement. In 1969 President Richard Nixon and his national security advisor Henry Kissinger decided to radically expand the bombings. In what was codenamed "Operation Menu," Nixon ordered B-52s to carpet-bomb eastern Cam- bodia. All told, between 1965 and 1973 U.S. bombs killed between 150,000 and 500,000 Cambodians.[3] During these eight years, the U.S. dropped 2,756,941 tons of munitions on Cambodia, exceeding the to- tal tonnage of such devices used during the six years of World War II and rendering the tiny nation the most heavily bombed in history.[4]

In 1970, the U.S. government also orchestrated a coup to prevent the Cambodian communist movement from gaining a foothold in Cambodia. The coup deposed Prince Norodom Sihanouk as the coun- try's leader and replaced him with former prime minister General Lon Nol, who was believed to be more amenable to America's anticom- munist interests. The bombings ended on August 15, 1973, when the U.S. House of Representatives cut off all funding for military action in Cambodia, but Lon Nol remained. His regime later came undone because of its close ties with the United States and the death and de- struction wrought by the U.S. bombings.

Prior to the country's bombardment, the Khmer Rouge had not been considered a major revolutionary threat in Cambodia. Led by

Saloth Sar, head of the underground Communist Party of Kampuchea (CPK), who took the *nom de guerre* Pol Pot, the Khmer Rouge
consisted of a few hundred regulars and a loose network of insur-
gents in villages around the countryside. Although it had received
tacit support from China since the mid-1960s, its attempts to launch
a national revolution were consistently hampered by Sihanouk's re-
pressive tactics as well as by Hanoi's reluctance to support an armed
uprising against the Sihanouk regime so long as North Vietnamese
fighters were allowed to operate in the Cambodian interior. All of this
changed with the 1970 coup.

The pro-American Lon Nol ended Cambodia's neutrality in the
Vietnam War and immediately ordered North Vietnamese troops to
be driven out; he also sanctioned mass violence against Vietnamese
civilians living in the country. Hanoi countered by pushing its armies
deeper into Cambodian territory and by supporting the build-up of
Pol Pot's forces. Thus began the Cambodian civil war that lasted from
1970 to 1975.

Between 1970 and 1972, Pol Pot rapidly expanded his army, bolstered by both North Vietnamese firepower and increased funding
from China. However, the Khmer Rouge's most vital recruitment
tool was the relentless U.S. bombing.[5] The mounting death toll legitimized Pol Pot's claim that the true enemies of the Cambodian people
were U.S. imperialists and their lackey, Lon Nol. According to Sydney
Schanberg, the *New York Times* journalist best known for his writings
about photojournalist and genocide survivor Dith Pran, the Khmer
Rouge "would point to the skies to the American planes that were
bombing, and say: there's your enemy. . . . At that time the estimates
of [Khmer Rouge] strength were 3–5000 unconnected gangs of guer-
rillas, no central control. By the end of the war they were 70–100,000,
a very different beast. . . . I think we gave them the enemy they needed
to build themselves."[6]

By the time the bombings ended in 1973, the Khmer Rouge controlled nearly two-thirds of Cambodia and Pol Pot was the movement's absolute ruler. As his stature grew, he purged those he believed
to be disloyal, particularly members of the CPK who maintained close
ties to Hanoi.[7] Pol Pot was determined to build his own brand of ultra-
Maoist agrarian socialism, one that was distinct from Vietnamese

Marxism. He was also wary of Vietnamese hegemony, reminding his followers of Hanoi's past betrayals of the Cambodian people. Pol Pot believed that Vietnamese communism had no true interest in Cambodia's liberation, that it would sooner take Cambodia for itself than see it fully independent. As historian Ben Kiernan argues, Pol Pot's anti-Vietnamese position was the ethnoracial logic behind the genocide; he distinguished the population as "true Khmers" and those contaminated by contact with Vietnamese and other foreign influences either by heritage or by geographic proximity.[8]

Warnings of the atrocities to come were apparent as early as 1972: cities were evacuated, forced labor was instituted in the countryside, currency was abolished in some areas, monks were defrocked, ethnic groups like the Islamic minority Cham were persecuted, and members of the Cambodian middle class—or those perceived to have class privilege—were prohibited from joining the Khmer Rouge. Between 1972 and 1975, as Pol Pot steadily conquered more territory, he expanded and intensified his experiments and pogroms, planting the seeds of what Dith Pran famously called the Cambodian "killing fields."[9]

On April 17, 1975, the Khmer Rouge took control of the entire country when it seized the capital, Phnom Penh. The genocidal reign of its Democratic Kampuchea (DK) regime was officially under way, and it immediately emptied the capital city, driving out approximately 2 million people over three days. Those who did not cooperate faced immediate execution. Pol Pot's goal was to eradicate the very notion of the modern city and move the urban population into a massive indentured agrarian state. His thinking was that, if Cambodia was to achieve its own genuine form of socialism, all vestiges of Western modernity had to be eradicated and the Khmer people had to return to the land. This ideology was often expressed through a temporal reference, with Pol Pot turning back the Cambodian calendar to "year zero." In effect, Cambodia was to start its history over.

During the zero years, from 1975 through 1979, approximately 1.7 million lives were lost, amounting to 21 percent of the Cambodian population.[10] The Khmer Rouge mass-murdered those it accused of being enemies of the revolution for ideological, religious, or ethnoracial reasons: professionals, scholars, teachers, monks, cultural workers, and ethnic minorities were exterminated. Many of those not immediately executed suffered slow deaths in re-education and labor camps. Pol Pot and his inner circle also oversaw the torture and execution of scores of former loyalists who, for various reasons, were accused of betraying the revolution.

Ra's home village of Snoeng, in the northeastern Cambodian province of Battambang, came under Khmer Rouge control in early 1975, shortly before the official rise of the DK regime. Ra witnessed firsthand the Khmer Rouge expropriating land, compelling labor, and wantonly persecuting those it perceived to be out of line. The regime described these acts as liberatory and valorized most of the inhabitants of Ra's village as "base people"—those who, owing to their peasant backgrounds and "pure" Khmer heritage, were natural supporters of the revolution. (Indeed, during the late 1960s, Battambang was the site of several important peasant uprisings that, although organized independently of the Khmer Rouge, proved a boon for Pol Pot.) Base people were said to be superior to "new people." These were city residents who arrived late to the revolution and whose loyalties were suspect.

Still, as Pol Pot's victory over Lon Nol became imminent, the Khmer Rouge grew increasingly irrational and violent even toward the base people. Shortly before the fall of Phnom Penh, some members of Ra's extended family were persecuted, having been falsely accused of crimes. Ra recalled the fate of an uncle, killed by Khmer Rouge officials who claimed that he had helped fellow villagers conceal their educational backgrounds from the regime. According to Ra, her uncle had extended an act of solidarity to these overly educated villagers, and this was a crime punishable by death.

> They killed him so that nobody can trust each other. You don't even trust yourself—you don't have your own mind about things. To survive the Khmer Rouge, you have to pretend you know nothing, to lose your mind. . . . But once they kill somebody from your family, then you really lose your mind.

Throughout most of the zero years, Ra was assigned to a unit that distributed medical supplies across several farming cooperatives.

In this capacity, she was able to check in on friends and neighbors. People that Ra had known her entire life were now unrecognizable, ghosts of their former selves. They had suffered cruelties they dared not speak of, and many had witnessed the murder of loved ones. Ra considered herself fortunate. None of her immediate family members had been killed, and she continued to live with her parents. However, in the spring of 1978 she was suddenly torn from her home and forced into a Khmer Rouge–arranged marriage with Heng, a complete stranger. Under the regime, Cambodians were not allowed to choose their own partners, so virtually all marriages were arranged by the state. Ra, only twenty at the time, had known that she could be selected for such a union but was still devastated. She contemplated either running away or accepting imprisonment, but her father warned her that she would be killed if she failed to go through with the marriage and she would be putting the rest of her family at risk—the Khmer Rouge would not hesitate to punish her loved ones if she resisted.

> *I had six brothers and one sister. My mother died when I was sixteen, a year before the Khmer Rouge took over my village. I eventually lost five of my six brothers. Only one of my brothers and my one sister and father are alive today. But I never saw the Khmer Rouge kill any of my family. One brother died as a child before the Khmer Rouge came. A second one died when he was electrocuted in an accident when working with his cooperative. Then another one was killed after 1979 during the fighting between the Khmer Rouge and the Vietnamese. He was killed in the war. A fourth brother died after he became very ill from being in a Thai prison for a long time. He had lived in Thailand after the war and got into trouble. When he got out [of prison], he was very sick and died in 1999. Then in 2005, my youngest brother was killed by a landmine. The landmine was left over from the war.*

To Ra, that she did not witness the murder of any of her immediate family members was important. It gave her some hope, allowing her to envision a possible future after "Pol Pot time." It also gave her some resolve as she entered her forced marriage with Heng. According to Ra, she was following orders that would keep her family alive. "I think they would kill my father, brothers, and sister if I said no; they would kill them that night."

In June 1978 Ra and Heng were married in a Khmer Rouge ceremony that included several couples who also were strangers to each other. Immediately after, she was sent to live with her new husband. Separated from her family for the first time in her life, she grew despondent. Each day she appeared more like the fellow villagers she no longer recognized. Before she slipped further into depression, however, the zero years reached a critical turning point, one that took her from her homeland.

Vietnam invaded Cambodia on December 25, 1978. Its stated goal was ending Pol Pot's atrocities as well as Khmer Rouge attacks on Vietnamese territories.[11] Between 1977 and 1978, Khmer Rouge military offenses in Vietnamese communities along the border had resulted in thousands of Vietnamese casualties. Yet there was no single, clear-eyed explanation for Hanoi's decision to go to war. As historian Stephen Morris argues, the invasion was driven by a combination of factors, including: Hanoi's overestimation of Cambodia's strength under the Khmer Rouge (which Morris refers to as a political culture of paranoia that afflicted Vietnamese and Cambodian communists alike); the rivalry between communist superpowers China and the Soviet Union (the former backed the Khmer Rouge; the latter, Hanoi); and Vietnam's desire to consecrate its military and political dominance in the former Indochina.[12] Within weeks of its invasion, the Vietnamese army toppled the DK regime in Phnom Penh, and by January 17, 1979, had installed the People's Republic of Kampuchea (PRK), led by Heng Samrin, a former Khmer Rouge official who had defected to Vietnam in early 1978.

The genocide had come to an end, but Pol Pot and the Khmer Rouge were far from vanquished. Khmer Rouge cadres were ordered to abandon their strongholds and retreat deep into the western countryside, taking captives with them. In late January 1979, Ra and Heng were rounded up in a group of several hundred villagers and taken into the surrounding forests of western Cambodia. They remained under Khmer Rouge control for nearly a year before finally escaping into Thailand. After three months in the Sa Kaeo UNHCR holding center, they were moved to the Khao-I-Dang refugee camp, where they spent four and a half years before resettling in the United States. During these years, the Khmer Rouge regrouped along the Thai-Cambodian border, rebuilding its strength and waging protracted guerilla warfare against the Vietnamese and the PRK. Once again, the United States was among Pol Pot's most influential supporters.

The 1965–1973 U.S. bombing of Cambodia solidified the Khmer Rouge's power. America's ongoing support of the regime after it was ousted by the Vietnamese similarly allowed Pol Pot's army to remain a relevant military threat in the region well into the 1980s and 1990s. The United States, the United Kingdom, and China, along with the Association of Southeast Asian Nations (ASEAN), denounced the Vietnamese invasion and continued to recognize the exiled DK regime as Cambodia's legitimate government despite being fully aware of its atrocities.[13] The United States was determined to curb Vietnamese hegemony at all costs, and this meant supporting the Khmer Rouge in fighting the Vietnamese-backed PRK. Indeed, throughout his term President Jimmy Carter aided Khmer Rouge fighters marooned along the Cambodian border while the CIA advised Khmer Rouge leaders from outposts in Thailand.[14] The United States' most public support for the Khmer Rouge came at the United Nations in 1979 and 1980, when President Carter twice voted for the DK to hold on to the Cambodian seat in the General Assembly. Remarkably, he cast his votes while referring to Pol Pot as the "worst violator of human rights in the world."[15]

Carter managed the contradiction of his anti-Vietnam foreign policy and his commitment to human rights using a two-pronged strategy. First, he asserted that all U.S. support to anti-Vietnamese forces in Cambodia was being channeled to a coalition of political factions that excluded the Khmer Rouge. Ample evidence that this was untrue has since emerged.[16] Second, he turned his administration's attention to a massive Southeast Asian refugee resettlement program, which he hoped would legitimize the United States as a leader in a new global humanitarian cause and simultaneously obscure its ongoing relationship with Pol Pot. For Carter, the figure of the refugee proved useful in answering the political quandaries of U.S. foreign policy.

Making the Refugee at the United Nations

In 1951 the United Nations adopted the Convention Relating to the Status of Refugees. Responding to the postwar European refugee crisis, in which thousands had fled fascist governments and their violences, the convention established a universal definition of refugees and outlined the obligations of asylum-granting nations to them. Refugees were now defined as individuals who cross national borders to escape persecution in their home countries. Only after crossing can they apply for asylum in either the country entered or a "third country of asylum." The success or failure of the asylum application hinges on whether not the refugee can successfully prove that he or she experienced persecution based on one of five criteria: race, religion, nationality, membership in a particular social group, or political opinion.[17] Moreover, the persecution had to come from the legitimate government of the individual's home country, not from an individual, family, or small group. In setting these criteria, the United Nations sought to distinguish refugees from economic migrants who cross national borders to escape poverty or seek better opportunities and who are not eligible for asylum. It also sought to differentiate the oppressors from the oppressed, given that war criminals often flee the scene of their crimes and embed themselves among those who are legitimately fleeing.

Although the convention's main goal was to protect universal human rights, the United States used it selectively to enforce an anticommunist Cold War agenda. Almost all of the 250,000 refugees granted asylum in the United States between 1956 and 1968 came from communist countries; fewer than one thousand came from noncommunist countries.[18] This practice was bolstered by the 1967 United Nations Protocol on the Status of Refugees, a supplemental measure aimed at expanding the reach of the convention to include recently decolonized states. As the focal point of the Cold War shifted to the Third World during the 1960s and 1970s, those fleeing communist regimes were often granted refugee status while those displaced by U.S.-supported regimes were denied.[19] Asylum thus became a key political tool that the United States used to demonize communist governments and celebrate those that were capitalist and/or anticommunist.

Ironically, Cambodian genocide survivors did not originally meet UN refugee standards as long as their asylum claims focused exclusively on persecution by the Khmer Rouge, because in the view of the most powerful nations on the UN Security Council—the United States, the United Kingdom, and China—the Vietnamese invasion and occupation of Cambodia were illegal acts of communist aggression. In this rendering, only those facing persecution by the illegitimate Vietnamese-installed PRK had an asylum claim. As Sucheng Chan notes, Khmer Rouge members, not those they tortured, were defined as the real refugees: "If the UN definition of 'refugee' were taken seriously, then the only persons who would have truly qualified as refugees with respect to the [PRK] Heng Samrin government would have been the Khmer Rouge."[20]

Nevertheless, President Carter and then President Ronald Reagan were determined to resettle Cambodian victims of the Khmer Rouge. The challenge for Carter's administration was to acknowledge the UN definition of "refugee" but work around it, which required emphasizing the general suffering rather than the specific histories that produced it. The shift from the specific to the general was evident in the political discourse leading up to the signing of the historic 1980 U.S. Refugee Act.

The 1980 U.S. Refugee Act

On March 17, 1980, Carter signed the Refugee Act into law. As an amendment to existing immigration legislation, its main provisions were threefold: (1) to increase the maximum number of refugees annually admitted from 17,400 to 50,000; (2) to align U.S. immigration law with the UN's Protocol on the Status of Refugees; and (3) to establish an Office of Refugee Resettlement (ORR) to oversee a comprehensive and uniform resettlement process.

In making his case for the act, Carter took pains to emphasize that the United States had a moral and political obligation to all Southeast Asian refugees because they faced a common persecution by communist governments that U.S. forces had failed to defeat. However, this assertion required that his administration lump Cambodian with Vietnamese, Laotian, and other asylum seekers who were said to be fleeing an undifferentiated Southeast Asian communist scourge. The Refugee Act abstracted Southeast Asian refugees from their precise national and ethnic contexts in order to justify a common political rationale for their resettlement in the United States.[21]

In constructing the deserving Southeast Asian refugee, Vice President Walter Mondale went so far as to liken them to victims of German fascism. During the 1979 UN conference in Geneva following the massacre at Mount Dangrek on the Thai-Cambodian border, Mondale urged world leaders to take up the cause of Southeast Asian refugee resettlement by recalling a similar conference that had taken place on Lake Geneva exactly forty-one years before. In 1938, thirty-two nations convened at Evian to discuss the resettlement of Jews from Nazi Germany and Austria. This was the international community's opportunity to act decisively before full implementation of Hitler's final solution. "If each nation at Evian had agreed on that day to take in 17,000 Jews at once," Mondale asserted, "every Jew in the Reich could have been saved."[22] Instead, those nations refused to act and "failed the test of civilization." Mondale implored the 1979 group "not [to] re-enact their error. Let us not be the heirs to their shame."[23]

According to Mondale, the Southeast Asian refugee was to be rescued from an old form of tyranny, the kind that once invoked Aryan supremacy to justify its conquest of Europe and the extermination of Jews. By equating the victims of the Third Reich (those whom we failed) and the Southeast Asian refugees (those who can redeem us), Mondale summoned a usable past—one in which the United States was featured as the main protagonist against global fascism—to foreclose any discussion on how the United States had generated the Southeast Asian refugee crisis to begin with.

Mondale's performance in Geneva is emblematic of what Cathy Schlund-Vials terms the "Cambodian syndrome," which has afflicted every U.S. president since Carter. She characterizes this syndrome as the "syncretic collapses of two distinct U.S. foreign policy moments"—the moment in which the United States gave rise to the Khmer Rouge and the moment in which it condemned its atrocities—which Schlund-Vials says is carried out in a "transnational set of amnesiac politics revealed through hegemonic modes of public policy and memory."[24] However, in selectively choosing which part of the past to remember and which part to forget, Mondale also narrated the future: He positioned the United States as the leader in a new global humanitarian effort of refugee resettlement. Standing before his counterparts in Geneva, the vice president stated that the United States would more than "do its part" in the resettlement of Southeast Asian refugees. Refugee resettlement in the United States was a matter of American largesse, not redress.

Following Geneva, the Thai government began its six-month open-border policy with Cambodia. Hundreds of thousands of refugees poured into Thailand, flooding the Sa Kaeo camp, where UN workers found themselves entirely unprepared. The site became a public health catastrophe, with journalists and refugee advocates pointing to the overcrowded, disease-ridden holding center as yet another example of how the world was failing the refugees.[25] The Carter administration seized on this as an opportunity to focus on the overall suffering of Southeast Asian refugees, promulgating the narrative of Cambodian refugees sacrificing everything to escape communism only to remain on the brink of death in UN camps because the international community was failing to act.[26] His underlying message was that the United States was compelled to save these refugees. In November 1979, First Lady Rosalynn Carter visited Sa Kaeo, and images of her cradling sick Cambodian infants made headlines around the world.[27] Four months later, the Refugee Act was signed into law, having received unanimous support in the U.S. Senate.

Refugees from Vietnam, Cambodia, and Laos represented the largest refugee resettlement program in the history of the United States. Indeed, some experts have suggested that the Southeast Asian refugees who resettled in the United States following the passage of the Refugee Act were the "largest non-white, non-Western, non-English-speaking group of people ever to enter the country at one time."[28] This major historical event was made possible by Schlund-Vials' Cambodian syndrome and other forms of state-sanctioned amnesia and selective memory, as well as by moral and affective claims of suffering that lumped Khmer Rouge genocide survivors in an unspecified lamentable communist "situation." Cambodian refugees were thus enlisted to serve several political agendas at once. For some, refugee resettlement restored the United States' global stature as a beacon of freedom. For others, it offered political vindication, justifying the much-maligned U.S. intervention in Southeast Asia. For still others, it was an opportunity to apply continued pressure on communist regimes.[29]

Despite these clear political motives, I do not suggest that the concern expressed by U.S. leaders for the rights and freedoms of Southeast Asian refugees was merely hypocritical. Certainly, there were some politicians who took the cause of human rights seriously and who genuinely believed it was the responsibility of the United States to deliver freedom to those living in the refugee camps, particularly genocide survivors. However, this notion of a "genuine" concern for rights and freedoms—the seeming opposite of political opportunism—demands scrutiny. What exactly does this freedom entail? What does it mean for the refugee to be the recipient of this freedom?

Liberal Warfare

In conceptualizing the post–World War II refugee, Hannah Arendt famously wrote, "The concept of the Rights of man based on the supposed existence of a human being as such, collapsed in ruins as soon as those who professed it found themselves for the first time before men who had truly lost every other specific quality and connection except for the mere fact of being humans."[30] Here she argues that, for the stateless subject, there are no such things as universal and inalienable rights—rights attributable to the "mere fact" that one is human. Indeed, when confronted with the stateless subject, governments cannot describe what exactly those rights are. Arendt suggests that human rights are a fallacy because they are always constructed and mediated by the nation-state itself.

Building on Arendt's argument, Giorgio Agamben proposes that, when the nation-state asserts its power to grant something like human rights, it simultaneously asserts its power to suspend them. That is, nation-states claim the power to determine who will be part of a political-juridical order of the nation and who will be stripped of all legal and political identity and status, cast into what Carl Schmidt refers to as the "state of exception."[31] According to Agamben, this is the very meaning of sovereignty: the exclusive power of the state to decide who is granted ascension to normative political life and who is relegated to the "bare life" in the state of exception.[32] From here, Agamben proposes that "the refugee" is constructed by the state as the subject who inhabits the state of exception, the figure poised to have rights restored. In this way, she at once protects and threatens to expose the "the original fiction of sovereignty."[33] The refugee protects this fiction by serving as the figure to be saved, thus upholding the illusion of universal rights and freedoms that exist independent of the state. She threatens to expose that fiction when the violence carried out by the state—often with the goal of securing the rights and freedoms of a population—inevitably produces more of those (non) subjects who stand outside of rights and legality.

Related to Agamben's argument is the concept of liberal warfare. This is war carried out in the name of delivering human rights and freedoms—including the right to peace. Indeed, according to Michael Dillon and Julian Reid, war is the precondition of a liberalism that cannot conceive of "its own global project of emancipation" without it[34] because "the practice of liberal rule itself becomes profoundly shaped by war."[35] In *The Gift of Freedom: War, Debt and Other Refugee Passages*, Mimi Thi Nguyen claims that the U.S. state's waging of a specific form of liberal warfare in Vietnam made U.S. liberalism globally hegemonic. Even when the United States lost the war, it nevertheless expanded its liberal empire through the waging of war itself. According to Nguyen, although the United States claimed that its war in Southeast Asia was an exceptional event meant to ensure delivery of freedoms to a population subjected to communist rule, war was never the exceptional feature of U.S. liberalism but always the necessary and indispensable one:

> Though liberalism names war as excessive and external to sociality, a violent event believed to happen "out there," liberal war avows an exception. War perpetuates deliberate violence to injure the bodies and properties of a named enemy; liberal war perpetuates violence that it claims is incidental to its exercise of power to free others from a named enemy who is in their midst (giving rise to the computational concept of

collateral damage [italics in original]). Such violence is vital to the genealogy of human freedom.[36]

Here Nguyen highlights two key elements of liberal warfare: (1) the named enemies of liberalism and (2) those said to be only "incidentally" destroyed in the process of being freed from that enemy—that is, the collateral damage of war. From here she shows that, following the official end of the U.S. war in Southeast Asia, Vietnamese refugees continued to serve both these functions of liberal warfare. On the one hand, they were routinely hailed as those to be saved from the enemies of U.S. liberalism, those who must remain forever indebted to the United States for the gift of freedom. On the other hand, as nonwhite subjects, they remained the collateral damage of unending liberal warfare, who in a society structured by racism were viewed as entirely expendable.[37]

Nguyen's radical reconceptualization of the Vietnamese refugee in relation to U.S. liberalism presents us with a generative way of understanding the Cambodian refugee in relation to the U.S. state after passage of the 1980 Refugee Act. If the act sought to make Cambodians the subject of liberalism, how do we now understand refugee resettlement not as a postwar measure or peacetime effort but as an act of liberal warfare? The enemies in this war are any number of parties who, at any given moment, conveniently serve to justify "interventions" on behalf of suffering Cambodians. As we have seen and will see, this enemy can take the form of a monolithic communism, of a timeless fascism, or of the racialized and criminalized captives of the U.S. hyperghetto. This rendering of the act invites a reconsideration of the seemingly contradictory policies, actions, and discourses that led to its passage and implementation. The selective memory and erroneous declarations about Cambodia and Cambodian refugees as apotheosized by Mondale's affective claims in Geneva can lead to the conclusion that Cambodian refugees were merely used to carry out ulterior motives: to justify new military interventions, to pressure Vietnam, to anoint the United States as a leader in a global humanitarian effort. However, through the lens of liberal warfare we see that ulterior motives are irrelevant or, at the very least, unnecessary. That is, we need not argue about whether the Carter administration truly cared for the human rights of Cambodian survivors or if it was only using refugee resettlement to obfuscate U.S. support for the reprehensible Khmer Rouge in its efforts to undermine a more threatening Vietnamese communism. According to the terms of liberal warfare, these two motives are not contradictory.

For the refugee, this implies that the moment she is said to cross into freedom—the moment in which the state claims to save her—is simultaneously a moment of danger because it is the very moment in which the terms of liberal warfare—violence, captivity, collateral damage—are reinvigorated. Thus, the unending nature of liberal warfare troubles the terms of transition on which the concepts of refugee "asylum" and "resettlement" are premised. With what certainty do we now speak of the refugee's liberation or her arrival to safety? More significant, how does the refugee herself know and give expression to these supposed turning-point moments?

Refugee Temporality

Ra spoke very little of her actual crossing into Thailand in December 1979. She was a superb storyteller, yet her narrative became remarkably devoid of detail when she approached the scenes in which she finally shed her Khmer Rouge captors and crossed the border. I invited Ra to say more about these moments, to provide me with a fuller account of the difference that crossing made, but she demurred. Thus, my interview notes appear riddled with holes: When exactly was she no longer under Khmer Rouge control? How did she convince Thai authorities to grant her entry into the refugee camp? My research seemed incomplete without this essential information. Over time, however, and with Ra's guidance, I began to understand that these apparent gaps in my pursuit of narrative completion were in fact indicators of continuity. Ra did not offer a clean recitation of past and present and the thresholds in between because they did not do justice to her sense of time and place; that is, they did not affirm her knowledge that with each apparent crossing her captive status was renewed.

Taken hostage by the Khmer Rouge following the toppling of the DK regime by Vietnamese forces on January 17, 1979, Ra and Heng traversed the forests of western Cambodia for approximately eleven months before she and others in her group finally crossed into Thailand to enter a UNHCR refugee camp. By then she had given birth to her first child Rann in October 1979. Throughout her time in the forests, Ra considered herself a Khmer Rouge prisoner, but her exact status at any given moment was ambiguous. She was by turns a hostage, a compelled laborer, and a reluctant follower who relied on her captors for survival. There were no clear dates to demarcate one state of captivity from the next:

> The Khmer Rouge controlled the entire group. We were the workers. We set up the camps, found food, and cooked for them. If another army attacked the Khmer Rouge, we would get killed in the fighting, too. There was no way [for enemies] to know who was Khmer Rouge and who was not. Heng's job was to transport food and the cooking supplies. I gathered food and cooked. This was a very difficult time. A lot of people died of illness and starvation. I saw dead bodies everywhere—even children. You didn't know who killed them or how they died. It was so bad that I didn't even care about the Khmer Rouge. I just wanted us to survive.

As Ra's time in the forest wore on, the grip of the Khmer Rouge soldiers began to loosen. Lacking provisions and reinforcements, the soldiers grew weak and desperate, susceptible to illness, starvation, and the occasional landmine. By the fall of 1979, they could hardly keep themselves, let alone their captives, alive. When Ra, Heng, and their newborn crossed into Thailand in December 1979, they were no longer held at gunpoint, but Ra claimed that they were never actually released because the Khmer Rouge soldiers were always close at hand. Many of them even crossed into Thailand with their erstwhile captives, disguising themselves as asylum seekers. Their attempts to blend in with other survivors required little subterfuge because they also appeared wounded and gaunt, indistinguishable from the masses.

According to Ra, there was no singular event—no turning point—that brought her captivity under the Khmer Rouge to its decisive end. One day in early December 1979, Ra and the remaining survivors of her group decided that it was time to cross the border. Never again would she step foot in Cambodia.

> *We decided it was time to go. We had stayed in the Cambodian border area for a long time. But there was no food, so many people were sick and I was afraid of the [anti–Khmer Rouge] forces on the border. I did not know what they would do to us. The whole time on the border we were afraid of being attacked. I think this is also why the Khmer Rouge tried to hide among the people. They didn't want to be attacked. Eventually our only choice was to cross into Thailand to stay alive. But some of us were more scared of the Thai soldiers. They can kill us, too. But there was no choice. We had to cross because the situation was so bad in Cambodia.*

Ra did not view her border crossing as deliverance into freedom. If, on crossing into a nation of asylum, the refugee is supposed to feel a moment of liberation, that moment never arrived for her. Instead, she described her crossing as uneventful. As soon as Ra crossed, she was immediately remanded to the Sa Kaeo refugee camp before being transferred to Khao-I-Dang, where she learned that her safety was far from guaranteed and that her captivity was ongoing. She found the Thai soldiers to be cold, if not outright cruel, and she sensed that neither the UN workers nor those attached to private humanitarian organizations (known as voluntary agencies or "volags") who processed asylum applications were in a position to check the authority of the Thai military.

Although Ra entered the Khao-I-Dang camp in January 1980, she and Heng were not interviewed for asylum until April 1983, long after many of those who entered with them had been interviewed and sent off for resettlement. The reason for the delay was Ra's original intention to go back to Cambodia. She was hopeful that the wars would soon end and that she would be reunited with her father and siblings. Ra recalled being asked by volag workers if she preferred to be resettled in Australia, France, or the United States. Her answer was "None."

Ra's initial decision struck some of her peers as foolishness and ingratitude because she and her family were among the lucky ones who had gained official entry into the UNHCR camp. The unlucky ones had been denied entry or had been removed from a camp for being "illegals." Thai forces routinely rounded up those in Khao-I-Dang who were suspected of being unauthorized, shipping them off to one of eight border camps that were governed by disparate and at times warring Cambodian factions, including the Khmer Rouge. Cambodians in these camps were slated for repatriation; they had little to no chance of permanent resettlement in a third country of asylum. Ra recalled witnessing heartrending scenes of families being separated after one or more members had been identified for removal.

"How could they possibly know?" Ra asked, referring to the Thai authorities who removed and transferred these refugees. Indeed, only the most cynical differentiated those who were granted official entry and those who entered without authorization. Most understood that the distinction was arbitrary. (The Northwest Bronx Cambodian community consists of both "official" and "unofficial" refugees, but this has never been a point of distinction among residents.) Moreover, bribery was commonplace, and, according to Ra, those rounded up and removed were likely those unable to pay off Thai soldiers.

The exclusion or removal of fellow refugees from Khao-I-Dang did not make Ra feel fortunate so much as certain that that there was no true safe haven, that those who claimed to ensure her safety could act just as arbitrarily as the forces she had fled from. Underscoring her ambivalence toward her ostensible saviors was the asylum process itself. Ra knew of refugees whose applications to the United States had been rejected even though their stories were identical to her own. Meanwhile, she knew that the United States had approved the applications of former Khmer Rouge soldiers who had lied about their pasts.

Still, Ra eventually came to the realization that her return to Cambodia was untenable. As her time in Khao-I-Dang wore on, the fighting in Cambodia continued. In Ra's assessment, the situation in the borderlands seemed to be getting worse. *Everyday you heard it: boom, boom, boom,* she said, referring to exploding mortar bombs and landmines. *By 1983, I knew that I could never go back to Cambodia.* Also, because she was now pregnant with her fourth child Rorth, she began to realize how difficult it would be for her to survive in war-ravaged Cambodia with four small children, even if the conflicts abated. "*I changed my mind. I realized that I could never bring the children back into Cambodia. It was too dangerous.*" Ra and Heng finally decided to go ahead with the asylum interview.

According to Ra, by the time they were interviewed, their only realistic opportunity for resettlement was to the United States, which had yet to fulfill its Cambodian refugee resettlement quota. The application process went as follows: the State Department contracted with the volags—known collectively as the Joint Voluntary Agency (JVA)—to conduct an initial interview with the asylum seeker. The JVA prepared a file on the applicant that was reviewed by a representative of the U.S. Immigration and Naturalization Service (INS). The INS field worker conducted a second interview with the applicant and made a final decision on whether or not he or she was admissible under U.S. immigration law.[38]

As Ra and Heng prepared for their first interview, they worried that the approximately eleven months they spent in Khmer Rouge captivity after the Vietnamese invasion would be scrutinized by their JVA interviewer. Because they feared that the interviewer would assume that they were members of the Khmer Rouge, not its captives, they decided to lie, saying that they had not been under Khmer Rouge control following the Vietnamese invasion, that they had made it to the border with a group that was politically unaffiliated, all the while avoiding the skirmishes between the various Cambodian factions.

On the day of their interview with the JVA, however, Ra noticed that Heng was extremely anxious: "*He was afraid of being caught in a lie.*" Knowing that they would be interviewed separately, Ra worried that Heng would crack under pressure:

> *They interviewed Heng first. I sat a few yards away in an area with Rann, who was about five years old. From there I could see Heng's face. He looked too nervous. At that moment I knew our story would not work. I knew it was a big mistake to lie.*

She made split-second decision:

> *I told Rann to go over to her father and tell him not to lie. I said to Rann: "Tell your father that mommy says to tell the truth.*

Tell him mommy says, 'If you fail the interview, then you fail. But don't lie.'"

But Rann refused to relay the message, so Ra incentivized her: "*Rann was eating a candy bar, so I said to her, 'If you go over to your father and give him the message I will buy you another candy.'*" Rann agreed (although to this day she insists that she was eating ice cream, not candy) and delivered the message. Rann recalled what happened next:

I walk over to my dad and I say, "Mommy says don't lie. If you *fall*, then you *fall*." My dad looked mad confused. He didn't know what I was saying. So I said it again: "Mommy said tell the truth and don't lie. If you fall down, you fall down." All of a sudden the translator busts out laughing. The white man interviewing my dad didn't know what was going on and he told the translator to tell him what I just said.

Ra picked up the story:

The interviewer says to Heng, "Ok, you're wife says tell the truth, so tell the truth." Heng then told the truth and so did I. When it was my turn to interview, the interviewer said to me, "You seem like people who want to be honest." So I think he wrote us a good report.

Ra's experiences of the camp and the asylum process reaffirmed what she had learned about arbitrary power under the Khmer Rouge: such power can never release, much less liberate, the refugee. Each time she was called before a given regime that determined she was worth saving while others were not, Ra knew that she was merely being transferred from one state of captivity to the next.

I term this knowledge *refugee temporality*. It is how Ra knew and gave expression to the persistence of past forms of power under seemingly new conditions. In this way, it also names how Ra knew and gave expression to unending liberal warfare: her recurring enlistment as one to be simultaneously saved and incidentally injured by the violence carried out in the name of human rights and freedom.

Refugee temporality challenges those who insist on the trans-figurative power of crossing the border. It calls to account dominant representations of Southeast Asian resettlement in the United States as caesura: whereas the refugee was once subjected to certain death, she is now officially granted the ascension to life—both literal and biopolitical. Refugee temporality challenges us to keep time with Ra in a different way. To illustrate this challenge, I turn to a scene from one of my interviews with Ra in 2009.

"Why didn't you run from them?" I asked her, considering the ever-deteriorating state of the Khmer Rouge. To gain a more detailed ac-count of Ra's final days with the Khmer Rouge, I wanted to know why she stayed with them for as long as she did. Why didn't she and others escape at the first opportunity? Ra asked me where I expected her to go: abandoning the group would have diminished her chances of survival; she would likely have starved to death within weeks or been attacked by bandits. She had been part of a survivor group that included fellow villagers she had grown to depend on as well as dying Khmer Rouge soldiers. She had found herself bound to them out of necessity, if not by gunpoint.

Ra's rejoinder to me was a serious one. She wanted to know not so much where but *why* I wanted her to have run. I responded by sug-gesting that the Khmer Rouge soldiers would never have granted her freedom; they would sooner have killed than released their captives. By escaping she could have restored a modicum of control over her life, even as she faced other imminent threats. Ra found my emphasis on self-deliverance vexing. I asked her if I was being naïve. No, just "strange." The premium I placed on her escape came across as a non sequitur. She didn't quite know where it was coming from or what to do with it. *Why did I want her to run?* Why was I invested in the refugee's clean break, even if she herself had deemed it untenable and irrelevant?

My exchange with Ra invokes Walter Benjamin's assertion that "a historical materialist cannot do without the notion of a present which is not a transition, but in which time stands still and has come to a stop."[39] Here Benjamin suggests that the desire for escape belongs primarily to the scholar. I needed it more than Ra did to make sense of her story, but she refused to grant me this indispensable transition, even if my stated intention was to represent her resilience at each new interval. My intention was an inaccurate reading of power, one that failed to account for how she experienced her captivity as one long interval—as a present that was never a transition but a long pause. Moreover, such a reading failed to account for how her captivity extended into the new conjuncture: her Bronx unsettlement.

2

Housed in the Hyperghetto

On May 26, 1986, Ra, Heng, and their five small children boarded a commercial flight from Manila to the United States. As Cambodian refugees, the family had spent the preceding four years in Khao-I-Dang, the largest of three UN international refugee camps in Thailand near the Cambodian border. In January 1986, the U.S. State Department approved Ra's request for asylum. Following a nearly year-long processing phase in the Philippines, the family made their way to the Bronx.

During a long layover at Los Angeles International Airport, Ra and her family were subjected to an additional set of clearances. For Ra, this latest screening was the last in a long line of them in Asia, and it followed the same pattern. Ra knew that the best way to clear nation-state processing was to ask few questions. She quietly produced for the gatekeepers all of the paperwork given to her during her processing in the Philippines. These documents included a "Statement of Understanding" issued by the American Council of Voluntary Associations (ACVA), the collective body of nongovernmental organizations, many of them national religious groups such as Catholic Charities. These organizations had been contracted by the State Department to serve as national sponsoring agencies to determine where in the United States to resettle the refugees approved for entry. The Statement was translated into Khmer, but Ra, who is semiliterate in her native language, was unable to read it. It contained the following line: "I will accept the initial housing arrangement provided for me and my family."

Having passed her final clearance, Ra was directed to a group of volunteers who were there to offer the refugees a reassuring word, advice on what to expect and what to avoid, and some clothing and dry goods. To Ra's surprise, these volunteers were Cambodians. It was evident to her that they had been living in the United States for some time: they spoke English and dressed like westerners.[1]

One volunteer, on learning that Ra was headed for New York City, rummaged through a bag of used clothes searching for winter coats. "New York is ice," she said in Khmer and insisted that Ra take the coats. That this was late May was beside the point. Until that moment, Ra had been surprisingly calm about crossing into the United States, but the worker's insistence made her anxious. Ra ordered her entire family to put on the coats before boarding a connecting flight to New York City's John F. Kennedy Airport. It was 80 degrees on the runway in Los Angeles that day, but as the plane taxied for takeoff Ra's family sat warmly bundled. One of her children began to complain, but Ra only tugged his zipper higher. The family sweltered through a nearly six-hour flight.

Sitting in her Bronx living room twenty-two years later, Ra laughed as she retold the story. Her grown children rolled their eyes, but before long managed to chuckle with their own memories of that day. "We had on big winter coats and flip flops," said one of her teenage sons. A robust sense of humor is an enduring characteristic of Ra's family. It has long sustained Ra in particular, helping her to survive two decades of Bronx unsettlement. However, the jokes began to sour when Ra revealed what happened in the months immediately after they landed in New York.

Ra and her family were placed in a two-bedroom apartment in the Northwest Bronx, one that few local renters would ever consider. As their first summer and fall gave way to the colder months, those donated winter coats in fact proved to be their only reliable protection against the elements. It was not the external climate but the internal housing conditions that posed the gravest challenge. During long stretches of winter, they had no heat or hot water because the building's owner refused to pay for fuel. Meanwhile, missing windowpanes kept frigid air circulating indoors. There was a moment when Ra seriously considered building an open fire in the apartment. As it happened, an electrical problem beat her to it. Soon after moving in, Ra noticed that an electrical outlet in her living room was emitting sparks. She told the landlord, who ordered a maintenance worker to obstruct the outlet with a sofa. Soon after, the sofa caught fire and flames quickly spread through the living room. The family evacuated unscathed, but their few possessions were ruined. Only eight months into their U.S. resettlement, they were once again displaced people. This was the first of many Bronx displacements to come.

I open with this story to illustrate the continued violence, uncertainty, and itinerancy that Ra and other Cambodian refugees experienced after being granted asylum and resettlement in the United States. Ra's multiple housing displacements during her initial years in the Bronx trouble the linear narrative that describes refugee resettlement: from captivity to rescue to freedom. Rather than being granted repose, Ra was delivered to a new site of liberal warfare: the hyperghetto. As discussed in the Introduction, Loïc Wacquant defines hyperghettos as inner-city neighborhoods that warehouse the poorest of the urban poor, particularly the Black subproletariat—those who, since the late 1960s urban insurrections, have been stripped of virtually every opportunity for livable-wage work. Cast aside by the state and by private capital as the permanently unemployable, residents of the hyperghetto are deemed worthy only of captivity. In this way, the hyperghetto reinstantiates forms of captivity and punishment endemic to U.S. slavery.[2]

Throughout the 1980s and 1990s, record numbers of new immigrants from around the world arrived in postindustrial cities in the United States, but only Cambodian and other Southeast Asian refugees resettled en masse in hyperghettos. We might say that they were the lone "new immigration" event to these urban communities where a new form of war, one genealogically linked to U.S. slavery, was being waged against those whose poverty and unemployability was criminalized and pathologized—those rendered as the irredeemable "underclass." And just as the refugees were once enlisted to play a specific role in the U.S. war in Southeast Asia, so they were enlisted as the hyperghetto's "exceptional" captives.

From One War Zone to Another

"When we first went to visit the refugee families at 193rd Street, the conditions were horrible," Blanca Ramirez recalled.[3] "There was no heat, no hot water. The windows were broken. It was freezing and you could see your breath in the air. It was like nothing I had seen before." In 1982, while Ra was living in Khao-I-Dang refugee camp, Ramirez was a housing organizer with the Northwest Bronx Community and Clergy Coalition (NWBCC), which was organizing Bronx tenants victimized by housing abuses, habitability violations, and bank redlining.[4] Ramirez was among the first to reach out to the Cambodian refugees who began arriving in the winter of 1982. She said that the properties the refugees were told to move into were "on the trouble list." Local organizers and Housing Preservation and Development (HPD) workers considered these buildings to be among the most derelict in the neighborhood.

"Who would be crazy enough to move into one of his buildings?" Ramirez asked her colleague. "I'm not sure," the colleague replied, "something about refugees from Thailand." While Ra was waiting to find out if she would be granted asylum in the United States, Ramirez was working with several Cambodian refugee families whose housing path Ra eventually followed on her arrival in 1986. Before long Ramirez learned that the refugees had no choice in selecting their new homes.

The ACVA organization assigned to Bronx Cambodians was responsible for the refugees' initial housing arrangements and for helping them to find employment and register their children for school. The federal Office of Refugee Resettlement (ORR), which was created as a provision of the Refugee Act, provided the funds for the ACVA to carry out these tasks. The ACVA subcontracted with local affiliate organizations (which I refer to as local resettlement agencies) that did the actual work of finding apartments and negotiating directly with landlords. According to Ramirez, the local resettlement agencies did this expeditiously, without prescreening apartments. They simply found buildings with the cheapest rents and multiple vacancies and moved the refugees in. Ramirez recalled her initial observations:

> I remember the first refugee apartment I visited. They had nothing. An entire family sharing mats in the middle of the living room floor. That was all the furniture they had. The rest of their belongings—clothes, some supplies—were neatly stacked against the wall. The first question that came to my mind was, Okay, you're from a war. But why come here? That's when I learned that they had been placed here by an agency. I mean, here we are—Blacks and Latinos—just trying to survive this crazy situation, and somebody thought to place them *here*? I recall an African American tenant saying to me, "Hey, that building was abandoned! Now they got Chinese people from the war moving in. What the hell's going on? Look, if they could put people from a war in *here*, then this world is a bad, bad place."

According to Ramirez, many local residents expressed compassion for the refugees (even though they showed little understanding of their nationalities), but they were bewildered by the refugees' arrival in the hyperghetto. They could hardly fathom why any government or private resettlement agency would decide to move those from war zones and refugee camps into these neighborhoods in crisis. Indeed, the residents of the Northwest Bronx had been living through a war of their own, one rooted in two kinds of conflagration: the Bronx arsons of the 1970s and the urban insurrections of the late 1960s.

Throughout the 1970s, arsonists set fire to buildings in the southeastern section surrounding the Bronx's once bustling industrial zone.[5] These fires begat more fires, and before long an epidemic took hold that destroyed much of the South Bronx's housing stock. From 1970 to 1980, some South Bronx areas lost up to 80 percent of their housing and population.[6] As the conflagrations spread northward, many Northwest Bronx residents feared that they were next in line and some began to flee the area.[7] Bronx tenants claimed that these fires were set by corrupt landlords for an insurance payout on buildings they no longer deemed profitable—abandoned and dilapidated properties that in the owners' views could not be turned around because of the intense poverty and crime that gripped the South Bronx. Landlords in turn blamed criminal elements in the neighborhood or brazen tenants who set fires to their own apartments to take advantage of a city program that promised to find them better housing if they had lost their home because of arson. As writer Jill Jonnes notes, city officials did little to stop the epidemic, rejecting numerous proposals offered by community leaders to deincentivize the arsonists.[8] Few landlords were criminally prosecuted for setting fire to their properties.

As neighborhood after neighborhood succumbed to the devastation, the Bronx became the national symbol of urban decline. Images of its charred buildings and whole city blocks reduced to rubble were ubiquitous. Over two weeks in August 1973, Charlotte Street was the site of a staggering fifty-six fires in twenty-two buildings. Local firefighters described the 1970s as the "war years."[9] On October 5, 1977, President Jimmy Carter, in New York City for a UN General Assembly meeting, paid a visit to the South Bronx. Standing amid the burnt-out buildings and mountains of rubble on Charlotte Street, he compared the scene to the bombed-out city of Dresden, Germany, in World War II. (Significantly, Carter was in New York City to sign two UN Covenants on Human Rights.)[10]

But the war that Bronx residents were experiencing was real, not metaphorical. Indeed, it was indelibly connected to the veritable warfare that had taken place in hundreds of U.S. cities in 1967 and 1968, when massive Black insurrections forever changed the fate of urban America, setting the stage for the hyperghetto. The state's response to these uprisings was militaristic: it called for ghetto dispersal and clearance measures derived from U.S. counterinsurgency efforts in Southeast Asia. As it happened, these strategies only exacerbated the Bronx arson epidemic, giving rise to hyperghettos.

In the two decades following World War II, Black residents took to the streets protesting poverty, segregation, and racial violence perpetrated by both white residents and urban police forces. By the mid-1960s, major cities such as Rochester, Philadelphia, and Los Angeles were beset by massive street protests, looting, the burning of public and private property, and violent confrontations between Black residents and police in what at first appeared to be sporadic incidents of unrest. By summer 1967, however, it was clear that a full-scale Black insurrectionary movement had taken hold as nearly two hundred eruptions shook cities throughout the country. Another outbreak in the spring of 1968 followed the assassination of Dr. Martin Luther King, Jr.

Although some reactionaries dismissed these events as senseless rioting among the hopeless and disorganized, the federal government recognized the wave of unrest in 1967 as nothing short of domestic warfare. At the urging of state governors, President Lyndon B. Johnson authorized the National Guard to occupy eight major U.S. cities where local and state forces had been unable to bring the insurrections under control.[11] The images of warfare were unmistakable: National Guardsmen pointing bayonets in the faces of Black marchers in Cambridge, Maryland, and firing shots at unarmed Black civilians in Newark; armored vehicles rolling down the streets of Detroit.

In response to the events of summer 1967, Johnson established the Kerner Commission to identify the root causes of the insurrections and develop recommendations for the prevention of future disturbances. The commission issued a final report critiquing U.S. structural racism that persisted despite the 1964 Civil Rights Act and calling for robust social welfare programs, massive job creation, and reforms in municipal policing.[12] Considering these recommendations to be a political betrayal by commission members (several of whom he had directly appointed), Johnson dismissed virtually all of the report's findings.[13] State and municipal governments followed suit, and so few if any of the transformative economic and social programs outlined in the report were undertaken. Indeed, the only ideas from the report that seemed to gain any traction with city officials were the ones in the concluding chapters relating to counterinsurgent measures.

One key recommendation called for the dispersal of large Black populations to avoid future insurrections. The reasoning was that urban unrest resulted from high geographic concentrations of African Americans and that, if these concentrations were broken apart, urban Black communities would lack the numbers and positioning they needed for insurrectionary activity. Although this overlooked other conditions that gave rise to unrest—including the political conscious-ness of a given community as well as its heterogeneity—the strategy nevertheless pointed to an incontrovertible fact.[14]

According to writer Joe Flood, the section of the commission report that focused on Black dispersal was drafted by Anthony Downs, a researcher who had previously worked at the RAND Institute.[15] RAND, a private research group, had been founded shortly after World War II to bring "order and rationality" to U.S. military endeavors through statistical analysis and game theory (developing mathematical formulas to weigh, analyze, and anticipate hitherto un-predictable human behavior).[16] With the U.S. invasion of Vietnam, its influence reached new heights in the development and rationaliza-tion of counterinsurgency tactics that would guide the U.S. strategic bombing raids, herbicidal warfare, and the relocation of populations.[17]

By the late 1960s, RAND had turned its sights to domestic issues, positioning itself as the think tank that could solve America's seem-ingly intractable urban dilemmas, including urban unrest. Downs, a researcher in RAND's new urban division, advocated the disper-sal of the Black ghetto as well as public and private divestment from Black neighborhoods to accelerate abandonment in already troubled areas.[18] Abandonment would in turn justify razing these neighbor-hoods once and for all. City officials euphemistically described these abandonment and divestment strategies as "planned shrinkage." Is it any coincidence that the RAND-inspired logic of planned shrinkage was strikingly reminiscent to that of the "search and destroy" tactics used by the U.S. military? Indeed, U.S. forces in Vietnam eviscerated troubled areas before quickly abandoning them; the goal was to kill the enemy and then destroy rather than rebuild their strongholds so that hostile forces could not reoccupy them. That RAND played a key role in Southeast Asian counterinsurgency and urban American postinsurrection research reveals the clear connections between U.S. liberal warfare abroad and at home.

The call for strategies of ghetto divestment and abandonment re-turns us to a discussion of the Bronx arson epidemic of the 1970s. According to Flood, during the 1970s Downs' proposals were carefully studied and championed by New York City housing commissioner

Roger Starr, who was responsible for developing proposals on the future of South Bronx neighborhoods devastated by arson. Specifically, Starr favored the withdrawal of "economic support from housing units that ought to be demolished. . . . Whole neighborhoods of high-school-district size would be demolished."[19] This partially explains both the city's failure to prevent the arson epidemic and its reluctance to reinvest in and rebuild neighborhoods the fires had destroyed. Once a neighborhood was deemed beyond saving, the city officials opted to accelerate the devastation and abandonment, thus incentivizing ghetto dispersal and demolition. Here, again, the terms of warfare in the hyperghetto exceeded mere metaphor.

As discussed in Chapter 1, collateral damage is a necessity of war, and the destruction of the Bronx proved no exception. Before the South Bronx neighborhoods targeted by planned shrinkage were completely destroyed, they continued to burn, and city officials called upon the fire companies of the nearby Northwest Bronx to extinguish these enduring flames. With their resources already stretched thin, firefighters were unable to respond quickly enough to fires in their own catchment, and many feared that the Northwest Bronx would see its own arson epidemic. This was the precarious context of the resettlement of Southeast Asian refugees, whom we might consider the collateral damage of U.S. counterinsurgent measures in Southeast Asia.[20]

The Organizer and the Refugees

Blanca Ramirez grew up in the shadows of the South Bronx fires, which most Americans viewed only on the television news. However, she "smelled the burning each morning, as I walked to school." A child of Puerto Rican migrants, Ramirez stood out among her South Bronx peers for having gained admission to a prestigious college. She "made it out," leaving the ghetto behind for an idyllic upstate campus. Four years later, however, with her bachelor's degree in hand, Ramirez chose to return to the Bronx as a community organizer: "Like a lot of young people, I wanted to live out my ideals. When I found out about community organizing, I knew this was the best way to do it."

The young organizer's idealism was immediately tested as the South Bronx arsons threatened to spread throughout the Northwest

Bronx. In her first stint as a community organizer in 1981, Ramirez was responsible for forming tenant associations in the most precarious buildings—properties that many feared could burn at any moment. Beginning in 1982, Southeast Asian refugees began to arrive and were assigned to these buildings. "I was absolutely shocked by the racism of it all," Ramirez said, recalling her initial visits to the refugee families. "How were the refugees going to fight for their rights? They had just arrived from war. Nobody spoke any English. But on their first day here, somebody had already figured out a way to take advantage of them."

She was referring specifically to landlords who maximized revenues by drastically reducing, if not outright eliminating, repair and fuel expenses because they saw the consequences of violating tenant habitability rights as preferable to defaulting on bank loans or taxes. Landlords made repairs only when housing court judges threatened them with fines or the transfer of property management to a third party. However, tenants were required to initiate such court action and attend lengthy judicial proceedings. Landlords knew full well that the vast majority of their renters possessed neither the time nor the resources to do so. This was especially true of recently resettled refugees. The apartments rented out to this group were especially egregious, riddled with the building's worst code violations. In Ramirez's opinion, these were units that would never be rented out to an established tenant.

According to Ramirez, the landlords' disregard for the refugees was reprehensible but hardly surprising. As a South Bronx tenant turned housing organizer, she was well aware of what property owners in the borough were capable of. She was taken aback, however, by the negligence of the resettlement agency that had placed the refugees in those uninhabitable units in the first place. She couldn't fathom how resettlement workers could so woefully fail the refugees who had been assigned to their care. "If they had just done their homework—if they had just come up once to see these units—then maybe a lot of these families would have been spared . . . but nobody bothered to check it out."

Even the city's bureaucrats were surprised by the agency's negligence. In 1985, after receiving repeated complaints, the New York City Department of Housing Preservation and Development (HPD) called for a meeting with tenants, the resettlement agency, and Ramirez and other community organizers. One HPD official spent much of the meeting excoriating the resettlement agency for placing the refugees in dilapidated buildings. According to Ramirez, "the official . . . looks directly at the [resettlement agency] representative and says to him, 'What the hell were you guys thinking?'" In its defense, the agency claimed that it had tried to keep refugee families close together to ensure that the newly arrived were not dispersed. Instead of scattering families into separate buildings throughout the Northwest Bronx, it had placed them into a few empty buildings. Of course, those vacancies had only been made possible because previous tenants had abandoned their homes, fleeing the buildings' egregious conditions, but this fact seemed to have been lost on agency workers.

Ramirez assumed that the agency, after its chastisement by the HPD, would be more supportive of her attempts to secure repairs for refugee apartments. Instead, it stymied her efforts to hold the landlord accountable. When Ramirez and her organizing team decided on a rent strike to force the landlord's hand, it looked to the agency's social workers for support. During the refugees' first resettlement year, the local agency paid their monthly rent directly to the landlord. Thus, without the agency's support Ramirez could not make the refugees part of the strike. Not only did the agency refuse to cooperate but its social workers persuaded refugees that the strike was not in their best interest and could mean eviction. One social worker finally told Ramirez, "Look, the Cambodians are living okay with the situation. They don't have the same problems [as the Black and Latino tenants]. The Cambodians don't want trouble."

On the one hand, it was a remarkable statement considering that the Cambodian tenants were living in the most precarious units—a fact never in dispute. On the other hand, the social worker's words and actions came across as a routine example of how Asian immigrant groups, cast as model minorities, were used to delegitimize claims of racial and economic injustice made by African Americans and Latinos. Model-minority representations cast Asian immigrants and Asian Americans as self-sufficient and industrious subjects who, unlike Blacks in particular, found ways to make ends meet even under the most difficult conditions without calling for redress or support from external parties. The assertion that Cambodian tenants did not have the "same problems" as African Americans and Puerto Ricans fell into line with this thinking.

However, in considering the war that was taking place in the hyperghetto, I question whether minority explanations fully account for the role that the refugees were enlisted to play. In the liberal war taking place in the 1980s hyperghetto, the agency social worker neither denied nor overlooked that refugees were experiencing hardships. She was not portraying them as some kind of success story in the hyperghetto. Her assertion that refugees did not "have the same problems" was not an objective evaluation of the conditions under which they were confined; rather, it was an expression of her deeply held belief that refugee suffering in this war should not be equated with the suffering of the hyperghetto's longstanding residents. She was suggesting that refugee suffering belonged to another time and place, that it was indeed "exceptional."

Refugee Exceptionalism

During the 1980s, reports of racial tensions between Southeast Asian refugees and established Black residents were common across the nation. In Houston's Allen Parkway Village public housing complex, Black tenants challenged the city housing authority's decision to "steer" Southeast Asian refugees to the complex, believing that it was a deliberate attempt to undermine tenant organizing.[21] Similarly, in New Orleans's Village d'Lest apartments, Black tenants protested a local Catholic Charities agency placement of Vietnamese refugees in this predominantly Black housing site without first consulting residents.[22] In some cities such as Philadelphia, resentments led to violent encounters as Black residents attacked Vietnamese and Cambodian newcomers.[23] Similarly, in Richmond, California, tensions ran high between the city's Black residents and the approximately 10,000 Laotian refugees who had been resettled in the area throughout the 1980s and 1990s.[24] Eventually, Southeast Asian and Black residents in cities such as Richmond and New Orleans overcame their conflicts and formed multiracial coalitions to address the common inequalities they faced.[25] However, during the initial years of refugee resettlement, the relationship between African Americans and refugees in poor neighborhoods was more often than not a difficult one.

During the 1980s and 1990s, racial divisions were exacerbated by popular and scholarly representations of a Black urban "underclass"— a term wielded by journalists and scholars as code for deviant behaviors and the "culture of poverty" among Black urban residents, particularly those of the hyperghetto, who were said to be at the root of chronic Black unemployment and criminal behavior. "Underclass" thus encoded the political shift from a discussion of structural inequality to one of "personal responsibility" and in so doing named new enemies of liberalism: the chronically unemployed and unemployable subjects of the hyperghetto. Southeast Asian refugee resettlement was often cast in contrast to underclass life. Refugees, although suffering some of the harshest conditions of U.S. urban poverty, were hailed as those who would eventually make it out of the hyperghetto, unlike their underclass neighbors. Several sociological studies conducted during the 1980s captured this sentiment, insisting on the inevitability of refugee economic self-sufficiency and adaptation to Anglo-American cultural norms.[26] When coupled with the tensions on the ground between Blacks and refugees, sociological research left little room for any discussion of ways in which refugees and African Americans might forge solidarities.

A decade after passage of the 1980 Refugee Act and the subsequent arrival of Southeast Asian refugees to U.S. hyperghettos, these predictions of refugee self-sufficiency proved false. The 1990 Census showed that Cambodians, along with Laotians and Hmongs, were among the poorest ethnic groups in the nation and that their average welfare participation and unemployment rates surpassed those of African Americans. Indeed, by the mid-1990s few could convincingly argue that model-minority status any longer applied. Here I agree with anthropologist Aihwa Ong, who, in *Buddha Is Hiding*, argues that journalists and policy makers in the 1990s began removing Cambodian and Laotian refugees from the model-minority category, separating them from "ethnic Chinese immigrants from Hong Kong, Taiwan, and China along with Vietnamese immigrants."[27]

Having been cast out of the model minority, where were these Southeast Asian refugee groups figured by hegemonic racism? That is, what was their new racial location? In Ong's assessment, Cambodians and Laotians were racialized as a "new underclass." Specifically, she claims that they were subjected to an "ideological blackening, in contrast to the whitening of Vietnamese and ethnic Chinese immigrants."[28] However, the terms of this blackening are unclear in Ong's rendering. On the one hand, she appears to equate blackening with a range of low-wage laborers mired in working poverty because they have few skills to succeed in the primary labor market. Among these are "Ethiopians, Afghans and even other Central Americans."[29] On the other hand, she uses blackening to refer to the way in which Cambodians and Laotians are associated, along with poor African Americans, with high unemployment, welfare dependency, and teenage pregnancy rates because of their "location and isolation in inner-city neighborhoods."[30] In making the case for a blackening of the refugee, Ong conflates two very distinct racial formations.[31]

Notwithstanding these conceptual dilemmas, Ong's analysis leads me to question how a blackening of this sort—the making of a new underclass out of refugees—was possible under the terms of liberal warfare in the hyperghetto. In other words, how was it possible for refugees to suddenly become the enemies of liberalism?[32] Were they now being targeted for dispersal, divestment, planned shrinkage, and other war tactics? Allow me to return to Mimi Nguyen's definition of liberal warfare as violence that claims to be "incidental to its exercise of power to free others from a named enemy who is in their midst."[33] I argue that in the Northwest Bronx and other hyperghettos of the early 1980s, Black (and to varying degrees Latino) tenants were targeted as the primary enemies of liberalism, to be dispersed by planned shrinkage or punished for staying behind in hollowed-out ghettos. Southeast Asians were inserted into this site of liberal warfare as those who should be rescued from it, as those deserving of freedom. To grant liberal warfare's continuance, however, their rescue could never be realized. Instead, the refugees were continuously positioned as collateral damage—those "incidentally" injured in the war to rescue them. Specifically, they were held in derelict housing conditions so that they could be targeted for a rescue that could never take place, a fictive rescue that justified liberal warfare. These and other forms of ongoing urban captivity rendered talk of a model minority irrelevant, but this did not mean that Southeast Asian refugees were subjected to the same forms of vilification and ridicule that were directed at the putative underclass.

Refugees were subjected to an alternative set of practices that I term *refugee exceptionalism,* which is a process whereby refugees were rendered as those necessarily *in* but never *of* the hyperghetto. More precisely, and in keeping with the notion of collateral damage, this distinction describes how refugees were subjected to violence that was said to be incidental to the cause of delivering them to freedom. In this way, refugee exceptionalism can only conceive of refugees as temporary inhabitants of the hyperghetto, as those who, decades after resettlement, continue to be framed as newcomers who are only passing through, momentarily caught in the crossfire of urban warfare. Put another way, refugee exceptionalism proclaims the long-term provisional status of refugees paradoxically as a way to carry out permanent forms of violence against them. To illustrate how refugee exceptionalism took shape in the Northwest Bronx, I turn to the first years of Ra's resettlement, which were marked by a series of housing crises and displacements.

Passing Through

Ra and her family arrived in the Northwest Bronx in May 1986, four years after Ramirez attempted to organize Cambodian tenants in one of the area's most troubled buildings. Ra's first apartment, the one that caught fire, was on University Avenue and 183rd Street, a section of the Northwest Bronx where only a small cluster of Cambodian refugees were settled. At first she felt reluctant to move into the apartment because few other refugee families lived in the building and she feared being removed from the vital networks that she believed would sustain her.[34] Then, too, lacking English proficiency and confused by the rental market, she had little hope of locating a place on her own. Landlords' continual refrain, "first month's rent and deposit upfront," seemed nonsensical to her. She knew that she was not free to act on her own, outside the resettlement agency's purview; in addition to arranging her housing, the agency controlled the rental payments that went directly to the landlord. It also dispersed stipends granted by the Office of Refugee Resettlement and processed welfare applications and recertifications.

After the fire, Ra felt she had no other option but to turn to the resettlement agency for help in her search for a new apartment. In July 1986, the agency placed her seven-member family in a basement apartment on the corner of Fordham Road and Andrews Avenue, a Cambodian community hub. Although this second home was more spacious than the first, the habitability problems were no less severe. Most longstanding Bronx tenants were unwilling to rent a basement apartment because of the potential for flooding, the proximity to the building's trash collection, and the absence of sunlight. However, Ra was desperate to find a new home as quickly as possible. Meanwhile, the agency assured her that the situation was temporary—that she, along with other recently resettled refugees, would not be staying in these apartments for long. Ra convinced herself that her family could make the most of it, and she took comfort in being close to other Cambodian families along Andrews Avenue:

> Andrews was a very hard place to be. The apartments were run down and small, and there was a lot of garbage everywhere. But there were also a lot of Khmer people. A lot of people from Khao-I-Dang and Battambang. I was happy to see so many Khmer people. But it was also hard to see how poor they were. It looked like everybody was struggling a lot.

What the resettlement agency claimed would be a temporary stay on Andrews Avenue turned into three years. The family endured the basement apartment and all that came with it: the rodents, the stench of trash, and the backflow of sewage water during storms. Ra quickly learned about Bronx slumlords, and knew that very little in her apartment would be voluntarily repaired. She recalled that in the Thai camps refugees were on their own, and each family had to create a habitat out of a space allotment. This rule seemed to apply in the Bronx as well. Ra's landlord did just enough maintenance to avoid government fines and legal action.

Concurring with Ramirez's assessment from years earlier, Ra claimed that the resettlement agency did nothing to hold the landlord accountable. It suggested to her that fighting was a waste of time and that she and others were better off spending their time looking for work and attending English classes:

> *Nobody helped us. The resettlement agency put us in the apartments and that was it. They never talked to the landlord. Once you moved in, you had to deal directly with the landlord and the super. You had to fight for yourself. The resettlement agency never said anything about our housing situation. The only thing they said to us was "apply for welfare" and "apply for a job."*

The agency's message was clear: the sooner Ra found gainful employment, the sooner she could leave her poor housing situation behind. This was despite the fact that most of Ra's Black and Puerto Rican neighbors were unemployed and living on welfare while piecing together whatever odd jobs they could find in the throes of an economic recession. In the agency's view, none of these conditions applied to Ra and other refugees; somehow, they were expected to achieve economic independence when all external economic conditions made self-sufficiency unlikely, if not impossible. To fulfill the expectation that they would be the exception to the rule meant that refugees had to attend job-training programs that were completely ineffective (as proven by the federal government's own longitudinal data). It also meant that they had to avoid confrontations with landlords, who could easily evict a troublesome tenant.

Ra was determined to get the landlord's attention, however. Her life in the camp had taught her the value of being boisterous, of being the type of captive who harangued administrators at every turn. So, drawing on what little English she possessed, she regularly launched into tirades about even relatively minor problems: clogged drains, broken doors, cracked windows, a broken toilet seat. When it suited her (or when she simply ran out of relevant things to say in English), she upbraided the landlord in Khmer even though he didn't understand a word of what she was saying. The landlord tried to dismiss Ra, blaming her for her own housing troubles. "You have too many children," he said. "They climb up on things, break everything. Why must you have so many kids?" That he chose this tack indicated to Ra that she had met her objective; she had found a way to frustrate him: "I wanted to stay in his ear to make sure if I have a real problem he has to deal with it." The strategy proved effective. The landlord made repairs if only to silence her. Ra was often surprised by her success, considering how little leverage she commanded. She had stepped out of the role of refugee who was said not to have the same problems as other tenants and who did not want trouble, and her transgression proved materially beneficial.

Still, the more serious housing problem that Ra had feared eventually occurred and she and her family were once again displaced. The constant pipe leaks had eroded the ceiling over her apartment and eventually a large section fell into her living room. The damage was so extensive that Ra didn't bother to ask for repairs but decided to find another apartment. As she packed her belongings, the landlord arrived to assess the damage. She asked him, "Did my children climb up there and break the ceiling, too?"

The agency helped Ra secure her third apartment, a one-bedroom on Valentine Avenue near 196th Street in a building that housed many of the first Cambodian families to arrive to the Bronx in 1982. Like the building that Ramirez had attempted to organize, this one was notoriously run down. Again, the resettlement agency intimated that in time her situation was bound to improve, but Ra felt the exact opposite to be true. The building was known for being one of the poorest-kept properties in the neighborhood, one that only the most vulnerable refugee families were compelled to live in. The move to Valentine Avenue was a clear step back. Ra had been in the United States for nearly four years, but her third relocation made her feel as if she were starting all over again.

The family lived on Valentine Avenue for just over four years, during which time Ra gave birth to two more children. In that apartment, too, rats terrorized the children at night and the lack of heat and hot water during the winter was unbearable. However, another form of violence was taking shape along their street that was more lethal than anything they had experienced in their previous two stops. Ra's stretch of Valentine Avenue was an open drug market. One summer day, when Cambodian tenants were gathered on the vast stoop for fresh air and socializing, a group of young men had a heated argument in front of the building. As the argument escalated, those on the stoop fearfully retreated into their apartments. Within moments shots were fired. From their apartment window, Ra and her children watched in horror as a young man, pleading for his life, was murdered by a group of assailants. Ra's son Rith, who was only seven at the time, recalled the scene: "They took bats to him and broke him open. They killed him in the street, in front of everybody." Three weeks later, Ra and her family moved out.

With each housing displacement, the resettlement agency failed to move Ra and her family to another neighborhood with better housing and less violence, and merely relocated them to the next vacant apartment in the same troubled area. Each placement seemed only to renew Ra's captivity in the liberal warfare that was the hyperghetto. However, those handling Ra engaged in refugee exceptionalism, telling her that her situation was only temporary, that the hardship of the Northwest Bronx was only a stop along the way to something better. To be sure, many Cambodians left the Bronx, but most did not find improved situations. They only moved laterally to other hyperghettos throughout the Northeast—Philadelphia, Providence, Lowell.

Many of those who stayed in the Bronx continued to live in the derelict apartments in which they were originally resettled. Others, like Ra, simply moved from one substandard apartment to the next within the same two square miles. All told, the Cambodians of the Northwest Bronx experienced no economic mobility even as the resettlement agency, landlords, and other keepers of the hyperghetto over three decades consistently hailed them as perpetual newcomers on the verge of something else, as those only passing through.

During the late 1990s, when I began working as a community organizer in the Northwest Bronx, I advocated for Cambodian refugee families in the very same buildings that Ramirez had attempted to organize over a decade earlier. I helped Cambodian tenants file complaints against building owners who were guilty of numerous habitability violations. The landlords accused me of being an interloper, an agitator. Echoing the social workers that stymied Ramirez's organizing efforts, they referred to Cambodian refugees as their "new tenants" who, unlike the longer established Black and Latino tenants, had never given them trouble until now. They seemed unable to fathom that the Cambodian tenants had been living in their buildings for over fifteen years, but they did not cast them as model-minority "strivers." The landlords knew full well that the Cambodians were not economically mobile. If they preferred Cambodians over African Americans and Puerto Ricans, it was because the newcomers were impoverished Third World subjects who made slum buildings solvent again; they paid the rent and rarely complained about the poor housing conditions they endured. This made them valuable not as model minorities but as continuous captives who did not transgress into hyperghetto status. In keeping with the terms of refugee exceptionalism, the Cambodian refugees constantly renewed their status as those who were only *in* but never *of* the hyperghetto.

The consistency with which numerous agents practiced it over several decades points to refugee exceptionalism's vast discursive power. It was not limited to the conscious actions of these agents as they attempted to meet certain political and economic ends. Rather, social workers, social scientists, and landlords were also drawing on and in turn reinforcing an implicit body of knowledge—what Michel Foucault refers to as a knowledge/power regime—that produced the refugee subject. As a community organizer, I noticed how refugee exceptionalism as subject-producing discourse was carried out in philanthropy: foundations that supported our work insisted that the poverty, joblessness, and poor health of Southeast Asian refugees were matters of immigrant "adaptation." In this way, they decoupled these violences from the broader war being waged against all inhabitants of the hyperghetto. Refugee exceptionalism came across similarly in my conversations with neighborhood schoolteachers, who attributed the struggles of their Cambodian students to their newcomer status (even though many of these students had been born in the Bronx). The suggestion was that the Cambodian students' poor grades and high dropout rates had little to do with the general assault on inner-city public education.

The discourse of refugee exceptionalism was particularly pronounced in the mainstream media's coverage of the Bronx Cambodian community. Since the mid-1980s, the *New York Times* has been one of the few major newspapers to periodically cover the borough's small Cambodian enclave.[35] A cursory review of some of its articles from 1994 through 2012 reveals the consistent representation of the Cambodian residents as perpetual newcomers to the Bronx hyperghetto. In October of 1994, the *Times* ran a profile of Bronx Cambodians in which Sister Jean Marshall, director of a local assistance group known as St. Rita's Refugee Center, gave her assessment of how long it takes a refugee to finally feel settled: ". . . between 10 and 15 years for a Southeast Asian refugee to become a nonrefugee," and she attributed this length of time to the various economic, cultural, and social obstacles that refugees must overcome.[36] According to Sister Jean's timeline, by 1994 the earliest refugee arrivals had either already transitioned to nonrefugee status or were on the cusp of doing so.

In 2000 the *Times* published another profile of the community that suggested that the refugees were nowhere near shedding their refugee past. "Children of the Killing Fields" focused on Cambodian teenagers, noting that "these young people also face a host of distinctive problems . . . [and] few community groups exist to help out new arrivals."[37] However, it had been eighteen years since the first wave of Cambodian resettlement in the Bronx, and most of the teenagers interviewed had been either born or raised there. Although they knew little to nothing of life in Cambodia or the Thai refugee camps, their problems were framed as those of newcomers, distinct from those of established residents. Even as late as 2012—thirty years after the arrival of the first wave of Cambodians to the Northwest Bronx— another *Times* piece commented that refugees were still struggling to "strike a balance between adopting American customs and holding fast to values from home."[38]

In these and similar *Times* articles, the refugees are frozen in time. Indeed, over three decades they are continually in a state of *arrival*; they are not allowed to be anything other than the hyperghetto's recurring newcomers. In this way, the articles are consistent with social workers' and landlords' insistence that refugees neither have nor create the problems of African Americans and Puerto Ricans, who are figured as the hyperghetto's long-term and intractable problem. At the same time, these articles refrain from casting refugees as model-minority paragons of liberalism. Instead, they appear as captives who must be repeatedly saved from the named enemies of liberalism: the postinsurrectionary underclass. Here, once again, the Cambodian refugees are enlisted as the collateral damage of liberal warfare.

"Somebody Is Always in Charge"

I asked Ra if she held the local resettlement agency ultimately responsible for her long-term housing troubles. After she left Valentine Avenue in 1990, she endured several more housing displacements over the next fifteen years.

"The refugees always pass through somebody's hands," Ra said dispassionately, "somebody is always in charge." Although she believed that the agency acted carelessly in its placement of refugee families, this didn't surprise her. In her view, the agency was merely the latest in her long string of handlers. She underscored this point by insisting that she could have joined other Cambodian families who moved out of the Bronx to hyperghettos in other Northeastern cities, but she chose not to. She failed to see that a move would make a difference.

This response bore a striking resemblance to her description of her final days under Khmer Rouge captivity. Ra and Heng stayed with their captors even when the soldiers no longer had either the strength to hold them or any interest in doing so. The couple simply had nowhere to run and had a better chance of surviving in the forests by sticking with their group of erstwhile captives and captors. Only when the couple saw an opportunity to cross safely into Thailand did they officially break from the Khmer Rouge. They were never liberated or delivered to safety. Instead, they were remanded to camps for the next six years. In telling this story, Ra was emphasizing that her captivity was never limited to a given regime or to its actors.

"Somebody is always in charge," she repeated. Not "The Khmer Rouge are always in charge" or "The soldiers are always in charge" but "somebody." They may be soldiers, UN humanitarian workers, the resettlement agency, social workers, landlords, welfare case workers, or, indeed, academic researchers. "Somebody is always in charge" was Ra's catechism, and it followed her into Thailand, where Thai military forces maintained control over the camps, often deporting or executing refugees, and it continued as the United Nations decided the fate of hundreds of thousands by establishing arbitrary standards to distinguish legitimate asylum seekers from economic refugees. Ra's catechism named the armed syndicates that controlled the informal economies operating along the Thai-Cambodian border and in the Thai camps. Then it traveled with her to the United States and would, Ra was certain, continue in the future. She felt it in the landlord's role as a keeper of the captive space, in the way in which the resettlement agency insisted that her woeful housing situation was temporary when all along Ra knew better.

In Chapter 1, I described the refugees' present that is unbroken from the past as refugee temporality. Refugee temporality names the knowledge system informing Ra that as she passes from one regime/handler to the next, as she is uprooted from one home and moved to another, an old and familiar power is being reinscribed. We might say that these crossings and housing displacements represent the moments in which refugee exceptionalism and refugee temporality converged. Each event reinscribed Ra's status as a captive, simultaneously reminding her that she had been there before. To illustrate this convergence, I return briefly to Ra's stay on Valentine Avenue.

According to Ra, the housing conditions on Valentine Avenue were so bad that she had considered moving out even before she and her children were witnesses to murder. She decided to stay because she appreciated the sense of community, reminiscent of Thai camp life, that the Cambodian tenants had created. Throughout the building, apartment doors were propped wide open as adjacent units were converted into communal space, and hallways, lobbies, and the stoop, neither public nor private, became threshold spheres connected by rugs and straw mats. Neighbors moved freely in and out of each other's apartments. To the passing observer, these arrangements seemed to defy common sense. Here, in one of the most crime-ridden sections of the Northwest Bronx hyperghetto, Cambodian families left themselves completely exposed. As it was, the threat of violent crime inspired these open arrangements, just as it had in the camps.

During the first few years of Cambodian Bronx resettlement, several families had been victims of home robberies. Armed assailants would send a decoy to knock on an apartment door and force his way inside, and others would follow. Once inside, they would hold family members hostage, forcing them to turn over their money and their life's possessions—these were generally jewelry and other heirlooms that they had been able to conceal from their captors at each stage of their sojourn or that they had acquired through the black markets of the camps. During the first years of resettlement, cash was kept in the home rather than in bank accounts. Local police officers implored the refugees to become more vigilant about security, to reinforce their doors and purchase stronger locks, but residents saw seclusion as only increasing the danger. Sealed away from one another—something they had never been in Cambodian villages or Thai refugee camps— each family was more vulnerable to attack.

Ra told me that the refugee camps in Thailand were largely controlled by criminal organizations, some of which had infiltrated her UN camp:

> There was a lot of crime in the camp. Everybody got something stolen. People from the outside were let into the camps and they stole from people and attacked people. I think they got into the camps because the Thai soldiers let them in. The Thai soldiers were corrupt. They got paid from the thieves, and they stole from people, too. Nobody could stop any of this. You just had to be careful and look out for each other.

There was very little that camp residents could do to fully secure their makeshift dwellings from thieves, so they did the exact opposite, living openly and communally to enhance their collective security. By moving freely between each other's quarters, they ensured that no resident was isolated. This practice proved vital in the Northwest Bronx.

One could easily interpret this strategy as a redeployment of earlier refugee survival skills. Much of the resettlement literature cites examples of refugees drawing on past cultural and social practices to survive present-day hardships. Valentine Avenue's spatial arrangements seem consistent with this trope, but such an interpretation is predicated on a clean break between past and present, here and there: Once upon a time, the refugee relied on such skills in her native country; then they were no longer needed on resettlement; now a new set of conditions required their retrieval.

However, Ra offered no indication that she was reaching back. Her captivity in derelict Bronx apartments presented her with conditions of captivity that resonated strikingly with her life in the camps, but she did not consider this a reversal of fortune or a betrayal of what life should have been like after escape. She never spoke of what it is like to *once again* inhabit spaces of violence because there had been no temporal break between past and present.

3

Welfare Resistance

When Ra and other Southeast Asian refugees began arriving in the 1980s, U.S. federal and local resettlement agencies struggled to fit them into existing economic, political, and cultural systems that could not account for them. They were told by social workers to apply for livable-wage jobs that did not exist or that were completely mismatched with the refugees' skill sets. They were also told that welfare programs—specifically, cash assistance and food stamps—were only stopgap measures, and that refugees were expected to become economically self-sufficient soon after their resettlement. However, as their years in the United States wore on (and as federally funded resettlement assistance programs either dried up or were discontinued), chronic unemployment among Bronx Cambodians persisted, and most of the refugees continued to subsist in the welfare state well into the 1990s.

By the fall of 1999, two of Ra's teenage children had joined the Southeast Asian Youth Leadership Project (YLP), and they encouraged Ra to see me about her welfare troubles.[1] YLP recorded the experiences of Southeast Asian refugee families who had been sanctioned and denied their benefits. It discovered that those who attempted to remedy their situations were being misinformed by caseworkers about their rights and due process. Making matters worse was the absence of interpreters at the welfare centers; refugees who did not speak English were unable to make headway.

When I first met with her about her welfare issues, Ra had just received a notice stating that her monthly welfare check would be discontinued because she had failed to properly declare who among her older children were dependents. The household welfare check would be discontinued until Ra brought her case "into compliance."

This was actually the second time in less than a year that Ra had been sanctioned by the HRA. Three months earlier, the HRA had withheld her food stamps, claiming that she had failed to properly recertify for them. "I did the same thing [then] that I do every time. The same exact paperwork," she told me. It was clear that in 1999–2000 Ra had more welfare problems than she had had in her prior fifteen years in the Bronx.

I suggested to Ra that her new troubles stemmed from the recent overhaul of the federal welfare system. President Bill Clinton had signed the 1996 welfare reform laws that radically reorganized and retrenched a modern welfare system in place since the Great Depression. The new federal law targeted poor women in the hyperghetto—particularly young Black women—who were demonized by both Republicans and Democrats as cheats and "welfare queens." They were accused of fraudulently collecting welfare benefits while hiding other income streams and birthing multiple children out of wedlock to augment their benefit checks. These racist and sexist tropes constructed women in the hyperghetto as the undeserving poor; their poverty was attributed to cultural deviance and criminality.

While the 1996 welfare act was designed to target those racialized and gendered as the underclass, refugee exceptionalism did not spare Southeast Asian refugees from its most damaging effects. Ra's experiences are but one example. I proposed that Ra pursue what is called a fair hearing in which she could argue her case before a state administrative law judge.[2] The city would also present its case, but I was confident that Ra's chances for a favorable ruling were good if she arrived with all of her documents in order. The city's representatives were often unprepared for fair hearings because they lacked the time and staff to carefully review every case in advance. They often won on technicalities, relying on mistakes made by welfare recipients who, unfamiliar with administrative law, either failed to bring the proper documentation or presented irrelevant arguments. I insisted that Ra could avoid these common pitfalls, and I would help her.

The more I explained, however, the more Ra withdrew. She wasn't intimidated by the fair-hearing process. She was simply unwilling to invest in what she considered a false negotiation. As example after example had shown her, from the Khmer Rouge soldiers in her village to the Thai military at the border to the aid workers in the refugee camp to the slumlords in the Bronx, those in power acted arbitrarily, withholding her means of subsistence at will. Although Ra would welcome a favorable ruling, she was not convinced that this would diminish the ability of those in power to act with impunity. In fact, she believed that the process only emboldened such power. Ra proposed that I manage the details of the case. In the meantime, she would do what she had always done—keep her family afloat by piecing together what the state was arbitrarily denying her.

U.S.-based community organizers insist that meaningful social change occurs only when the oppressed confront institutional power directly. This confrontation is expressly *political*, distinguishing community organizing from "direct services" programs set up to assist those in need but which fail to challenge the forms of power and systemic inequality that created the adverse conditions to begin with.[3] The assertion of one's statutory rights is considered the crucial first step in community organizing: the oppressed must complete the know-your-rights phase before they can adequately speak truth to power. For this reason, my initial meeting with Ra left me feeling uneasy. By agreeing to her proposal that I take care of the hearing without her participation, was I preventing her from moving from victim of the welfare state to agent of change?

Or was I instead being challenged to question the rigid line between political action and daily survival? In other words, was Ra making a more deft critique than I had initially realized of how state power actually operates arbitrarily? She recognized that the law's purpose was to punish and that this foreclosed fair negotiation, whether at the hands of a craven regime in Southeast Asia or a racist and sexist welfare system in the United States. Ever the consummate organic intellectual, she arrived at her own assessment of what Loïc Wacquant, in his conceptualization of the hyperghetto, refers to as the fusing of the penal and social-welfare wings of the state.[4]

By exploring the ways that Ra and other Cambodian refugee welfare recipients resisted the U.S. state's arbitrary abuses in the wake of the 1996 welfare overhaul, this and the following chapter return to refugee temporality—the refugee's knowledge that her present hardships are a reinscription of her past captivities. In this, Ra and others challenged the periodization of welfare reform as emblematic of a new turn in late capitalism. Scholars and activists often describe welfare reform as the paragon of neoliberal domestic policy in the United States. Neoliberalism indexes a new, transnational alignment of economic and social policies aimed at dismantling the main barriers to an unfettered global free market: organized labor, market regulation, environmental protection, and social welfare. However, as Wacquant notes, welfare's rapid retrenchment worked hand in hand with the expansion of state apparatuses aimed at managing poverty through penal statutes and geographic enclosure in the hyperghetto.

Cambodian refugees in the Bronx like Ra certainly understood this. It came across in the way they referred to the welfare state as a distinct site of captivity, one that welfare organizers' political strategies, tactics, and statutory demands did not often account for. Indeed, what some considered a new neoliberal turn in social and economic policy did not adequately explain Ra's and other refugees' distinct sense of subjection. Were they experiencing a *new* moment in statecraft or merely the continuation of a form of captivity from which they had never been fully released?

Rethinking the Neoliberal Turn

That a Southeast Asian youth program became a welfare advocacy group surprised me. It was not my original intention to become a welfare-rights advocate and organizer. The role grew directly out of my work with neighborhood youth. I was part of developing a leadership program for Southeast Asian refugee teens like Ra's children, to develop their skills as community organizers.

When I asked the youth organizers to identify and mobilize around an issue that commonly affected refugee teens, I assumed that they would pick school reform or juvenile justice—something traditionally youth-focused. Instead, many spoke of their families' sanctioning by city welfare programs and of being pulled from school and other activities to accompany their parents to welfare offices to serve as interpreters and advocates. Before reaching puberty, many of these youths were already adept at filling out welfare applications and explaining the recertification process to their parents.[5] They seemed to take their role in stride and often joked about welfare-office escapades, but their anger was palpable. As long as these teenagers could remember, their families had been subjected to the whims of welfare bureaucrats.

Their families had originally been placed on welfare by local resettlement agencies immediately after their arrival in the Bronx. Following the mandate of the federal Office of Refugee Resettlement (ORR), the agencies insisted that the refugees use welfare only as a temporary and adaptive measure, predicting that they would inevitably secure gainful employment and economic independence. After more than a decade, however, no such jobs had materialized. Refugees remained on the welfare rolls, illegally supplementing their meager monthly checks with a string of informal, off-the-books jobs. The resettlement agencies and the ORR never admitted to the failures of a resettlement program that once boldly predicted refugee self-sufficiency. Nor, in keeping with the terms of refugee exceptionalism, did the state alter its narrative to suggest that Cambodian refugees had become shiftless, unmotivated, or deviant—terms reserved for the vilification and ridicule of Black welfare dependents. Instead, Cambodian and other Southeast Asian families were simply forgotten, left to linger in the welfare state indefinitely. Every so often a refugee family faced harassment from a bureaucrat who claimed that the household was no longer eligible for welfare but, with the help of a bilingual child, managed to keep their benefits. This common routine would undergo a major change, however, with the passage of the 1996 welfare reform law.

Reflecting the new consensus that welfare contributed to social irresponsibility and complacency among the chronically unemployed, the 1996 law was suggestively titled the Personal Responsibility and Work Opportunity Reconciliation Act (PRWORA), and its main provisions were unmistakably punitive. It introduced mandatory work programs known as "workfare" in which recipients were required to work 30 hours a week in no-wage city-approved jobs that took time away from off-the-books jobs; it limited the total number of years for which recipients could receive welfare to five; and it changed the name Aid to Families with Dependent Children (AFDC) to Temporary Aid to Needy Families (TANF). The new law also originally called for the denial of food stamps and Supplemental Security Income to permanent residents, and it tightened eligibility and verification requirements across the board.[6] Local caseworkers in the Bronx and elsewhere were often unsure how to implement the new rules because the federal government allowed state agencies to interpret the provisions in a variety of ways. Confused, misinformed, or simply overwhelmed, caseworkers could easily forget to ask for required papers or request the wrong ones. Either way, recipients like Ra and other Cambodian refugees paid the price in the form of sanctions.

Once the new law went into effect, even before families had reached their lifetime limits or entered workfare programs, many found themselves summarily removed from the welfare rolls. This happened because welfare reform was an exercise in political devolution—"devolution" being code for "state's rights"—which underscored the extent to which welfare's rollback was part of the dismantling of New Deal– and Civil Rights–era entitlement programs.[7] By granting state and municipal agencies wide latitude, the law allowed them to tighten eligibility criteria and create more onerous verification requirements that dropped many recipients from welfare programs, particularly TANF.[8] If a local agency acted precipitously, if it went too far, the burden fell on welfare recipients and their advocates to prove that the original intentions of the federal law had been transgressed.

New York City Mayor Rudolph Giuliani took full advantage of devolution. As the first Republican mayor to govern New York City in twenty-five years, he garnered national attention for how quickly his administration cut the city's welfare rolls in half.[9] In addition to wielding the mandatory workfare requirement as his primary welfare deterrent (a point I elaborate on subsequently), he also sanctioned those who failed to meet the city's strict verification standards. A culture of sanctions soon defined the city's welfare regime in the wake of PROWRA, and this deterred many refugees and others from submitting recertifications and new applications. Welfare recipients were constantly threatened with benefits cuts for failing to provide paperwork: proof of income, utility bills, school records, and medical records. Even when such paperwork was properly and promptly submitted, the recipient was often told that something wasn't quite right, which of course resulted in a sanction.

It was difficult enough for fluent English speakers to advocate for themselves under these conditions. For non-English speakers, the task proved insurmountable. If not for the Cambodian community's bilingual and bicultural teenagers, many refugee households would have been unjustly denied crucial benefits.

One of the first youth organizers to join YLP was Chhaya Chhoum, a seventeen-year-old Cambodian woman whose family had resettled in the Bronx in 1984. At barely five feet tall, she stood out immediately with the latest in mid-1990s hip hop couture and an impeccable Puerto-Rican–inflected Bronx accent. Like many of the Cambodian teens old enough to recall life in the camps, Chhaya was fully bilingual in both Khmer and English, but for one as fully steeped in Bronx youth culture as she, her Khmer was unusually strong. This had much to do with the language skills passed on to her by her mother Sara, who worked full-time for Montefiore Hospital's Indochinese Mental Health Program—the only such program in the city. Sara had studied English intensively during her years in the camps, and by the time she arrived in the Bronx she was one of few refugees over the age of thirty who spoke fluent English. Her bilingualism, combined with her deep solidarity with fellow Cambodian survivors, made Sara a vital community resource. She spent countless hours accompanying friends and neighbors to meetings with welfare caseworkers, medical appointments, and parent-teacher conferences. When Montefiore Hospital decided to create a mental health program dedicated specifically to Southeast Asian refugees, it knew exactly who to hire as part of its counseling team.

Considering what her mother did for a living, one might assume that Chhaya had never had to step foot in a welfare office as an interpreter, but quite the opposite was true. Following in Sara's foot-steps, Chhaya had volunteered her time to help the adults in her community, providing translation for them in a number of settings. Although my efforts must have seemed redundant when I began re-cruiting in her neighborhood, offering teenagers an opportunity to serve their broader community, she was one of the first to join YLP and quickly became a leader.

From the outset, youth organizers such as Chhaya challenged the notion that YLP should organize around "youth issues" such as school reforms and funding for neighborhood youth programs.[10] Instead, they wanted to focus on the economic issues that affected the community at large, recognizing that such matters had a di-rect impact on their own lives. The amount of time many of them were already spending at welfare centers advocating for their par-ents underscored this point. YLP decided to turn its full attention to welfare-rights organizing, and in so doing it moved beyond the narrow purview of youth issues to face head-on a nationwide, cross-generational crisis.

Moreover, YLP joined a movement that was an extension of the Civil Rights, Black Power, and feminist movements of the 1960s and 1970s. The very concept of "welfare rights" had been spawned in 1966 by the National Welfare Rights Organization (NWRO), which had organized nearly 25,000 members—90 percent of whom were Black women—into a movement demanding adequate income as a right, not merely as a charitable state benefit.[11]

According to the NWRO, because capitalism necessitated extreme poverty it was the state's responsibility to establish antipoverty mea-sures. A guaranteed adequate income also would compensate poor women for their unpaid labor in the domestic sphere.[12] NWRO's anal-ysis of racialized and gendered capitalism placed it at the cutting edge of U.S. racial justice and feminist struggles of the time. Dr. Martin Luther King, Jr., drew on its ideas as he developed his poor people's campaign in 1968. We might say that intersectionality politics writ large, emphasizing the inseparability of race, gender, and class op-pressions, owes a debt to the NWRO's theoretical and practical work.

Our group joined a national welfare-rights coalition, Grassroots Organizing for Welfare Leadership (GROWL), which saw itself in the tradition of the NWRO.[13] GROWL developed a national strategy of coordinated direct action against local welfare agencies that were implementing the 1996 welfare reform law in ways that violated recipients' civil rights. Thirty years earlier, the NWRO had pioneered an organizing model that promoted local chapters, providing resources to those on the ground in order to promote coordinated actions across different cities. GROWL adopted a similar model, working with local organizations to implement a national organizing campaign that would expose the most damaging effects of the 1996 law.

YLP began by protesting the lack of translators at Bronx welfare centers. By failing to provide adequate interpreter services, the centers violated federal equal-access laws designed to protect people with limited English proficiency from national-origins discrimination. We challenged New York City's workfare program on similar grounds, arguing that if participants could not communicate with their supervisors, equal program participation was impossible and the program goals fundamentally unachievable. In both instances, our tactics included threatening civil rights complaints, flooding the system with fair-hearing requests, organizing direct action protests, and conducting media exposés.

However, there was a discernable difference between our organizing efforts and those of the NWRO. Whereas the NWRO had spoken of the right to a guaranteed adequate income as a means of redress, our efforts exposed the extent to which refugee welfare recipients were being treated unequally and abusively through federal welfare reform's local implementation. Our efforts were less about restoring Keynesian policy than about "equal access" and the recognition of difference and plurality in the welfare state. What did it mean to demand such things from a state that so readily conveyed its racialized and gendered contempt for the poor and chronically unemployed? Indeed, welfare reform was the coda to nearly three decades of relentless racist and sexist portrayals of the poorest of the urban poor that were embedded in terms such as "welfare queen," "culture of poverty," and of course "underclass."[14] By the mid-1990s, public poverty discourse was so implicitly (and often explicitly) racist and sexist that it left no room for compassionate discussion of the poor, much less for talk of redress.

In light of these conditions, the demand for interpreters seemed only to mask the deeper economic, racial, and gendered violences being carried out through welfare reform. In other words, the focus on interpreters seemed to imply that the "postreform" welfare state had the potential to treat all parties fairly if only it made adjustments aimed at granting everybody equal access as mandated by civil rights. Looked at from that angle, our efforts appeared to conform to a logic in which the state was respected as a redresser of all manner of social and cultural inequalities so long as such inequalities were abstracted from a critique of capitalism and its violent uses of difference (racism, sexism, homophobia, xenophobia). During the 1990s, a key term emerged among labor and community organizers to name this logic: "neoliberalism."

Neoliberalism generally describes new global economic and social policies, driven primarily by the United States and Western Europe, that guarantee global capitalism's unimpeded growth. From the 1970s onward, the hallmarks of neoliberalism have been market deregulation, privatization of public resources and public space, an assault on organized labor, and the dismantling of the welfare state.[15] In carrying out these measures, neoliberal regimes avow the language of equality for all: because unfettered market growth is said to grant every sector of society an equal opportunity to accumulate resources, to improve its quality of life, it follows that neoliberalism must simultaneously disavow the statutory discrimination of difference, specifically that based on race, gender, ethnicity, or religion (sexuality has been left largely unprotected by the neoliberal regime). This disavowal is precisely what distinguishes the expansion of the U.S. empire through liberal warfare: the protection of supposed universal rights and freedoms that serves as justification for the state to carry out all forms of violence—often against those it claims are the subjects of such rights and freedoms.

In the late twentieth century, the neoliberal assertion of equality often took the form of multiculturalism, the celebration of ethnoracial difference accompanied by calls for legal nondiscrimination against minority groups. In some instances, multiculturalists advocated special state protections for certain groups to ensure their equal treatment and inclusion, but under the neoliberal regime such protections must steer clear of the market because the market is said to be neutral. Multiculturalism as policy and practice can only conceive of "culture" when it is abstracted from the political economy; as soon as issues of race, gender, and sexual difference are coupled with a critique of capitalism's dependency on the exploitation of difference, these issues lose their status as cultural categories to be celebrated and protected.

As Lisa Lowe notes, this splitting of culture and capitalism is the very *raison d'être* of multiculturalism during neoliberal times: it "asserts that American culture is a democratic terrain to which every variety of constituency has equal access and in which all are represented, while simultaneously masking the existence of exclusions by recuperating dissent, conflict, and otherness through the promise of inclusion."[16] In other words, within the multiculturalist frame, the assertion of difference—including a dissident's call for a specific set of group rights—can immediately be re-presented as reinforcing hegemonic claims about the unwavering promise of American plurality and inclusion.

To what extent, then, did our efforts at asserting language accessibility rights for Southeast Asian refugees actually reinforce the very power we sought to challenge? Was our campaign for interpreter services at welfare centers merely a call for inclusion, a piece of the neoliberal multicultural pie, that foreclosed a critique of the fundamental, irrevocable racism and sexism undergirding welfare reform? These challenging questions had to be posed, even if they did not jibe well with community organizing's daily exigencies. To a certain extent, YLP could put off the challenge by arguing that our efforts were aimed only at holding on to whatever remained of the welfare safety net, that we were biding our time to wage a more comprehensive fight down the road. However, this line of argument failed to account for the fact that, in "winning" our short-term demands we actually bolstered the welfare regime we sought to resist.

As it happened, Ra and other Southeast Asian refugee welfare recipients—many of them the mothers of the youth organizers—felt ambivalent about YLP's demands. Even as they participated in the YLP campaign, testifying about the abuses they experienced or protesting on the front lines, I often sensed that their activism had less to do with a firm investment in our specific demands than in their desire to engage in some form of collective dissent. Moreover, their political critique had little to do with the neoliberal turn, a dubious multiculturalism, or even the shifting role of the state. Instead, it emerged out of their distinct transnational and decades-long experiences with a power that operates arbitrarily yet presents the illusion of a negotiation.

Organizing the Adults

Knockoff designer handbags, the ones sold in Chinatown, were popular among the Cambodian mothers of the Northwest Bronx in the early 2000s. A faux Gucci or Prada was a status symbol—although not the type one normally associates with designer wear. Such bags were the preferred carrying cases of the mothers who "worked" the welfare state. Unusually large, they provided ample room for a multitude of welfare documents, identification cards, and health records. "It's their welfare bag," Chhaya joked.

When these women took their seats in YLP meetings, their welfare bags were often propped prominently on their laps. The Cambodian mothers were a formidable group. YLP members spoke to them of strategies, of pressuring those in power. Such strategies required people to believe in a set of rights and have faith that civil society could deliver them. Ra and the other welfare mothers seemed unconvinced.

According to the youth organizers, the hardest part for them wasn't the direct confrontation with those in power—welfare center directors, workfare supervisors, local elected officials—nor was it speaking to the media once they had overcome their initial anxieties. Rather, the hardest part was organizing the adults, in many instances their own parents. It was hard for the obvious reasons: family dynamics, ageism, and patriarchy. It was also hard because of the older generation's understanding of its relationship to state power.

The youth refugee organizers drew up thoughtful agendas that included icebreakers and small-group discussions. They created flowcharts of the welfare bureaucracy so that the adults could differentiate between those in power and those who merely did the bidding of high-level administrators. They went through detailed scenarios and role-plays to distill common grievances among adult refugees. All told, they worked diligently to develop a process for adult community members to arrive at a clear strategy.

Rarely did the youth organizers make it through an entire meeting agenda. Somewhere along the way, a small mutiny would occur and the agenda would be discarded as the adults took the conversation in their own direction. This was especially true when it came time to discuss campaign demands. Deciding on concrete demands was the crux of the agenda—the main "takeaway" in community-organizing parlance—but the adults did not grant it easily. They carried on elliptical conversations of being misled by caseworkers and sanctioned and their plans to make ends meet in the interim. They reached into their welfare bags to share letters from the welfare agency that had little to do with the topic at hand.

Some YLP members found these moments frustrating. I did, too, feeling that we had lost control of the meeting and were failing to make headway. Chhaya, however, saw it differently. In her view there was something politically productive in the way the adults took the meeting in their own direction to give expression to their own understanding of welfare-state power. Indeed, Chhaya interpreted it as a sign of their investment, not necessarily in the precise demands, strategies, and tactics proposed by YLP but in the opportunity to collectively reflect on what was happening to them and to explore the possibilities of resistance. Chhaya reflected back on those years:

> Sometimes it seemed like the meeting got out of hand, and people were confused. But I never saw it that way. I saw that people were angry, but they knew exactly what was happening to them. You had to let them take it. They came to these meetings and they wanted to express that anger, to talk about their mistreatment. For them, the goal of the meeting was [to] express their frustrations and tell the story of what was happening to them. You can't always facilitate that as part of your agenda.

Ra seemed to affirm Chhaya's assessment. She did not attend these meetings consistently, but when she did she made important contributions. Her outspokenness and sharp wit were on full display—

qualities she seemed to pass on to her three children, who each took a leadership role among the youth organizers. Ra was supportive of the youth, commending them for their efforts even as she offered criticisms. Her critiques were not always explicit, but came across in muted responses, in the way that she and the other adults interrupted discussion of our "concrete" demands.

I raised this point with Ra during one of our interviews years later. Why were she and the others reluctant to assert their statutory rights? "Because they [welfare agency workers] will tell you anything," she said. "They make a mistake, but it's your fault. Then they do it again." According to Ra, it was impossible to hold the welfare regime accountable:

> They cut the welfare first, and you can't do anything to stop it. You have to wait until they correct the mistake. You can hand in the right papers and show them everything, but it doesn't matter. You still have to wait. Even if they make a big mistake, it doesn't matter. Nobody gets in trouble.

Here Ra was acknowledging that, even if welfare bureaucrats conceded that a particular sanction was unjustified, they did not admit to the damage it unnecessarily inflicted on the welfare recipient. Benefit discontinuance, which could last anywhere from one to three months before resolution, took a serious toll on poor families. It determined whether they had enough to eat, if their utilities were shut off, or if they could afford winter coats. If the welfare agency was proven to be in error, the recipients' benefits were simply restored (with losses recouped), and the matter was closed. None of what the family had suffered, however, was subject to redress. The welfare agency, in other words, had the power to throw the most vulnerable families deeper into crisis and to do so with impunity. Ra refused to be naïve about those terms. Just as the state and its adjuncts once arbitrarily placed the refugees on welfare (at first insisting that it was a temporary and adaptive measure before leaving them there indefinitely), so it arbitrarily removed them if those in power decided that the system was broken. Moreover, Ra and other welfare recipients who made supplemental income through off-the-books jobs were scrutinized and sanctioned by the welfare state for doing precisely what the state, specifically the Office of Refugee Resettlement and local agencies, had promised yet failed to do years earlier: find a way for refugees to scrape together a living in an environment that offered few opportunities for livable-wage work. How, she wondered, could anybody negotiate with power that acts so arbitrarily?

> *They [welfare state] can't make up their mind. First they say apply for welfare, you need it. You can't live without it. Then they say "okay, no more welfare"—you have to get out, find a job. Okay, there's no job so now you go to workfare. But then they will still cut your welfare. You can't believe anything about welfare.*

Although Ra thought it was futile to negotiate with the state, she did not object to YLP's organizing strategies; rather, she signaled that such efforts would not be her primary mode of engagement with welfare-state abuses. Instead, she believed that she had to keep things moving when confronted with arbitrary power. This meant finding alternative sources of income—homework, factory work, and odd jobs.

Other adults who attended our meetings shared Ra's perspective. Over the years, many of them had grown accustomed to the occasional sanction that resulted from language barriers, a caseworker's clerical error, a notice to attend an interview that went astray in the mail, or sudden changes in local welfare regulations. These sanctions chastened welfare recipients. However, after 1996 they sensed that something qualitatively different had taken hold; something akin to abuse and calculated malfeasance that left no room for negotiation.

One of the adults whom YLP worked with was Linh, a sixty-year-old Vietnamese woman who cleaned the streets each morning for the workfare program. In critiquing the welfare state, she assigned it a gender: "*He* is pushing me too far," she said of workfare. "I cannot survive the program. If I stay, I don't survive. If I am kicked out [of welfare], I will not survive. I don't know what to do." Working through the idiom of domestic violence, Linh proposed that the welfare state ensnared women in an economically and legally abusive relationship. She was confronted with an impossible choice: tolerate the conditions or get out. She had no rights to claim; the terms of civil society were as irrelevant in the welfare state as they were in the domestic sphere.[17]

Trevy, another woman with whom YLP worked, was a mother of five and among the first Cambodian refugees to resettle in the Bronx. She contrasted her post-1996 experience of welfare with her experience under the previous regulations. After 1996, she felt certain that she was being driven from the welfare state. When she first arrived in the Bronx, she recalled, social workers seemed overly eager to sign her to a range of benefits programs. Trevy survived on some of these programs for nearly two decades, yet always wondered how long the support would last. "They want us out," she said. "[It's] not like before . . . when we first came. They want to hurt us now. I remember they once said to us, 'Apply for this [program], apply for that one. You need to *eat welfare* to survive.' Now, they want to put us out." According to Trevy, welfare reform was forcing refugees off welfare arbitrarily.

Both Linh and Trevy spoke of welfare-state abuse in terms of confinement and forced removal. That is, they related to it in spatial terms: across the public and private spheres, welfare was not so much a set of benefits and regulations as it was a *location*. It followed that Linh, Trevy, and Ra responded by moving through space—by hustling to find alternative sources of income and in-kind donations. In addition to homeworking and factory work, some sold homemade food in local parks, others collected and redeemed aluminum cans, and all sought extra "rations" from local food pantries. Indeed, if Ra and others preferred to rely primarily on their own movements as opposed to community-organizing strategies to survive and resist the welfare state, these were tactics they refined while living in the camps. Ra recalled that, although she received rations and was told by camp workers that her basic needs would be met, she was never under the illusion that she could rely on what they were offering, that she could rest. She always had a side operation and it was invariably one that violated camp rules: peddling rice wine or betel nut (an addictive chew popular among Cambodian women).

> I wasn't allowed to sell these things, but I had to make sure that we had enough in case something didn't go right. You're like a prisoner in there, so you can't believe what they [those running

the camps] tell you. You just find work. What if there wasn't
enough food? Sometimes other people tried to get me in trouble
for doing these things. They wanted wine and I wouldn't give it
to them so they tried to give me trouble. But I had to be tough
and stand up to them.

In returning to her camp experiences while reflecting on her problems with the U.S. welfare state, Ra was suggesting that she did not
conceive of the neoliberal welfare regime as a *new* historical period in
U.S. capitalism and statecraft. Rather, welfare was yet another location in the ongoing cycle of rupture, displacement, and confinement
that characterized her unclosed sojourn. Her hustles in the camps and
in the Bronx were a direct response to her unambiguous status as a
captive. In this sense, Ra, along with Linh and Trevy, exposed a key
truth about the hyperghetto: it, too, functioned primarily as a site of
captivity and stigmatization.

Loïc Wacquant argues that the welfare regime of the past four
decades, and particularly since the passage of welfare reform, has fully
meshed with the penal state. The revolving door between prison and
the urban neighborhood—the defining feature of the hyperghetto—
has been constructed primarily through social-welfare policies. The
objective of this construction is not merely to maintain and regulate
capitalism's surplus labor pool but also to renew specific social strati-
fications and symbolic orders—namely, the captivity of Black bodies that serves as both a continual "fount of social instability" and a
symbol of racial domination.[18] This side of neoliberalism is too often
misunderstood or overlooked, according to Wacquant. He notes that
most analyses tend toward the "thin conception of the economists"
rather than a "thick sociological characterization of neoliberalism"
that discusses welfare discipline (particularly supervisory workfare),
the police and prison apparatus, and racial stigmatization.[19]

The difference between the thin and the thick, I argue, is not
merely scholarly or conceptual but epistemological. In other words,
it marks the distance between the scholar's (or activist's) rendering
of new developments in capitalism and the captive's *knowledge* that
what is happening is not a new phenomenon but a reinscription of
her captive status, a return to a familiar place. For the Cambodian

refugees in particular, their experiences of captivity and forced labor allowed them to intimately know what Wacquant describes as that "double regulation" of the poor—the merging of the penal and social-welfare arms of the state—that is endemic to the hyperghetto.[20] This knowledge ultimately determines the refugees' survival and resistance strategies as well as their relationship to the notion of rights.

I often asked Ra and other refugees how they pulled it off. After fleeing Cambodia, they made their way into the Thai camps (often unauthorized), secured dwellings and rations, convinced UN workers to grant them an asylum interview, applied for and received resettlement in a third and final nation of asylum, landed in the United States, and now had to navigate a racist, sexist, and classist power matrix that just wanted them to disappear. How had they survived when so many others had not?

Ra and the others refrained from heroic recounting: there were no saviors, no major turning points in their stories. They spoke only of steady movement. They hardly spoke of rights at all—of the supposed restoration of legal personhood that finally grants refuge and resettlement. In their telling, the manner in which a given regime—the Khmer Rouge, Thai soldiers, the United Nations—shuttled refugees between near death and the granting of asylum had nothing to do with right and legality. It was unattributable. The refugees never possessed anything with which to negotiate. *Demands? What could one possibly demand from these spaces?* All they could do was *move.* They never stopped looking for the next opening that might grant them a reprieve—a commutation of final capture. This is not to say that Ra and the others evaded power. They were always its unequivocal subjects. They just never stayed in one place long enough for arbitrary state power to make a final determination on what to do with them.

Nowhere was the refugees' reliance on movement more relevant than in their dealings with the city's mandatory workfare program. In the next chapter, I describe the experience of a Cambodian welfare recipient who survived a Bronx workfare program while holding on to her job as a low-wage factory worker. Her survival strategies worked at cross-purposes with YLP's attempts to challenge the workfare regime, however, and this dissonance ultimately proved productive, compelling YLP to reconsider how resistance takes shape among refugees.

Figure 1 Ra Pronh in 1980 at the Khao-I-Dang refugee camp, Thailand. *(Collection of Ra Pronh.)*

LEFT: **Figure 2** Ra Pronh, her ex-husband, and their two oldest children at the Khao-I-Dang refugee camp ca. 1982. *(Collection of Ra Pronh.)*

BOTTOM: **Figure 3** Ra in 1986 selling porridge at the U.S. Refugee Processing Center in the Philippines and visibly pregnant with her son Rith, her fifth child. Throughout her time in the refugee camps and her life in the Bronx, Ra supplemented camp rations and welfare benefits with income generated from her informal labors. *(Collection of Ra Pronh.)*

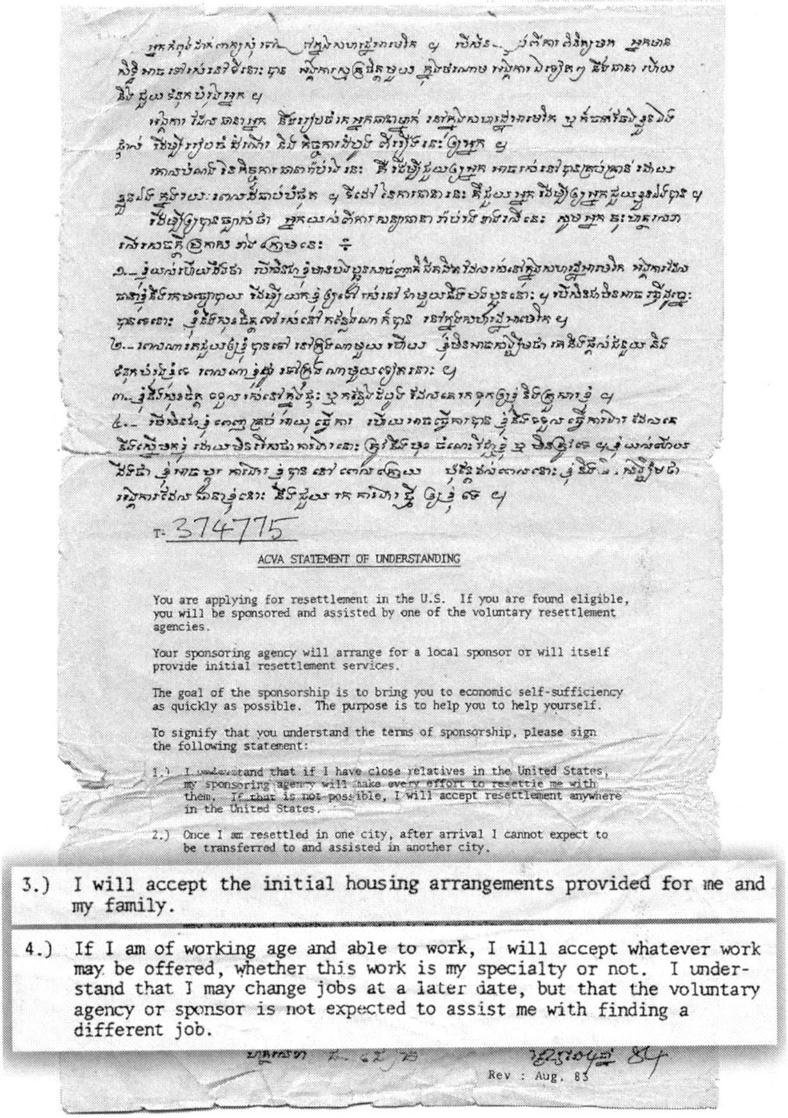

T-374775

ACVA STATEMENT OF UNDERSTANDING

You are applying for resettlement in the U.S. If you are found eligible, you will be sponsored and assisted by one of the voluntary resettlement agencies.

Your sponsoring agency will arrange for a local sponsor or will itself provide initial resettlement services.

The goal of the sponsorship is to bring you to economic self-sufficiency as quickly as possible. The purpose is to help you to help yourself.

To signify that you understand the terms of sponsorship, please sign the following statement:

1.) I understand that if I have close relatives in the United States, my sponsoring agency will make every effort to resettle me with them. If that is not possible, I will accept resettlement anywhere in the United States.

2.) Once I am resettled in one city, after arrival I cannot expect to be transferred to and assisted in another city.

3.) I will accept the initial housing arrangements provided for me and my family.

4.) If I am of working age and able to work, I will accept whatever work may be offered, whether this work is my specialty or not. I understand that I may change jobs at a later date, but that the voluntary agency or sponsor is not expected to assist me with finding a different job.

Rev : Aug. 83

Figure 4 ACVA Statement of Understanding. Before departing for the United States, Ra was issued this document by the American Council of Voluntary Associations (ACVA), the collective body of nongovernmental organizations contracted by the U.S. State Department to manage the resettlement of Cambodian refugees in U.S. cities. ACVA's main task was to arrange housing and assist refugees in finding employment. *(Collection of Ra Pronh.)*

FACING PAGE: **Figure 5** Broken Promises/Falsas Promesas, 1980. Charlotte Street stencils by John Fekner. Charlotte Street was decimated by the South Bronx arson epidemic of the 1970s. In October 1977, President Jimmy Carter stood amid the rubble, pledging to rebuild America's forsaken inner cities. *(Photo © John Fekner Research Archive.)*

BELOW: **Figure 6** Cambodian residents of the Northwest Bronx protesting cuts in translation services at a local health clinic, 1998. The protest was organized by members of the Youth Leadership Project (YLP) of CAAAV: Organizing Asian Communities. *(Collection of Chhaya Chhoum.)*

ABOVE: **Figure 7** Chhaya Chhoum and members of Mekong NYC in 2013. From left to right: Alicia Rivera, Khamaly Srey, Thanna Son, Chhaya, Khamarin Nhann. *(Photo © True Yee Thao.)*

LEFT: **Figure 8** Ra Pronh and her granddaughter Jade in 2008. *(Photo © Bud Glick.)*

RIGHT: **Figure 9** Ra with four of her children in 2014. Standing (from left to right): Rann, Sonya, Rith, Rorth.

4

Workfare Encampments

Several of the Cambodian mothers who participated in the Youth Leadership Project (YLP) insisted that welfare "rights" were just another fiction that the refugee was asked to accept and uphold. It was a fiction that masked their persistent state of captivity in the context of the U.S. welfare state, particularly one undergoing radical retrenchment, if not complete collapse, following the implementation of new federal policies in 1996. The refugees exposed this fallacy by revealing how the political and economic time in which they were resettled—characterized by the scholar and activist as neoliberalism, postindustrialism, late capitalism, and so forth—was continuous with the time from which they came: the time of the camps.

Community organizer Chhaya Chhoum clearly understood this. During one of my interviews with her, she posed the following question: "What does it mean to organize a group of people who have never really left the camp?" Her question was neither rhetorical nor metaphorical, nor was it blithe commentary on the refugees' inability to let go of the past. Rather, it offered an accurate reading of the refugees' condition, acknowledging their belief that they were living under a regime that wielded its power arbitrarily, just as power was wielded in the camps. At the same time, her question genuinely sought an understanding of what it takes for the community organizer to never-theless engage refugees in collective action. It suggested that, although the refugees had little use for the discourse of rights, they believed that resistance remained both necessary and within their power.

To explore the complex meanings and practices of refugee resis-tance during times of ongoing captivity, I begin this chapter by de-scribing the entrapment of the refugee by the Bronx welfare state of the late 1990s, particularly within the confines of the city's mandatory workfare program. Here I draw on the experiences of Kun Thea, a Cambodian refugee mother and widower who worked thirty hours per week as a part of a sanitation crew in exchange for her monthly welfare check. Kun Thea was well aware that the point of the workfare program was not job training but to compel her self-removal from the welfare rolls by burdening her with unreasonable work demands. She refused to capitulate, deciding instead to attend workfare while also keeping her off-the-books job as a factory worker. In addition, she continued to raise her five children. To some, her strategy for eco-nomic survival could hardly be construed as resistance. In Chhaya's view, however, the difference between survival and resistance for those who had never left the camp was rarely as simple as it seemed.

The Welfare Trap Revisited

Beginning in the late 1960s, New York City welfare offices were called "income support centers." In 1998 they were conspicuously renamed "job centers" to reflect the city's "bold re-organization of NYC's welfare system and emphasis on work first."[1] Although wel-fare-to-work programs had existed in the city since the 1980s, they had been reserved mainly for adults with no dependent children. The 1996 welfare reform law, however, mandated that everyone receiving a monthly welfare check be required to participate in workfare. Mayor Rudolph Giuliani was determined to make New York City a national model for how quickly and effectively a municipal agency could re-duce its welfare rolls by leveraging this mandatory requirement.[2] His administration proclaimed that the city's Work Experience Program (WEP), in which participants worked thirty hours per week cleaning city parks and offices, would encourage thousands to quit welfare.

Others would be removed because of noncompliance with WEP.[3] By 2001, the mayor's strategy seemed to be a remarkable success: more than 50 percent of those receiving Temporary Aid to Needy Families (monthly cash assistance) prior to the "work-first" doctrine had been removed from the rolls.

Not everybody quit WEP so readily, however. Kun Thea was a mother of five: two teenage boys and three grade-school-aged daughters when I met her in 1999. She and her family were living in a small two-bedroom apartment on 193rd Street. Vietnamese by nationality, she considered herself "Khmer Krom"—a name given to a region of southern Vietnam that remains contested territory. Most Cambodians view it as land stolen from them by the Vietnamese. Many of those from Khmer Krom, including Kun Thea, speak Vietnamese, Khmer, and the Khmer Krom dialect. Along with her parents, Kun Thea fled Khmer Krom for Cambodia in 1970 to escape the escalating U.S. war in Vietnam. She never anticipated the nightmare that would befall Cambodia when the Khmer Rouge took power in 1975. As a teenager, Kun Thea spent two years in a Khmer Rouge labor camp before escaping to Thailand in 1979. She was granted entry into Khao-I-Dang, where she later met her husband. The two of them applied for and were approved for asylum in the United States and settled in the Bronx in 1984.

Since her early days in the Bronx, Kun Thea and her family had survived on a combination of welfare benefits and under-the-table wages earned from factory jobs in neighboring New Jersey. In these light manufacturing firms, they sorted and packed small merchandise: pet supplies, perfumes, and candies. During the early 1990s, Kun Thea's husband became gravely ill with a liver disease, and he was no longer able to work. Kun Thea had no choice but to pick up extra shifts at the factories in order to make up for his lost wages; she also earned supplemental income by assisting neighbors who were "homeworking"—subcontracting themselves as home-based garment workers. (As I discuss in Chapter 5, Ra participated in this economy as well.) As her husband's condition worsened, Kun Thea worked anywhere from twelve to fourteen hours per day at an array of factories. She jumped from one to the next, depending on where she could find the best wages, keeping up this pace even after her husband passed away in 1996.

In the fall of 1999, Kun Thea received a letter from the city's welfare agency stating that she was required to report to WEP. She was assigned to the Department of Parks and Recreation to clean parks in the Bronx's Belmont neighborhood, an area once known as the borough's Little Italy. She was ordered to work thirty hours per week in exchange for a monthly $1,000 welfare check.

The letter from the welfare agency intimated that she could avoid WEP by going without her monthly check. To be sure, one of the objectives of mandatory workfare was to encourage welfare recipients to remove themselves from welfare and to enter the low-wage labor market full-time. Kun Thea, unwilling to make this deal, became determined to keep both her welfare benefits and her factory job. She described her daily routine:

> I walk three miles each day to and from WEP. It's very good to walk, better than taking the bus. The city gives me a Metrocard but I save that for my son. At seven in the morning it's a very peaceful time to walk. This is my one time alone all day. The supervisor arrives late on most days. We're supposed to start at seven-thirty, but he comes close to eight. One time, he asked me why I got there so early. He said that I was trying to make him look bad. I don't know if he was joking. I told him I have to start on time so that I can leave by two thirty in the afternoon. But I don't think he understood what I said. I don't think he cares. My daughters come home from school by three thirty, and I need at least one hour to cook for them. That is the only time I have to cook. After I cook, I go to Devoe Park and wait for the factory van. It comes at five. If you arrive to the park late, the van will leave without you. The nightshift at the factory goes from six to one in the morning. On a night with no problems, I get back home by two. I sleep for four hours, and then get up with my youngest daughter. At seven, I leave again [for WEP].[4]

Kun Thea's daily routine sheds new light on the notion of "welfare trap," the phenomenon of welfare recipients caught between the vagaries of the unskilled-labor market and an inflexible welfare bureaucracy. Often they refuse to find work because their welfare will be reduced by the amount they earn from official employment. They fear being dropped from benefits such as food stamps and Medicaid if they "overearn." To understand why more people do not escape the welfare trap, ask yourself a few questions: Why would anybody voluntarily enter conditions of working poverty when the welfare state offers more protections? Why would anybody opt for official employment when they have the chance to earn unreported income that does not reduce their monthly welfare grants (even if these are informal jobs that pay below the minimum wage)?[5]

State-driven countermeasures to the trap—such as raising the minimum wage or the wage-income threshold for welfare recipients— are of course anathema to neoliberal logics. The 1996 welfare reform law took a punitive approach to "resolving" the trap. Although the new law claimed that the purpose of the mandatory workfare requirement was to move welfare recipients from dependency to economic self-sufficiency, it completely failed to deliver on this goal. New York City's own data revealed that only a miniscule number of WEP participants were actually trained in a new skill and fewer still transitioned from workfare into stable, nonpoverty-wage jobs.[6]

It was clear to YLP that the point of mandatory workfare was, unequivocally, to entrap recipients more effectively by making life in the welfare state as difficult as life on poverty wages. Moreover, because workfare consumed so much time, it purposefully made refugee adults unavailable for work at the off-the-book jobs that supplemented their welfare benefits. Simply stated, after 1996 entrapment took on a more literal meaning: welfare recipients were ostracized, punished, and confined to a designated space of compelled labor. Because the youth organizers saw nothing redeeming in the WEP program, they decided against an organizing campaign focused on reforming it, taking the position that workfare should ultimately be abolished. Our immediate efforts focused on moving as many refugee adults out of WEP as possible, either by securing medical exemptions or by exploiting loopholes such as alternative educational programs to satisfy the workfare requirement.

YLP's stance on WEP stood in contrast to that of some groups in the welfare-rights and labor organizing community who proposed that workfare participants should be unionized. These groups sought to take city officials at their word: they insisted that those in workfare were truly "workers" (or at least workers in training) who should be compensated and protected as such.[7] However, this position failed to recognize that the undergirding logic of workfare was to discipline and punish, not to exploit vulnerable workers for profit. Although the state certainly took advantage of the low-to-no-wage labor provided by WEP participants, it wasn't motivated by purely economic incentives—capitalism's unfettered drive for profit. Here I argue that economic reductionism effaces the central role of racialized punishment and stigmatization in establishing the social order. As Loïc Wacquant suggests, such reductionism can mislead us into believing that U.S. neoliberalism was rationally designed by a few pulling the strings, when in fact it is a pervasive racial and spatial logic of enclosure that extends from slavery into the postindustrial landscape.[8] Contemporary permutations of this logic are now mediated through the social welfare programs once spawned by the New Deal, the Great Society, and the Civil Rights movement.

Kun Thea, in her own way, recognized this broader logic of entrapment to which she was subjected and from which she could see no true exit, no outside. Perhaps this is why she chose to keep both workfare and factory work, recognizing that neither would ever be capable of pulling her out of poverty. It would be all too easy to read her actions through the model-minority stereotype, to reduce her to the trope of the Asian immigrant who, even under intense welfare-state scrutiny, maintained her knack for generating income at any cost and under any conditions. This facile reading, however, ignores the epistemological standpoints of Cambodian refugees for whom captivity and forced labor were not new phenomena.

Kun Thea seemed unsurprised by any aspect of the trap in which she found herself. As she described her daily routine of shuttling between workfare, home, and factory, she gave the impression of having been there before—indeed, of one who had never quite left captivity. By this I mean that she possessed an intimate knowledge of the spaces to which she was confined and knew what she had to do to survive them. The challenge for YLP organizers was to recognize this knowledge as the basis of political action, but we often occluded it in our attempts to outmaneuver and outwit neoliberal governance.

The Workfare Workaround

In its effort to release refugee welfare recipients from the WEP requirement, YLP pursued several avenues: medical exemptions for those suffering from war's lingering physical and emotional effects, childcare exemptions for those with small children, and educational exemptions for those who might be better served by an alternative job-training program. The first two exemptions were contingent on individual circumstances, but the educational exemption potentially applied to all adult refugees being called into WEP.

Kun Thea, along with the majority of workfare participants, bridled at the suggestion that WEP provided on-the-job training. "What kind of training or instructions do I need?" she laughed. "You just sweep the sidewalk and the streets, and then gather the trash inside the parks. Who doesn't know how to sweep?" It puzzled her that the WEP supervisor talked as much as he did, barking what seemed like orders and complaints to a crew of Black, Latina, and Asian women. Kun Thea felt fortunate that her limited English shielded her from understanding most of it.

> He yells at them to do this and that. His tone is bad. But he leaves me alone because I don't speak English. Even if I understand what he is saying, I pretend I don't understand, and I just keep doing what I'm doing. But why is he yelling? What can he really teach us?

Kun Thea described the futility of it all; she seemed amused by these daily workfare interactions, but such scenes of miscommunication presented a unique organizing opportunity for YLP. Because WEP was funded in part by a federal grant, it was required to ensure equal access to participants as mandated by federal civil rights law. That Kun Thea and other limited-English speakers were unable to communicate effectively with their supervisors meant that they were not treated equally. What possible training could take place in the absence of basic verbal communication? YLP's initial exploration into the issue suggested that the city's workfare program violated the 1964 Civil Rights Act Title VI ban on "national origins discrimination."[9] If this could be proven, the city would be required to either hire translators (or supervisors who could adequately communicate with all participants) or grant refugees an alternative to workfare that accommodated their language needs. The first option, of course, spelled self-defeat. Certainly YLP's goal was not to *enhance* workfare with translators, but the Giuliani administration was unlikely to increase workfare resources by hiring them. There were far too many languages spoken by New York City welfare recipients, and hiring interpreters for all of them would have been incredibly costly.

In our view, the city's only logical choice was to offer limited-English-speaking refugees an alternative—in all likelihood an educational program. Some of our allies in the welfare rights and labor organizing community saw this as a narrow solution that helped only refugees and other immigrants while leaving nonimmigrants unprotected.[10] YLP responded that dismantling the workfare behemoth required multiple "small hits" from numerous contributors—labor unions, community groups, immigrant and refugee groups, and so forth. Securing workfare exemptions and alternatives was not YLP's ultimate goal but a finite tactic to frustrate the system while temporarily alleviating the workfare burden for some. However, we were so singularly focused on workfare's punitive nature—"anything but WEP" was the line that guided us—that we never considered the dangers of alternatives.

In response to YLP's language discrimination complaints, the city proposed that non-English speakers, in lieu of workfare, attend a welfare-to-work program called Begin Employment Gain Independence Now (BEGIN). BEGIN programs were managed by nonprofits and community colleges and offered job training, basic literacy, and GED preparation classes. Because of the Bronx's large Latino population, many BEGIN classes were taught by certified English-as-a-second-language (ESL) instructors, and the city suggested that the refugees avail themselves of this resource. Whether or not the Cambodian refugee and the ESL instructor could effectively communicate was irrelevant to the bureaucrats. The city needed only to demonstrate that it had made an effort to match the non-English speaker with a certified ESL instructor to satisfy any federal complaint.

It was a vexing proposition. On the one hand, YLP did not consider this a political victory. On the other hand, it seemed to have met the short-term objective of temporarily challenging the mandatory workfare requirement. From here, we rationalized: the BEGIN program appeared less taxing than workfare, and it involved no physical labor; also, it required slightly fewer hours than WEP, which would free up participants for factory or homeworking jobs. However, many refugees, including Kun Thea, took the opposite view.

Kun Thea was familiar with BEGIN. In 1998, a year prior to her workfare placement, she had been sent to a BEGIN program at a local community college. At the time, her caseworker claimed that new policies mandated that recipients attend job-training sessions. Kun Thea complied, and thus began several difficult months of confinement:

> They wanted me to go to classes where I would learn English. They also had counselors who would help me look for a job. I went to the classes, and of course I didn't understand anything. I know how to speak three languages—Chinese, Khmer, and Vietnamese—but not English. Most of the other students spoke Spanish, and so did the teacher. There was another Vietnamese woman there. She spoke English much better than me. I think she even spoke it better than the Spanish students.
>
> The teacher didn't know what he should do with me. And the counselor gave up on me the very first day. Finally they decided that every day I would sit in front of an English-learners video. "At the end of this video, tell me three new phrases you learned."

Kun Thea felt detained. Her testimony suggests that there are different forms of captivity: the kind that restricts movements and the kind that grants mobility within a given confine. The BEGIN program was certainly the former:

> I felt like I was being locked in a room for "reeducation." I had a lot of bad experiences like this before. You sit in rooms and you wait. You listen to somebody speak, but you don't understand. You are not allowed to leave. But I would just stare out of the window. The BEGIN program gave me a lot of time to think. This was soon after my husband died, so I would just stare out the window and think about [him]. I would think too much, and I couldn't stop. Around the same time we got the news that Pol Pot died. And then I think a lot about my family back in Vietnam and Cambodia, about everything . . . the Khmer Rouge, the camps. I became very sad, so I just stopped going.

Kun Thea described feelings of isolation and stasis—immobility that led her to "think too much," to become overwhelmed by the weight of her past. She desired movement, but was denied it not only by ostensibly "kinder" social welfare policy but also, potentially, by community organizers determined to challenge neoliberalism.

The classroom proved no less a space of captivity than the workfare site. A genocide survivor, Kun Thea found the "educational" space intolerable because it summoned specters of the past. Although the educational exemption was supposed to provide a useful skill, it also functioned punitively because Southeast Asian refugees were scolded for not knowing enough English to catch up and for not being able to communicate with the mostly Spanish-speaking students and instructors.

Kun Thea and other refugees possessed a wealth of knowledge about compelled labor and captivity, and this is precisely what informed them as they navigated the radically transformed post-1996 welfare state. In this they read the bureaucratic field of the Bronx welfare state as yet another location along an unclosed sojourn of captivity, one that required them to remain mobile and resourceful and to avoid being lured into an arrangement in which they were complicit in their own punishment.

YLP's attempt to secure a potential workaround for Kun Thea and others trapped in workfare yielded several lessons on community organizing. The most immediate one concerned the pitfalls that organizers encounter when they pursue a short-term remedy for a problem they already consider irredeemable, a problem for which the only solution is abolition, not reform. Indeed, at what point should YLP have determined that no alternative was suitable? Should it have refused to pursue any alternative, recognizing that any negotiation only legitimized the workfare regime? This conundrum was similar to the situation discussed in Chapter 3, where YLP demanded language interpretation services at welfare centers. In that example, a successful organizing campaign for interpreters certainly addressed an important community need but also potentially reinforced a form of neoliberal multiculturalism that, in its affirmation of plurality, equal access, and inclusion for all, obscured the more profound economic, racial, and gendered violences of welfare reform. In the end, the demand for interpreters did not work at cross-purposes with the daily needs and desires of the refugees. (To the contrary, I would argue that most refugees benefited from the reform even as they remained skeptical of the notion of "welfare rights.") Kun Thea's situation with BEGIN was different in that it brought into sharp focus a situation in which the organizers' pursuit of an alternative had the potential of deepening her daily crisis.

All of this points to an existential problem for community organizers: What kind of organizing refrains from concrete demands of power? Community organizing, as a distinct methodology, centers on a clear demand issued against a specific powerbroker or target: the director of a welfare center, the commissioner of the Human Resources Administration, the mayor. On identifying the demand and the target, organizers plot measured strategies and tactics that put them in the best position to "win." However, as Kun Thea's quandary exemplified, there are moments when there is nothing to be won.

Sometimes a particular political demand suddenly proves to be a liability, if not an impossibility, because of an unexpected shift in political conditions. In these instances, organizers are left without a core issue on which to focus. Such was the case for YLP and its allies in the movement for national welfare rights discussed in Chapter 3.

In the fall of 2001, Grassroots Organizing for Welfare Leadership (GROWL), of which YLP was a member, was at the height of its national campaign to challenge reauthorization of the 1996 welfare reform laws. Its efforts were suddenly neutralized by the events of September 11, 2001. Indeed, in the post-9/11 era, GROWL's demands could no longer gain traction in a public sphere that had turned its attention entirely to the issue of national security. For the coalition to pursue its agenda in this context would have proven not only futile but politically costly, delegitimizing the group as politically tone deaf and considerably setting its work back.

Responding to the new reality of post-9/11, some in the welfare rights movement believed it was best to take a hiatus, to wait for the exceptional moment to pass, but for Chhaya and other young Cambodian community organizers, moments such as these—marked by war and crisis—represented not the exception but the rule. They saw this moment of disjuncture as an opportunity to address the most challenging contradictions the community organizer could confront.

Giving Up the Demand

The national movement for welfare rights came to an abrupt halt on September 11, 2001. GROWL had scheduled a briefing that morning for members of the House of Representatives on Capitol Hill on the adverse impacts of federal welfare reform. The data had been culled from various member organizations, including YLP, and Chhaya was slated to testify. However, as we approached the steps of the Rayburn House Office Building, we encountered congressional staff running in the opposite direction. One stopped just long enough to explain to us why everyone was evacuating the building: "The Pentagon was hit by a plane. I think we're under attack." Less than an hour earlier, two commercial airplanes had crashed into the towers of the World Trade Center.

Needless to say, the hearing did not take place that day. Although GROWL continued to exist as a coalition, the national political climate had shifted so dramatically that the group's original strategy of changing public opinion on welfare reform—moving the discussion from vilification and ridicule of the poor to a critique of an ineffective and unconstitutional policy—no longer seemed tenable. In the wake of 9/11, there was simply no room in the national dialogue for the plight of the urban poor and the policies that affected them. The welfare reform law was reauthorized by Congress in 2002.

In this context, many local activists and community-organizing groups, particularly those in New York City, were forced to rethink their work. In the four years between the 1997 implementation of federal welfare reform and September 11, 2001, YLP had carried out several protests and sit-ins at local welfare agencies and one impromptu sit-in at the offices of the regional health and human services agency, located only blocks away from the World Trade Center. In the years to follow, however, such actions became inconceivable. Not only were these buildings now on virtual lockdown but, in the climate of fear and insecurity that gripped the city, the public had little tolerance, much less sympathy, for direct political action of this sort. In light of these conditions, what was one to make of the concrete political demands so central to community organizing?

According to Chhaya, at times one had to be willing to let go of strategies that amounted to a set of discrete demands. Chhaya became director of YLP in 2004, and under her leadership the group initiated several new programs focused on refugees' holistic health—economic, physical, and emotional. These programs were not always centered on making key demands of those in power, nor were they based solely on an organizing model of identifying and applying pressure on targets that could concede to certain measures. Instead, they met the direct needs of community members by providing welfare and housing advocacy, locating legal and health resources, and creating space for peer-to-peer reflection and storytelling about past traumas.

To the passing observer, such programs might have appeared identical to the those offered by "direct service" organizations that seek to help people cope with life's challenges without addressing (or even acknowledging) the systemic inequalities that are at the root of those challenges. For Chhaya, however, these initiatives were expressly political in both form and content. They reflected her belief that those who sought to organize refugees had to first account for the refugees' complex daily realities. She was convinced that meaningful participation flowed from the organizer's deeper appreciation for the ways in which refugees "move through their day-to-day reality with dignity" despite all they had suffered:

> For me, the question isn't about community organizing versus direct services. What I care about is doing things that support and restore the dignity of people—especially people as traumatized as Cambodians. The community organizer says, "Come to meetings. Go to protests. Now you're part of something." But how true is that? If you really want people to feel part of something—and keep in mind some of these people have never felt part of anything in their entire lives—then you need to have respect for their day-to-day situation. . . . Show them this respect by supporting them with their immediate needs [and by] just stopping and listening to what they have to say. That's how you support them—just hang out and listen to them, let them go on. See what kind of political action comes out of that.

Here Chhaya was echoing some of the principles and methods of popular education theorized by Paulo Freire, who argues that resistance is a matter of liberatory praxis—a cycle of critical reflections followed by actions that yield deeper, more pointed reflections. In Freire's view, meaningful political action is measured not by stated goals but by the extent to which oppressed peoples engage in praxis collectively, by their capacity to think critically with each other about their common condition and then enact/create an alternative to that reality.[11] When Chhaya said, "Just hang out and listen to them," she was describing a very important political activity, the very challenge to power. During my tenure as director of YLP, we sometimes used popular education methods. The youth organizers facilitated small-group discussions to draw out community members' political analyses of the welfare state. They also used scenario and role-playing exercises to explore the political tactics that were most appropriate for a given situation. At the time, I viewed these methods only as means to an end, relying on them to move the organizing campaign along, to grant our efforts the ostensible "consensus" needed to press forward with a specific demand or a certain tactic. Chhaya, however, seemed to be saying that the organizer should create room for praxis without the guarantee of an immediate takeaway, of "concreteness." The work of grasping the refugee welfare recipient's understanding of power and affirming that understanding is politically urgent in itself. Perhaps the organizer who carefully plots out a campaign strategy cannot see its immediate benefits, but such praxis nevertheless stands as a necessary challenge to power.

This difference in perspective might explain why YLP's most effective welfare center protest was the one that I felt most uncertain about. In August 2000, YLP carried out an action against a local welfare center known as "Bainbridge" (located on the corner of Bainbridge Avenue and Fordham Road). The caseworkers there had discontinued the benefits of numerous refugee families that summer. Several of those sanctioned blamed language discrimination because they did not have a bilingual family member to interpret for them, believing that they could get by with their limited English. As it turned out, however, they were unable to effectively answer the caseworkers' questions during routine recertification interviews. On behalf of YLP, I left messages and sent letters to the director of Bainbridge calling for a meeting on the issue. All of these communications went unanswered.

YLP held a series of meetings with adult welfare recipients to gauge their support for a direct-action protest at Bainbridge. We proposed marching on the welfare center and then occupying the waiting area just outside the director's office until she agreed to negotiate with us in person. As discussed in Chapter 3, however, these planning meetings were often unfocused and inefficient—at least by traditional community-organizing standards. The adult participants preferred to engage each other and not the meeting agenda, sharing stories about their current financial and familial predicaments that did not deal squarely with welfare. Youth organizers had to squeeze in their questions: What should we do if the director of the welfare center refuses to meet with us? What if somebody other than the director is sent to negotiate on the director's behalf? What if the police are called in to have us removed? None of these questions were sufficiently answered, but the adults assured us that we should go ahead with the action and that they would back us up.

The adult refugees turned out in strong numbers for the Bainbridge action, exceeding my expectations. They never balked when the director initially refused to negotiate with us or even when the police were called in to "observe" the situation. Because the center was a public space, and because virtually all of the protesters were families with cases at the center, the police had no grounds to remove or arrest anyone for trespassing. However, they remained throughout the sit-in, at times threatening to arrest YLP members for disorderly conduct if they continued to display their placards.

To my surprise, the adults suggested upping the ante by holding the sit-in for as long as possible. This buoyed the youth organizers, granting YLP greater leverage so that in the end the director agreed to meet YLP's demand for interpreters. She would either reassign Cambodian recipients to a welfare center with a Khmer-speaking caseworker or provide interpreters at Bainbridge over the phone through a third-party service.

Such reforms—limited to the framework and logic of neoliberal multicultural inclusion—did not necessarily diminish the local welfare state's ability to implement draconian federal welfare reform measures, particularly removal from the welfare rolls. Indeed, YLP's larger concern was that refugee families not be sanctioned arbitrarily by caseworkers—a concern that did not lend itself to a precise policy demand. But, as it were, the resolve of the protestors that day— particularly the adults—seemed enough to make a difference in how caseworkers would handle refugee cases moving forward. It appeared to have put the administrators on notice that the refugees could effectively mobilize around an issue. Immediately following our action, YLP members observed a drop in the number of reported sanctionings at Bainbridge.

Going into the action at Bainbridge, I was convinced that our group was unprepared, that our demands were not specific enough, and that we lacked solid contingency plans. However, the space that the adult community members created for themselves during the planning meetings proved a vital form of political preparation that allowed them the time and space to frame questions about state power on their own terms, not on those circumscribed by the organizer's agenda. These questions were a form of meaningful participation through which the refugees began to see political possibilities that, although inchoate, pushed the action at Bainbridge ahead in ways that I had not anticipated. Freire might describe this as the moment when the oppressed begin to approach the "untested feasibility" of political action: "Untested feasibility [is] the future which we have to create by transforming today, the present reality. It is something not yet here, but a potential, something beyond the 'limit-situation' we face now."[12] Freire is proposing that a group's movement toward this "potential" is carried out through the enactment of a new reality—in this instance, a group's collective reflection on conditions followed by their occupation of a space that they previously associated with arbitrary rule. Such movement is at times enough to achieve the political objective at hand.

This is not to say that Frederick Douglass's well-worn adage "Power concedes nothing without a demand" is incorrect; rather, it is to say that a demand does not always have to be clearly articulated, finite, and measurable to *move* power. This lesson guided Chhaya in her years as director of YLP, and it would form the basis of her new initiative in the Southeast Asian refugee neighborhoods of the Bronx.

In 2011 Chhaya started an independent organization, Mekong NYC, many of whose core programs are carryovers from YLP (as are many of its members). However, the new organization makes no distinction between youth organizers and adult community members and, according to Chhaya, it is entirely intergenerational. Through Mekong, Chhaya has developed a slate of arts-focused programs that encourage the kinds of collective reflection, action, and imagining that had been the foundation of YLP's most productive political actions. Mekong partners with local artists who conduct photography and mask-making workshops, and there is a community theater project. Taken together, these initiatives provide an opportunity for the refugee community to express its understanding and analysis of its present condition in creative ways that do not privilege the autobiographical statement or traditional testimony. This is crucially important for a community that is semiliterate and for whom storytelling is not only a cultural practice but a means of healing from trauma. According to Chhaya, telling one's story is not so much about "setting the record straight"—indeed, she notes that with each retelling of a particular survivor's story certain dates, sequences, and locations may change—as it is about "truth telling" that counters the official, state-sanctioned accounts of what happened to the genocide survivor:

> First the war, then the genocide, then the camp, and now here in the Bronx. Sometimes I sit in my office and wonder, *How are they supposed to come out of all of this?* I mean, what do we expect them to say after all of this? Making things worse are all the people who try to speak for them, all those people along the way who said to them, "This is what happened to you" and "I'm here to save you"—soldiers, camp people, the social workers. These people only made [the survivor] crazier. The very least we can do now is give our people a space to give language to their own trauma. Provide them some programs where they can tell their stories.

Cathy J. Schlund-Vials speaks to something very similar in her analysis of Cambodian "memory work." She notes that Cambodian genocide survivors and their progeny in the post–killing fields era have been subjected to state-sanctioned narratives and representations of the genocide that do not square with what survivors know to be true. Schlund-Vials calls attention to diasporic Cambodian visual, literary, and performance artists who tell a different story, who produce a different memory through their work that opposes nationalist abstractions and erasures.[13] She quotes Cambodian American political scientist Khatharya Um, who asserts that, for survivors of the genocide, remembering is "the ultimate resistance."[14]

Considering Chhaya's turn to this form of resistance, I asked her if she has given up on community organizing: "No, not at all. You always need the part where you demand something from those in power. You don't ever give that up." After pausing, she added, "What I have given up is my fear of losing. I think community organizers are too often motivated by a fear of losing. I want to be motivated by something else." This alternative motivation is a keener understanding of resistance that does not assume the organizer's role is to bring adult community members to a given political project (enlisting them for training in organizing, bringing them up to speed on the working of neoliberalism, helping them to understand a law or policy that must be demanded from the state). Such an approach assumes that political action is external to the refugees' routine acts of survival or that these acts of survival, on their own, are insufficiently political. Mekong's arts-based programs allow the community organizer to see the terms of justice, reconciliation, and ultimately resistance embedded in the refugees' stories and movements. Before charging headlong into any new organizing campaign, Chhaya and others give these stories and movements full expression. This helps the members of Mekong to determine what, if any, demands should be made of those in power in a given situation. Indeed, they allow for a clearer rendering of what refugees such as Kun Thea *already know* about their present condition—about this camp that they have yet to leave behind.

5

Sweatshops of the Neoplantation

While Southeast Asian Youth Leadership Project (YLP) organizers were challenging the state's attempt to summarily remove their families from the welfare rolls or to entrap them in workfare following the passage of the 1996 federal welfare reform laws, welfare mothers such as Ra were attempting an overlapping resistance strategy. Ra stepped up her efforts to secure additional income through her off-the-books jobs as a home-based garment worker. The 1996 welfare law was promulgated, in part, on the vilification (and in some instances criminalization) of "welfare cheats"—those who earned unreported and unauthorized income while also drawing their monthly welfare checks. Ra's experience as a homeworker, however, dispels this image.

When Ra and her family moved into their first Bronx apartment in July 1986, the local resettlement agency immediately signed her up for welfare benefits. These were supposed to be her sole income source in her new country. Soon after, however, for the reasons analyzed in previous chapters, Ra began to realize that this sanctioned income was severely insufficient. Only a few months after her arrival—in the summer of 1986—she began homeworking to supplement her welfare income and continued it steadily for the next fifteen years. According to Ra, this work was never an option but always a necessity because neither source alone enabled her to adequately feed, clothe, and shelter her family. She was caught in the welfare trap: unable to survive only on welfare but penalized with reduced welfare benefits or dropped from welfare entirely if she earned aboveboard income. The myth of the welfare cheat was simply neoliberalism's way of masking trap economics while justifying the removal of the poorest families from the nation's welfare rolls.

Ra refused to fold. She did not acquiesce to the demands of a radically reformed welfare state that implemented new measures to either prevent (through workfare) or punish (through sanctions) those earning supplemental income. To the contrary, she *increased* her output as a garment worker, in this way carrying out what community organizer Chhaya Chhoum described in Chapter 4 as acts of refugee resistance that are indistinguishable from acts of daily survival. Indeed, such acts can be thought of as political *movements* of a different sort—the kind that refugees have always relied on to create the next opening, to find a way out when confronted by a seemingly inviolable power that renders political negotiation irrelevant. While the community organizers of YLP negotiated with the state, Ra kept things moving by turning her apartment into a veritable factory.

This chapter focuses on Ra's experiences in the home-based garment industry—in what could easily be described as her apartment sweatshop, which was not unlike the garment sweatshops in the immigrant enclaves of major U.S. cities. Indeed, in exploring this particular form of labor and resistance, I make sense of what some might consider a sociological improbability: the refugee who produces goods for multinational corporations from the spaces of the hyperghetto— that is, from the site of slavery's urban afterlife. This practice seems improbable because the sociology of globalization often assumes that the global assembly line only passes through contemporary U.S. cities via the immigrant ethnic economy: the Chinatowns and Koreatowns where ethnic business owners, as subcontractors for the garment industry, exploit the labors of mostly undocumented immigrant workers.

The low wages, long hours, and downgraded working conditions of the immigrant sweatshop allow subcontractors to stay competitive with their overseas counterparts. Meanwhile, the hyperghetto is often left out of the globalization discussion, with globalization scholars routinely failing to recognize that, much like the ethnic economy, the hyperghetto is also "globally integrated." Instead, these scholars treat the forms of liberal warfare carried out there as strictly domestic phenomena. The hyperghetto, in other words, is considered by some to be unworldly, even though the output from Ra's various Bronx apartments highlights the multiple and complex ways in which transnational capitalism's crude production processes are indeed inscribed in what has been termed the "neoplantation"—a terrain of liberal warfare, rooted in U.S. slavery, that has always been central to the global economy.

Home as Sweatshop

Just a few months after moving in to her first Bronx apartment in July 1986, Ra was approached by a garment-manufacturing middleman. A refugee from Vietnam who had resettled in the Bronx during the early 1980s, he was fluent in Vietnamese, Khmer, and Mandarin, and served as one link in a chain made up of garment subcontractors and the burgeoning Bronx refugee community. This middleman worked for a Chinatown firm contracted by a larger manufacturer that in turn was contracted by a major retail corporation to produce hair accessories, specifically bows and scrunchies. In the subcontractor's view, it was not cost-effective to produce these smaller items in downtown shops that came with high rents and other overhead costs. Accessories were most profitable when subcontracted out to home-based workers who owned their own sewing machines and paid for their own space and utilities.[1]

Since the earliest days of Southeast Asian refugee resettlement in the Bronx, the middleman had been a common fixture. On a weekly basis he transported his accessory materials to the refugee neighborhoods, offering assembly work to residents interested in earning cash. In exchange for their labor, he paid his refugee homeworkers rates that were comparable to those in many Third World outposts.

The middleman knocked on Ra's door, offering her work, "You need something to do?" Ra recalled him asking. "I have work for you." Ra, however, did not have access to a sewing machine. Undeterred, the middleman offered her work assembling belts. He said she needed only pliers and hole punchers, which he would supply upfront and deduct the cost from her first paycheck. Ra described her average workday assembling belts:

> I worked early in the morning 'til midnight. My husband worked, too. Two of us—we worked about thirteen hours. We used the pliers—everything done by hand. In thirteen hours he made only three dozen. Maybe thirty-six or forty belts. [The middleman] paid three dollars per dozen. So we made about ten dollars after thirteen hours.

According to Ra, the belts were more difficult to assemble than the middleman had let on and she found working with pliers painful and tedious. In wage terms, Ra and her husband each earned approximately 39 cents per hour.

By summer 1987, as the anniversary of her first year in the United States approached, Ra had saved enough to buy her first sewing machine. She could now assemble hair bows, clips, and scrunchies. Among the refugees, homeworking was simply described as "doing bow." Ra and others were paid 90 cents per dozen for scrunchies, $1.50 per dozen for hair bows, and $2.00 per dozen for hair clips. This was slightly less money than belt production offered, but doing bow yielded far more pieces per labor hour. According to Ra, she and her family could average 30 dozen scrunchies in twelve hours. "We once made one thousand scrunchies . . . in a single weekend," recalled her daughter Rorth.

By the late 1990s, Ra and her family were spending up to eighty hours per week assembling accessories for some of the nation's largest retail companies. Her children recalled sewing on brand-name labels. They also recalled sewing on labels that read, "Made In China," which probably meant that the family was producing an order that was originally to have been assembled overseas—in all likelihood a restocking order for a popular item that required a quick turnaround. To meet the retailer's demand, the manufacturer decided to have the scrunchies assembled in the United States and hired a subcontractor to fulfill the order in local sweatshops. Those sweatshops were found in the apartments of Bronx Cambodians.

That the manufacturers and subcontractors had the original "Made in China" label sewn on may strike some as surprising. However, I would argue that there was little if any contradiction for the manufacturers (legality notwithstanding) because in their view the U.S. sweatshop was just an extension of the Third World outpost. Beginning in the 1960s in the United States, the term "Third World peoples" served as a political signifier. It pointed to the parallel struggles and political solidarities between racially oppressed groups in the United States—particularly those who inhabited the insurrectionary ghettos—and the anticolonial and antiimperialist efforts in Asia, Africa, Latin America, and the Caribbean. However, by the late 1990s—as Ra and her children were sewing on "Made in China" labels—that expression had long fallen out of favor. By then, the "Third Worlding" of the U.S. city primarily referred to the way in which the ethnic economy functioned as a simulacrum of the free trade zones of Asia, Latin America, and the Caribbean, where labor lacked protections and big business did as it pleased.

As it happened, however, Ra and her family were actually producing from the site of the postinsurrectionist ghettos—what we might call the U.S. Third World site *of old*—not from the immigrant ethnic economy. In this sense, their homeworking represented the convergence of at least three Third World genealogies: the actual Third World outpost, the insurrectionary ghetto turned hyperghetto, and the immigrant ethnic economy. This convergence was brought into sharp focus in the summer of 2000, when Ra's then sixteen-year-old daughter Rorth video recorded her family's life as hyperghetto homeworkers.

That summer YLP organizers were filming interviews with refugee community members struggling to hold on to their benefits in the face of punitive welfare reform measures. They interviewed welfare mothers who had been unfairly sanctioned, teens who had no choice but to translate for their parents at local welfare centers, and workfare workers who cleaned city streets and parks. Rorth, a YLP youth organizer at the time, came up with an alternative idea. She wanted to film the side of the welfare struggle that few ever see—where poor families convert their homes into sweatshops to supplement welfare benefits that never provide enough to meet basic needs. The footage she captured, which would later be included in the documentary film *Eating Welfare*,[2] constitutes one of the film's most compelling scenes

In the film, Rorth swings open the door of her apartment to reveal a world in which the contradictions of refugee resettlement, the punitive welfare state, and the global sweatshop collide. She uses a point-of-view shot, allowing viewers to see what she sees as she walks through her apartment. She steps through a small foyer that leads directly into the kitchen, and there is Ra, working at a sewing machine while speaking with a friend on the phone. The sewing machine table is placed against the wall of the kitchen, where a small breakfast table should be. Rorth pans right to reveal the rest of the kitchen and points to a box fan that sits on the windowsill, deadpanning "That's what you call an air conditioner."[3] She then points to two sewing machines against the far wall of the kitchen. One of the sewing machine tables doubles as a counter for dishes, a rice cooker, and a crate of eggs. The observant viewer notices the absence of a major kitchen appliance: the refrigerator. By now, Ra has grown impatient with her daughter. She chides Rorth in Khmer, telling her to take the camera elsewhere. Rorth steps into the adjacent living room.

The first thing the viewer notices is that the living room does not have a single piece of typical living room furniture. Against one wall to Rorth's left stand a black filing cabinet and a tall stereo speaker (but no stereo player). Between them is a small television set resting on a folding tray table. Cartoons are playing. The wall directly across from the television, to Rorth's right, consists of a single bookshelf holding a Buddha. Rorth says, "We never forget religion, no matter how poor we get."[4] In the near corner of the room is the refrigerator. Rorth explains: "We don't have enough space [in the kitchen] to put our machines so we put the [refrigerator] out here."[5]

The rest of the room is barren save for a few straw mats on the floor. Sitting on the mats are two eight-year-old boys. One of them is Rorth's youngest brother Vanna; the other is his friend. Between them sits a mound of grey scrunchies. Vanna is in the midst of working his part of the scrunchie assembly line—threading elastic through a fabric hose. His friend is keeping him company. Fixated on cartoons, the boys never look up to acknowledge Rorth and her camera.

Before the scene fades to black, Rorth explains to viewers what they are witnessing:

> There are nine people living here. It's not enough space. We can't afford to get any furniture. . . . This is what we gotta live through because we're on welfare. And they say welfare is supposed to help us. It's not. It's not at all. Because if it was, we wouldn't be living in these [types] of conditions.[6]

In this two-minute unedited sequence of *Eating Welfare*, Rorth dispels the myth of the "welfare cheat" who drains public coffers while enjoying multiple streams of income. Welfare cheats are said to live in housing conditions superior to those of the average working-class person. They are also said to purchase items that nobody on welfare alone could possibly afford: brand-name clothes, new furniture, jewelry, appliances. None of this is in evidence in Rorth's apartment.

To the contrary, Rorth exposes the drastic effects of the welfare trap: substandard housing conditions, furniture-less apartments and long hours of labor. She gives viewers a rare glimpse of the home-working conditions typically endured by many refugee families in the Northwest Bronx and of the particular role that children play in the production process. Building off of this scene in *Eating Welfare*, allow me to briefly elaborate on that process.

Among Cambodian refugees of the Northwest Bronx, homeworking was a family affair: It began with a parent at the sewing machine who converted a rectangular piece of fabric into a simple hose with one fold and a connecting seam. A grade-school-aged child took the fabric hose and pulled it over a rod, usually the leg of an inverted folding chair. The child drew the ends of the hose together, creating folds like the bellows on an accordion for that scrunched effect. From here, a preteen threaded an elastic band through the hose using a chopstick, notched at one end to hold the band in place. Next, one of the teenagers carefully knotted the elastic at its ends, completing the loop before removing the entire piece from the rod and returning it to the parent, who finalized the product by sewing the ends together.

There were of course gendered and generational variations to this division of labor. If a particular child proved prodigious at a certain step, he or she was promoted to that station. Some children were even skilled enough to replace their parents at the sewing machine. I recall stories told to me by teenage brothers Bunroeun and Bona, who were renowned for being one of the fastest scrunchie-making teams among Bronx Cambodians. Bona had a smooth touch on the sewing machine, a skill rarely attributed to boys.

"Nobody ever beat us," Bona boasted, referring to the brothers' firm belief that they had once produced more scrunchies over a given weekend than had any household in the same amount of time—ever. On occasion, they playfully inquired if any other homeworking families had closed in on their unofficial record. In the boys' bedroom hung a photo of them standing defiantly next to a pile of scrunchies that nearly touched the ceiling.

Despite the pride they took in their skill and pace, Bunroeun and Bona, who both became members of YLP, did not enjoy the work or see it as anything other than a burden that took them away from schoolwork, friends, and weekend activities. They understood clearly the terms of exploitation—how little their family made compared to the middleman and the garment manufacturer, to say nothing of the retailers—and they were angry about it. They were also motivated by resentment of their father, who had recently abandoned the family, leaving behind a wife with five children, the youngest only a toddler. They were contemptuous of a welfare state that granted them only enough to cover the rent and threatened to punish them for doing anything aboveboard to make other ends meet. If the brothers took jobs at McDonald's, their family risked losing welfare benefits entirely.

Bunroeun and Bona were the oldest of the children, and they wanted nothing more than to protect their mother. They talked earnestly of becoming "men of the household." If this seems problematically cliché, consider their interesting twist on the patriarchal trope. Becoming men of the household meant mastering the sewing machine and achieving a blazing piece-per-hour rate. They never downplayed their role as homeworkers. They owned it. They "flossed," as the expression goes.

Similarly, as Ra's children mastered a particular task, they took on monikers. Rasmey, for instance, referred to himself as the "elastic master." As they grew older, the children used their workloads as currency; one of them picked up another's work in exchange for material goods or a favor. They also became familiar with one another's work habits; the siblings joked that they all kept a close eye on Rith, who was adept at siphoning off his materials to the others' piles. Ra's children looked back on their homeworking years with regret that they had been trapped in working poverty but also with nostalgia because they considered those years to be the time when they were the closest to one another—the time before their family was broken apart by the state, as I discuss in Chapter 6. Sonya, Ra's youngest daughter, associated the family's completion of large homeworking orders with the few outings they took. "That's when we all went to the beach," Sonya said. "We finished a big order and my mom took us all to Coney Island. That was our reward. We got on the train with all this food, spent the whole day there."

In fashioning these identities and associations out of homeworking, Ra's children, and Bunroeun and Bona, exerted a modicum of control over an impossible situation. In the face of an unscrupulous garment industry and a callous welfare state, they gave alternative meanings to their work as a way to engage forms of power that were overwhelming and out of reach. As historian Robin D. G. Kelley reminds us in his analysis of Black working-class politics and culture, the most highly exploited workers neither fully succumb to nor collectively revolt against their oppressive conditions. Rather, they engage in daily forms of individualized and creative resistance—what Kelley, borrowing from anthropologist James C. Scott, describes as "infrapolitics." "Like Scott," he says, "I use the concept of infrapolitics to describe the daily confrontations, evasive actions, and stifled thoughts that often inform organized political movements."[7] Although this is not a substitute for organized resistance, Kelley suggests that "the political history of oppressed peoples cannot be understood *without* reference to infrapolitics, for these daily acts have a cumulative effect on power relations."[8]

Infrapolitics invites a nuanced analysis of the ways that young Bronx Cambodians understood their lives as workers. It compels us to deal at once with their sense of exploitation, their sense of identity, and the subtle forms of resistance they engaged in. So, too, it encourages us to treat with greater complexity the ways in which Ra and other homeworkers arranged their hyperghetto living quarters as sites of production. How might infrapolitics grant us a more layered reading of the scene captured by Rorth in *Eating Welfare*? The scene immediately reads as an example of a poor family completely capitulating to the productive needs of capitalism, compelled to turn their domestic/private sphere into a sweatshop while turning family relations into work ones. In this it is emblematic of the way in which neoliberalism is said to impose the collapse of the worker's public and private domains into one to shift more of the production costs onto the worker, rendering most labor rights (including occupational safety regulations) irrelevant because homeworkers are technically independent contractors working at a piece-per-hour rate.

Years later Ra offered a more complex picture of the homeworking environment. She certainly agreed with her daughter's assessment of the facts: the family was too poor to purchase furniture. Equally true was the fact that the family had to make room for multiple, industrial-sized sewing machines and create an open space in the living room to assemble products. Still, Ra never believed that she had relinquished control of her living/working space. Nor did she consider homeworking to be an entirely new form of production that signaled the arrival of the neoliberal moment. Indeed, just as the newness of neoliberal welfare reform escaped her, so, too, did the supposed newness of the collapse of the public/private divide. Ra found homeworking to be familiar and routine, if not retrograde. It was completely consistent with past modes of survival that required her to remain mobile and versatile. In other words, it affirmed her refugee temporality—her distinct knowledge that her time and space in the hyperghetto were consistent with the times and spaces of her past captivities.

Homeworking in Refugee Time and Space

As discussed in previous chapters, Ra was used to living on the threshold—in times that were neither past nor present, in spaces that were neither public nor private. This is exactly how she described the time and space of homeworking itself. In 2011, I asked Ra to review her homeworking apartment from the *Eating Welfare* scenes. Here is her interpretation:

> The refrigerator goes out of the kitchen. That's the first thing. Take it out and put it in the living room. Now I put the sewing machine in the kitchen where the refrigerator used to be. From this place, you can see everything when you sew. You can see the front door of the apartment—who comes in and out. You can watch the food on the stove and sew at the same time. The kitchen is where I work. The living room has no furniture. No sofa. No table. No chairs. I only have the refrigerator. The children sit on the floor and do bow. The baby can play around them. I wanted to see everything in front of me because I never knew how long I was going to be in one place. I don't put anything away because you have to take everything with you when you leave.

Here Ra was describing a space of constant, fluid movement in which one activity bled into the next. This movement was deliberate, not random or chaotic. There was an intentional disavowal of compartmentalizing domestic and waged work, living space and working space. Ra spoke as if she had no need for these binaries, which only slowed her down. In this way, she affirmed the notion that the labors of women of color and Third World women in the domestic sphere are never fully distinct from their waged/public work and, inversely, that their work in the public sphere consistently relies on gendered modes of privatization, domesticity, and flexibility.[9] Ra's description of her dynamic and fluid working/living quarters seemed to epitomize this feminist precept.

At the same time, Ra's description was consistent with the specific epistemological standpoint of the refugee, with refugee temporality. Her apartment revealed the unsettledness of the refugee condition; its sparseness conveyed the refugee's belief in mobility as a means of survival in this new territory. Previous chapters discussed the forms of this mobility: multiple apartment relocations and constant shuttling between welfare office, workfare, and factory. Here I propose that mobility was also to be found in the fluid activities taking place in the homeworking apartment. Indeed, Ra was achieving movement through the arrangement of space itself. She set up her apartment in a way that allowed her to continue to maneuver, to manipulate a given terrain where she could produce goods, give care, and socialize with others. Although her homeworking apartment was set up to meet garment production demands, it also afforded her some control over a life of constant uprooting.

As Ra said, "I wanted to see everything in front of me because I never knew how long I was going to be in one place. I don't put anything away because you have to take everything with you when you leave." She sat at the sewing machine in the corner of the kitchen where she had clear line of sight to the apartment door and the living room entrance. She physically positioned herself at the threshold to command control over her environs. Such control was not about domination but about versatility and maneuverability. From her perch, she could sew and manage household tasks such as preparing meals, all the while keeping a watchful eye on the comings and goings of family, friends, and neighbors. This recalls my discussion in Chapter 2 about Cambodian refugees who, resettled to some of the most troubled buildings in the Northwest Bronx, kept their doors open to each other and converted hallways and lobbies into common spaces as a way to enhance collective security. They blurred the lines between public and private to better look after each other.

Visitors constantly streamed in and out of Ra's homeworking apartment. Other homeworkers in the building and throughout the neighborhood routinely called on her for support, and she helped them with instructions, shared materials and tools, and was known in the neighborhood as one of few workers who could repair all three of the major industrial sewing machine brands. Ra's apartment bustled with energy, and its bare living room functioned as more than just a shop floor for scrunchies. She saw her ascetic living space as ideal for small children to play or nap in, and from her sewing station she provided countless hours of childcare for family and friends.

Did any of this amount to resistance and, if so, what kind? There was no evidence of a direct labor-capital confrontation. The owning class was not even indirectly challenged or frustrated, and their profits and interests were never threatened. To the contrary, one could argue that Ra's efficient command of her space only yielded greater returns for the garment industry. However, she clearly refused to succumb to capitalism's demands and constraints. She determined the time and space of her production, simultaneously placing herself in a position to look after others, to extend meaningful acts of solidarity in the hyperghetto.[10]

Unworldly Ghettos

Based in her Bronx apartment, Ra was part of an integrated, if geographically dispersed, assembly line that included other immigrant women workers who toiled in garment sweatshops in New York City and elsewhere. The companies that sold the scrunchies made by Ra and her family also profited from the output of immigrant sweatshop workers in major cities throughout the United States. Unlike Ra, however, these workers, many of whom were undocumented immigrants, were said to live and work in "ethnic economies"—the Chinatowns, Koreatowns, and barrios that mirrored the unregulated and exploitative conditions of their homelands. Returning to the notion of the Third Worlding of the U.S. cities, these sweatshop workers of the ethnic economy represented a new moment in what Immanuel Wallerstein and others have defined as a "world system analysis." According to Wallerstein, the core/Western nations of the world have long dominated and exploited peripheral/Third World nations that are dependent on capital investments. However, during the mid-to-late twentieth century the difference between core and periphery became less relevant[11] because the production functions of the periphery were increasingly being carried out within the core and vice versa. The immigrant sweatshop of the ethnic economy was a salient example of the collapsing of the core and the periphery into one entity.

In many ways, the collapse of the core-periphery divide was consonant with Ra's understanding of her own situation of refugee temporality: she, too, was living in a U.S. urban environment that strikingly resembled her past life in the camps. Just as immigrant workers were routed to U.S. production sites that mirrored those of their homelands, refugees were deliberately placed in a space where the terms of their past experiences with liberal warfare were granted a renewal by landlords, welfare bureaucrats, and now those who managed the global sweatshop chain. This suggests that refugee resettlement can be understood within a world-systems framework, that it conforms to a logic of global migration under late capitalism.

However, scholars of globalization have by and large failed to draw these parallels. In particular, sociologists of globalization have tended to view the immigrant ethnic economy and the hyperghetto as distinct, if not incommensurable, spaces. I would be hard-pressed to find a sociological rendering that recognizes the refugee camp as the periphery and the hyperghetto as its core. My point in calling for this kind of world-systems interpretation is to insist not on a one-size-fits-all rendering of global migration but on an analysis that accounts for the refugee's deliberate routing to the hyperghetto. In other words, I call for an analysis of refugee migration that moves beyond refugee exceptionalism's suggestion that the refugee is only incidentally in the hyperghetto toward a serious consideration of the centrality of the hyperghetto to the global circuit of advanced capitalism. Such an analysis also encourages us to take seriously the liberal warfare carried out in the hyperghetto—to understand that housing, punitive welfare, policing, and mass incarceration are not merely domestic problems but global contradictions. It is precisely this global perspective of the hyperghetto that is absent—or disarticulated—in the main currents of the sociology of globalization. To expound on this critique, I briefly turn to the work of one of the field's pioneering scholars.

Saskia Sassen, who coined the term "global cities," has studied the process whereby the immigrant ethnic economy becomes a Third World within the urban centers of the United States.[12] She sees the globalization of capitalism as the spatial and social reorganization of production across the globe, which requires not only the ongoing exploitation of land and labor in the periphery but also the dispersion of laboring bodies from these poorer and darker nations to the industrialized core. This outmigration has spurred exploitation in the periphery that creates internal disruptions: evictions, debt, unemployment, poverty. Again, all of this explains the movement of Chinese workers to New York's Chinatown sweatshops and, similarly, the revolving door of workers between Mexican *maquiladoras* and downtown Los Angeles manufacturing firms. According to Sassen, this phenomenon has led to a global decline in wages in which "sweatshop production in New York or London has become price competitive with cheap imports from Asia."[13] Global wage suppression, combined with neoliberal austerity, represents the downside of globalization.

However, Sassen also sees important social and political opportunities in the new moment. She is particularly sanguine about the potential for a new kind of resistance taking shape in global cities— major urban centers to which both multinational corporations and a multinational workforce have resettled and converged; these are represented primarily by New York City and Los Angeles. In Sassen's view, a new working class has emerged in these cities whose proximity to the major nodes of global capitalism has given it a political presence not seen in core U.S. cities for some time. She writes:

> [The] disadvantaged in global cities can gain "presence" in their engagement with power but also vis-à-vis each other. . . . Historically this is different from the 1950s–70s period in the United States, for example, when white flight and the significant departure of major corporate headquarters left cities hollowed out and the disadvantaged abandoned. Today the localization of the global creates a set of objective conditions of engagement.[14]

Sassen suggests that even the most vulnerable, marginalized workers of the global city have the potential for resistance. One would assume that this workforce includes homeworkers like Ra, who appear to be distanced from power but are in fact within reach of multinational corporations. However, Sassen's contrasting of the global city of today against the "hollowed out" cities of yesterday leaves one to wonder about the global status of the residents of today's hyperghetto, who live in the remains of this supposedly hollowed out past. Are hyperghetto residents a part of what Sassen describes as the "localization of the global" or do they stand outside of it? One infers from Sassen's body of work that the working class of the global city are low-wage service workers, particularly new immigrants (the subjects of the "subnational unit") who are overworked in the ethnic and broader service economies.[15] These unprotected, contingent workers have never been underemployed, nor have they been the primary recipients of welfare benefits or any state subsidies for that matter; thus they are globalization's overworked, not its "underclass." Yet what are we to make of the overworked Third World migrant such as Ra who lives in and labors from the hyperghetto? They seem to simultaneously fit the description of global sweatshop worker and sociology's problematic dependent and unemployable subproletariat. I propose that if the sociologists of globalization were to "discover" Cambodian refugee homeworkers in the Bronx hyperghetto, they would likely engage in their own form of refugee exceptionalism, making these homeworkers a satellite extension of the ethnic immigrant labor networks (Chinatowns, Little Saigons, etc.). Their labor would be said to *belong* to the subnational unit, not to the hyperghetto. This is because the sociology of globalization does not account for globally integrated labor within the hyperghetto itself.

Perhaps this elision stems from a misreading of the origins of the hyperghetto, particularly of the urban insurrections that gave rise to it. Consider Sassen's take on the difference she sees between today's working-class struggles and the ghetto insurrections of the 1960s. She writes that the latter were "short, intense eruptions confined to the ghettos and causing most of the damage in the neighborhoods of the disadvantaged themselves." Her suggestion here is that the frustrations of African Americans were turned inward as opposed to being outwardly directed at capitalist and state institutions. "In these ghetto uprisings there was no engagement with power," Sassen concludes.[16] This is a rather remarkable statement, considering that the approximately 200 insurrections in 1967 alone forever changed the geographic and demographic fates of some of the largest U.S. cities, forcing business leaders and state officials to negotiate the redistribution of political power (something that nonviolent protest alone never quite achieved). It also ignores the role these insurrections played in compelling the federal government to finally recognize that de facto segregation in the North could be just as insidious as statutory white supremacy in the South. The federal commission that investigated the events of 1967 called for transformative social policies in policing, housing, employment, urban renewal, public education, and small business development.[17] That President Lyndon B. Johnson ignored these recommendations does not diminish the role of mass insurrection in changing national and international discourses on American apartheid.

Even if Sassen is merely referring to what she perceives to be the failure of the ghetto uprisings to directly confront corporate capitalism, her statement proves equally misinformed. One of the first major urban uprisings during the Civil Rights era—and arguably the one that gave rise to the late-1960s insurrectionary period—took place in Rochester, New York, in 1964. Although sparked by police brutality, the unrest addressed the profound race and class inequalities exacerbated by some of the nation's most profitable corporations.[18] These were companies such as Kodak, Xerox, and Bausch and Lomb, which were headquartered in Rochester and made it a premiere industrial town for white workers and professionals. During the postwar years, Rochester was dubbed "Smugtown" because of its high wages, negligible unemployment rate, and ever increasing standard of living. However, none of these economic goods trickled down to the city's Black residents. On the contrary, as Rochester's economy grew, its race and class inequality deepened. The 1964 uprising was a direct response to these globally influenced conditions.

Similarly, the 1967 Detroit uprising was led by Black autoworkers who understood that their radical organizing efforts against the Big Three automakers—Ford, Chrysler, and General Motors—were ineluctably tied to the revolution in the streets.[19] They challenged the racism of a global industry that paid Black workers the least, forced them into the most menial of jobs, and made them the last hired and the first fired. Movement leaders were not interested in collective bargaining agreements but in building a Black workers' revolution. It came as no surprise that many of the militant Black workers held leadership positions in Detroit's Black Power movement, which set the tone for the July 1967 insurrection.[20] They understood that the racial and economic revolutions were inseparable from one another.

Although these urban insurrections of the 1960s forged a new militancy in the Black Freedom movement, they suffered overwhelming defeats. In the end, many of the sites of major urban insurrections were restructured in the 1970s as hyperghettos in a process accelerated by divestment of state and private capital from inner cities. Meanwhile, many of the grassroots leaders guiding the movement beyond insurrection were politically co-opted, incarcerated, or crushed by state violence. Throughout the 1970s, the postinsurrectionary ghetto remained devoid of capital investments (domestic or transnational) because even the most exploitative of industries failed to invest within its boundaries, choosing instead to set up shop in other areas of the city, including the immigrant enclaves. This might explain why the sociology of globalization is generally silent on matters of Black subproletarian life and death in the global city. The hyperghetto—without new immigrant influxes, shop floors, small ethnic firms, or anything resembling a vertically integrated ethnic economy—leaves this sociological subfield very little to say on the matter, and so it chooses not to speak at all.

The Neoplantation

The consequences of the silence of globalization sociologists are significant. In failing to account for the hyperghetto, globalization theorists overlook the ways in which global capitalism continues to reap tremendous rewards from laborers such as Ra, as well as from the multiple forms of liberal warfare endemic to this space: housing displacements, police violence, mass incarceration, and the drug wars.[21] Perhaps a more inclusive sociological paradigm is order, one that can simultaneously account for these acts of warfare and for the ways in which the global assembly line cuts through the hyperghetto.

In theorizing the centrality of Black life and death in the development of global capitalism, geographer Clyde Woods points to such an alternative in his conceptualization of the "neoplantation." The term refers to the Black punishment, capture, disenfranchisement, and displacement endemic to the U.S. plantation that have "grown to become the dominant national and *international* regime."[22]

U.S. slavery was always globally integrated, the plantation economy playing a key role in the development of the world economy throughout the eighteenth and nineteenth centuries. In addition to profits from the global slave trade itself, the cotton produced on Southern plantations spurred the growth of U.S. financial and shipping industries and made them globally competitive. However, Woods maintains that there is more to the globalization of the plantation than the extraction of surplus value. The multiple violences of plantation society—violences that, for example, made the Mississippi Delta one of the poorest regions in North America—have been replicated nationally and internationally as a model of racial punishment, enclosure, and displacement. According to Woods, the contemporary policies and practices carried out in virtually every major modern city which we normally associate with neoliberalism, such as "renewal and gentrification, revitalization, new urbanism, and smart growth," are rooted in the plantation system.[23] In this way, Woods suggests, the neoplantation regime anticipates and perhaps exceeds the neoliberal regime.

The most devastating features of the neoplantation are to be found in the hyperghetto, particularly in its mass incarceration and drug wars. The hyperghetto functions as gateway to the former and theater of the latter. The global economic reach and lucrativeness of both are undeniable. Mass incarceration, much of it managed by private multinational corporations, is among the most profitable industries in the world. According to Ruth Wilson Gilmore, the warehousing of Black bodies serves as the economic engine for many a postindustrial town.[24] Incarceration puts the unemployed back to work in the prison interior and in a range of ancillary industries. (Not incidentally, the Rochester area has particularly benefited from economic growth driven by prison expansion.)

The mass incarceration rate is also accelerated by the so-called war on drugs. Although most research reveals that this war has been lost—or, more accurately, that it was never meant to be won—it remains extremely profitable. In addition to pouring billions of dollars into public law enforcement and the private multinational corporations that support and provision the state (communications, weaponry, surveillance), it has spawned a range of ancillary industries, including drug testing, rehabilitation counseling, and scientific research.[25]

The globally integrated hyperghetto clearly evinces the multiple permutations of the neoplantation. The question remains how this worldly space accounts for the Third World migrant who labors in its interiors. How does it make room for homeworking refugees such as Ra? According to Woods, the answers to these questions might be found in the blues.

In making the case for the neoplantation, Woods introduces the concept of "blues epistemology," which he describes as a dynamic knowledge system of Black survival and resistance in the neoplantation context.[26] This system consistently informs African Americans of slavery's continuance and unending Black dehumanization and underdevelopment. To illustrate, he refers to the unprecedented death, destruction, and displacement visited on African Americans during Hurricane Katrina in 2005 as a "blues moment."[27] Blues epistemology names what the Katrina survivor knows but does not always articulate—at least not through direct statement or inscription—about his or her status as a captive, as one yet to be freed. Such knowledge comes across in music, bodily movement, and acts of survival and solidarity. In this, blues epistemology shares much with refugee temporality. Following the music, it critiques linear, progressive narratives proclaiming that in due time the contradictions of capitalism, white supremacy, and patriarchy will resolve through liberalism. It identifies the multiple ongoing permutations of the past, proving to the survivor that he or she has not crossed over into something new but that terms such as "post-emancipation," "post–Civil Rights," and "postracial" mask slavery's continuance.

Finally, Woods defines blues epistemology as "open," meaning that, although it derives from the specific experiences of those genealogically linked to U.S. slavery, it is at moments partially accessible to others.[28] Other oppressed peoples might sometimes glimpse something of themselves—something resonant—in the blues. Here Woods provides us with a way of understanding the Cambodian refugee's presence in the hyperghetto beyond refugee exceptionalism. How might refugee temporality find a measure of reciprocity in the blues? How does the space that Ra has entered more accurately reflect her own knowledge that liberal war is unending and that resettlement is impossible? Blues epistemology makes room for the refugee: she can work on the global assembly line from any number of places in the world, and yet she works it from *here*.

By way of conclusion, I offer a vignette of all that blues epistemology makes room for. In the winter of 1999, at the height of her family's homeworking years, Rorth took the subway from the Bronx to Times Square. By then, the area had been thoroughly "Disneyfied," converted from what was once a heterogeneous hub of bars, sex shops, and adult theaters from the 1960s through the 1980s into one of the world's largest corporate tourist traps. Indeed, Times Square at the end of the twentieth century stood as the apotheosis of global capitalism's drastic geographic and spatial changes in this global city. Each block housed one or more of the world's largest retail companies, and at the center of it all was the Disney Store.[29]

Rorth entered the store and was immediately drawn to a pile of grey scrunchies in the far corner. "They were of Tigger—from Winnie the Pooh," she recalled and knew them well. Rorth studied one carefully, certain that it was one she had made. She was mesmerized. Perhaps she glimpsed her true place in the world, a position unaccounted for by a sociological imagination that can only conceive of her in fragments: refugee, sweatshop worker, welfare dependent. Or perhaps Rorth saw, for a moment, beyond these boundaries, weaving together what Woods describes as that "coherent system of 'geographical wisdom'" so deftly captured by the blues.[30] Or maybe it wasn't so much what she saw but what she heard. In making the case for the vastness of the blues, Woods poses a rhetorical question: "Is [the blues] profoundly open?" He immediately answers, "Has it not been the soundtrack to successive waves of globalization for nearly a century?"[31]

6
Motherhood

"I stabbed him. I hurt him," Ra said softly. "But I did not want to kill him." The police officer was so startled by Ra's confession that he hardly noticed when she linked arms with him. "I was so scared. I didn't want to let go." It was late January 1998, and the stabbing victim was a middle-aged Cambodian man from the Pelham Bay section of the Bronx. Ra had never met him before their violent encounter. For several weeks prior to the incident, he had repeatedly called Ra's apartment, attempting to speak to Rann, her eighteen-year-old daughter. The man hung up if anybody other than Rann answered. Ra knew something was wrong, and she began investigating. Before long she discovered that his name was Samorn and that he was married with a reputation for harassing young Cambodian women.

At the time, Ra and her family were living on the third floor of an old house on Sedgwick Avenue near Fordham Road, in the University Heights section of the Northwest Bronx. They had moved there in January 1995, shortly after witnessing a homicide on Valentine Avenue. Desperate to leave the apartment on Valentine, Ra jumped at the first opportunity she found. The house was located on the outskirts of University Heights, close to the Major Deegan Expressway and far away from subway stations. Ra and her family had to walk considerable distances to get to schools and grocery stores, but Ra was attracted to the idea of living in a house (the only one she has ever lived in) as well as the prospect of being away from all of the commotion in the heart of the refugee neighborhoods. She described her first three years of living on Sedgwick as relatively peaceful compared to what she had experienced during her first nine years of living in the Bronx. This respite ended abruptly in the winter of 1998.

Ra devised a plan to confront Samorn and tell him to stay away from her daughter. When he called again, she pretended to be Rann and arranged a meeting. She directed Samorn to a friend's apartment on Andrews Avenue in University Heights, one of the main hubs of the Cambodian community and the site of a major drug market where the police maintained a heavy presence. Ra arrived early and positioned herself just outside her friend's door, waiting patiently for Samorn. Once he arrived, she verbally accosted him. She did not intend to use the kitchen knife tucked inside her winter coat unless he attacked her first. Samorn tried to deny everything, and when this proved futile he ridiculed Ra and threatened Rann. Moments later Samorn was on the floor, the kitchen knife lodged in his midsection. Ra stepped into her friend's apartment to call the police.

Perhaps afterwards Ra clung to the police officer because from that moment forward she knew nothing would ever be the same. She was bracing herself for what would happen next. Over the next seven years, from the beginning of 1998 through the end of 2005, Ra faced an attempted murder charge, was investigated by the city's child welfare agency, lost her home, and was forced into homeless shelters. During this time, her marriage ended. Ra's confrontation with Samorn was a confrontation with those who, since her days under the Khmer Rouge, sought control over her as a mother. Just like her home-based garment work and her ongoing struggles with the city's welfare agencies, Ra's labor as a mother was a racialized and gendered practice through which her ongoing captivity was maintained. On that fateful night, however, Ra took action—she made her break—and it resulted in the most volatile period of her Bronx unsettlement. She reflected on the incident:

> I said to myself "I'm not afraid of this man." I experienced the Khmer Rouge and I went through the camps, so I'm not afraid

of him. . . . I couldn't allow anything to happen to Rann. Deep inside I was scared, but I had to do it. If that man did something to Rann, she would have no future in this community.

In this chapter, I trace the unbroken line of patriarchal power shaping Ra's movements from Southeast Asia to the Bronx. I explore her seemingly idiosyncratic experiences and their structural linkages: from a marriage arranged by the Khmer Rouge to the interpersonal and street-level violence of the Bronx to state agencies that criminalize motherhood in the hyperghetto. I demonstrate that Ra's captivity was maintained not only by those who controlled the terms of her housing, welfare, and work but also by the patriarchal relationships to which she was bound.

Refugee women are often said to enter a new relationship with patriarchy on resettlement as the "Americanization" process shifts gender roles within the traditional Southeast Asian family. At first glance, this seemed to have been true for Ra and her husband Heng. Heng was quiet and unassuming. A rail-thin figure, he mostly kept to himself after arriving in the Bronx, rarely participating in the weekend gambling and drinking common among the men in the neighborhood. Heng spent a good amount of his time helping Ra with the homeworking orders, and when the welfare system demanded that the head of the household attend workfare, he was the one to go. In many ways, he did not present as a traditional patriarch. Some community members even described him as passive—a notion that augmented Ra's reputation as assertive and domineering.

On the surface, the couple appeared to fulfill an Asian refugee version of Daniel P. Moynihan's fantasy of a ghetto inhabited by emasculated Black men and Black matriarchs. Just as the "Moynihan Report" was sociological fiction, however, so a facile reading of Ra and Heng's seemingly reversed gendered roles belied the definitively patriarchal nature of their relationship.

Forced Marriage under the Khmer Rouge

It started with a missing vial of medicine. Under the Khmer Rouge, Cambodian villagers were divided into work cooperatives, and in spring 1978 Ra was temporarily assigned to a medical unit caring for the sick and infirmed. One day the unit's inventory came up short. According to Ra, this was common but on this occasion it sparked an investigation. Ra was caught with the vial of medicine she had stolen for an ill family member and was immediately called before the nurse supervising her unit and the head of her local cooperative, a low-ranking Khmer Rouge officer. Ra steeled herself for severe punishment, but, to her surprise, the nurse explained to her and to the officer that Ra had stolen the medicine for her suitor who had fallen ill, a man from another cooperative. Turning to Ra, the soldier said that he would grant leniency if Ra would immediately consecrate her relationship with the man in question. The two would be married in a Khmer Rouge ceremony.

This story was complete fabrication, as convoluted as it was bizarre. Ra had no such suitor nor had she ever seen or heard of the man who would turn out to be Heng. She could not tell if the nurse was trying to protect her or if she was simply doing the bidding of the officer, who routinely arranged marriages throughout the village using whatever pretext he could find to justify a forced union. Still, Ra offered no defense. For a moment she considered pleading for punishment in lieu of the marriage—perhaps a jail sentence—but then she remembered something her father once told her when the Khmer Rouge first took control of her village in 1975: "This is the new Cambodia. There are no more jails." Ra knew that the only way she would come out of this situation alive and be able to protect her immediate family from reprisal was to marry a man chosen by *ankgar*.

During its 1975–1979 reign in Cambodia, the Khmer Rouge claimed several titles, including Democratic Kampuchea and Communist Party of Kampuchea. On a daily basis, however, it referred to itself as *ankgar*, the organization, which evoked a singular, depersonalized omnipotence. *Ankgar* was the state, the culture, and the substitute for religion. It was also the family. Under the Khmer Rouge regime *ankgar* even supplanted parents in the sanctioning of marriages.[1]

Forced marriage under the Khmer Rouge was a particular form of gender and sexual violence that served several objectives. It was one of the primary tools to ensure the dividing line between "base people" and "new people." The former were those identified as "true" Khmers owing to what the regime considered their pure ethnoracial stock and their peasant backgrounds. According to the regime, these were the people on whose behalf the revolution had been waged. New people, by contrast, were considered inauthentic, becoming part of the revolution only after the Khmer Rouge took power in 1975. Among the new people were those from urban areas, ethnic minorities, professionals, Buddhist monks, and the educated. New people who were not immediately liquidated served as the regime's scapegoats, "capitalist-imperialists traitors" who could be blamed for the revolution's failures while also justifying its most extreme measures. This was an essential role that the Khmer Rouge preserved by strictly prohibiting marriages between base people and new people. It enforced this prohibition by arranging all base marriages.

In addition to preserving the social caste system, the Khmer Rouge used forced marriage to replenish the population with loyal subjects and workers because they believed that, when complete strangers were forced into unions, they and their progeny remained more loyal to the Khmer Rouge than to one another. Also, it allowed more effective control of the terms of sexual violence in the new Cambodia. Khmer Rouge soldiers routinely raped Cambodian women. On occasion the regime leaders denounced such rape as a crime against the masses, which they "fixed" by sometimes allowing male cadres to choose women to wed. Of course, these women had no choice in the matter. Forced marriages legitimized—indeed, ceremonialized—forced sexual relations. In the view of the Khmer Rouge, rape happened outside of marriage, so it was not rape when a male soldier forcibly married and had sex with his wife. Studies on Khmer Rouge forced marriages are replete with the testimonies of women who were raped by their husbands, with the assistance of the men's comrades, after refusing sex on their wedding nights.[2]

Ra met Heng on their wedding day in April 1978. Although never recruited as a Khmer Rouge soldier, he was the prototypical base person—an agricultural worker who toiled for the Khmer Rouge's massive indentured agrarian state. At twenty-four, he was also considered by the regime to be at the perfect age for a marriage arranged by *ankgar*. Following a ceremony that lasted only a few minutes, Ra was immediately sent to live with Heng in his home and was never again to share a home with her parents and siblings.

> I was only twenty. The Khmer Rouge—they put women who were twenty with the men twenty-five and up. I didn't even know what was going to happen that day. They called me into the room. I waited there for two hours. Two hours later, that's when he came. That's when I saw Heng. They told us to sit next to each other, [and then] they married us: "Stand up. Say your name. Now shake the hand. Now [you are] husband and wife."

As Ra shared this memory with me, she joked that this was a "new-style" Cambodian wedding and certainly more efficient than the traditional Khmer ceremony that could last for days. Such was the gallows humor she often deployed when there were no words to adequately express the terror and shame she felt under the Khmer Rouge. Indeed, Ra had no illusions that her wedding was anything but a sentencing: "If you say no, they'll kill you that night." She described the walk to Heng's house after the ceremony:

> I don't want to go to his house. But if I don't go, I think they're going to kill me. I walked over there, but I don't want nobody to see me. I don't look to the people around me. I want to cry. I want to close my eyes because I don't want nobody to see me.

Shortly after the marriage, the Vietnamese invasion of Cambodia commenced, and in January 1979 Ra and Heng were driven into exodus with Khmer Rouge soldiers who had taken them hostage. Held at gunpoint, the couple traipsed the forests of western Cambodia as captives throughout most of that year. During this time, Ra discovered that she was pregnant and gave birth to Rann in October 1979, two months before she and Heng were finally able to escape their captors and cross into Thailand. Many Cambodian couples ended their forced marriages following the ousting of the Khmer Rouge regime and its replacement by the Vietnam-backed People's Republic of Kampuchea (PRK), but Ra and Heng stayed together; their situation presented few other options for Ra. In the forests, single women, particularly mothers, were vulnerable to attack by Khmer Rouge soldiers, paramilitary forces, and bandits. Marriage provided Ra some protection from these threats.

In early the 1980s, Ra and Heng would have three more children together while living in the Khao-I-Dang refugee camp in Thailand: two sons, Rasmey and Rom, born in 1981 and 1982, and their daughter Rorth, born in 1984. When they decided to apply for asylum, the couple discovered that their status as a nuclear family would prove beneficial to their application and eventually their resettlement. The Office of the United Nations High Commissioner for Refugees and U.S. refugee resettlement policies prioritized the protection and resettlement of nuclear families with small children. In contrast, single adults, multigenerational households, and nonheteronormative families had a difficult time building their asylum cases.[3] Moreover, the humanitarian workers and soldiers who ran the camps allocated resources, particularly food, according to the number of people in each family. For this reason, polyamory was common. Married men pursued single women, including widows with children, to claim more than one family and thus more rations.

Once Ra, Heng, and their children resettled in the Bronx, the nuclear family incentive persisted through their two income streams: the welfare agency paid them more as a two-parent household, and two adult assembly line workers meant more homeworking income. However, nearly fifteen years after resettlement, Ra questioned whether or not her marriage could still fulfill her goal of protection for herself and her children. The fallout from the stabbing incident suggested to her that it could not.

Waiting Out Captivity

As news of the stabbing reverberated throughout the Bronx Cambodian community, Heng refused to defend his wife and daughter; nor did he publicly condemn Samorn. Instead, he stayed quiet and remained out of sight. At home, in private, however, he blamed Ra for shaming him and blamed Rann for drawing Samorn's attention: Ra should have looked after their daughter more carefully.

Heng's reaction was Ra's breaking point. Following her arrest and conviction, she decided to leave him, to do whatever she could to "bring the children *out* from this man":

> I decided I can't be with him anymore. It was right after my arrest. Everybody was talking about me and Rann. Everybody in the community was saying I was crazy. They gave the younger children a hard time. "Why did your mother do that? Is she crazy?" But [Heng] didn't say anything. He didn't defend the family. He told me I brought him shame. That's when I decided I was going to leave him and take the children away.

This would not be easy or quick. Divorcing Heng meant finding a new home and fighting for custody. On both counts, Ra's timing could not have been worse. Her public defender told her that a jury conviction would result in a lengthy prison sentence, but he anticipated that the prosecutor would offer a plea bargain to avoid trial. In fact, during negotiations the prosecutor offered three years of supervised probation in lieu of prison for a plea of guilty to aggravated assault. Ra's lawyer advised her to accept the plea in return for a shorter sentence. His explanation was simple, if unsettling: Samorn was himself facing sexual assault charges related to another incident. The prosecutor seemed eager to close the case against Ra, realizing that going to trial with Samorn as his complainant and key witness would be disastrous. Ra accepted.

From 1998 to 2001, Ra served her probation and regularly checked in with her probation officer. She was also subjected to unannounced probation visits as well as rules prescribing where and with whom she could socialize. Finally, she was required to seek counseling from a social worker. Under such intense scrutiny, Ra felt that she had no choice but to defer her plans to leave her husband. On top of all of this, in August 1999 she and her family were victims of yet another housing calamity. A fire on the first floor of the house they lived in—according to Ra, the result of the first-floor tenant's unextinguished cigarette—caused enough smoke damage to her third-floor unit that she and her family were forced to move out. They immediately moved into an apartment building on 193rd Street that housed numerous Cambodian refugee families.

Ra was now back in the neighborhood she had so eagerly left behind four years earlier. She thought of moving out on her own and then sending for her children, but she feared that any such move would be misconstrued as an attempt to evade authorities, which would result in a probation violation and prison. She also feared that Heng could easily retaliate against her. If Ra decided to leave and take their children, he could falsely accuse her of something that could send her to prison for violating probation. If that happened, Ra knew, she would be in no position to fight for custody.

So she decided to wait, reasoning that the three years would pass quickly. She continued to share the apartment with Heng, but kept to herself. She no longer shared a bedroom with him, choosing to sleep in the living room, which doubled as a small garment factory. Ra focused entirely on her children and homeworking during this period. She was relieved that Heng was on a mandatory workfare assignment so they would not be partnering on homeworking orders. "We were completely separated. I was living with him, but I was done."

Ra's capture by the criminal justice system, combined with her capture by the city welfare and resettlement systems and her marriage, took a toll on her self-confidence. For the first time in nearly two decades of motherhood, she felt insecure about her ability to protect her children. What if one of them were threatened again? How could she defend that child without being arrested? Ra also felt a growing sense of danger, a fear that the violence in her neighborhood was escalating. Each week seemed to bring news of another beating, stabbing, or shooting of a Cambodian refugee youth. Some of the victims were children she knew; she had witnessed their quick transition from childhood to a cruel adolescence marked by emergency rooms, courtrooms, and prisons. Their stories fed Ra's growing sense of helplessness that made enduring her probation and her marriage increasingly difficult. Nevertheless, she was determined to outlast these trials, and she claimed that she would have had new problems not arisen with her son Vanna.

Child Welfare

Vanna, Ra's youngest child, was only six years old when Ra was convicted of aggravated assault in 1998. When prison seemed imminent, she worried most about the impact it would have on "the baby." Although she was spared prison, over the course of her three-year probation her fears for Vanna continued.

No sooner had Vanna started fourth grade in 2001 than the truancy letters began arriving. He left in the morning and returned in the evening, but his real whereabouts were a mystery. Sometimes when he returned home he was scraped and bruised, his clothing torn. This continued for a month before Ra realized that he was skipping school and falling into all sorts of trouble—getting into fights and running from truancy officers. Vanna returned to school for a period of time before going astray once more. Ra believed that before long he would fall in with one of the local gangs that robbed or dealt drugs. She was so consumed by her fears for him that she barely noticed when her probation came to an end. No longer focused on leaving her husband, Ra now focused on saving her son. She tried both reprimand and reward to change his behavior, but nothing proved effective. She felt she had lost control.

"I don't want it anymore," Ra said to her social worker in May 2002. "I don't want to be a mother." Then came another life-altering confession. "I hit him," she said, "With a belt. I hit Vanna very hard." The irony was that by then Ra had already served her probation and so counseling was no longer required. During her probation years, she had found the sessions helpful, and she continued with them. Each week, she traveled ninety minutes by subway to Chinatown for a forty-five-minute session. She chose that particular social worker, a young Vietnamese American, because her interpreter was a friend; Ra felt she could trust her. "I wanted her to help me. I needed to tell somebody that I couldn't do it."

After Ra's confession that she had hit Vanna with a belt, the social worker asked some follow-up questions: How badly was he injured? Were marks left on his body? Did anybody else witness the beating? Ra answered each question honestly. The following evening, a caseworker from the city's child welfare agency arrived at Ra's apartment, accompanied by the police, to interview and examine Vanna. She took photographs of his back while the officers detained Ra in the hallway. The caseworker then interviewed other members of the family.

Ra was placed in handcuffs and taken to Bronx central booking. She spent two nights in jail before being arraigned on charges of battery and endangering the welfare of a child. The judge also issued an order of protection prohibiting Ra from seeing or making unauthorized contact with Vanna, and she was ordered to move out of the family's apartment immediately. Ra believes that had this arrest occurred less than a year earlier—while she was still on probation—she would have been sent to prison.

It was May 2002, and Ra had waited more than three years to break free of the husband whom the Khmer Rouge had ordered her to marry. Now she was forced out of her home by the state, charged with a crime against her youngest child. At that point, Ra and Heng stopped living together. Two decades earlier, *ankgar* had compelled their marriage. Now, and just as abruptly, the state intervened to bring that union to its decisive end by displacing Ra from her home:

> The judge and police—they told me I had to leave the house. I couldn't live with Vanna or Sonya anymore. For a long time I wanted to separate from their father and take all the children with me. But now I couldn't be with the children because I was being thrown out. I had no home for five years.

From 2002 to 2007, Ra led a nomadic life. She moved in and out of multiple apartments, rarely staying in any of them for more than a month or two. She moved so many times she lost count. Displaced from her family home, she lost her two main sources of income. Because she was no longer counted as part of the family's welfare grant, Heng was listed as sole head of household and the dependent children were budgeted entirely under him. Lacking a permanent place to live, Ra could no longer take homeworking orders.

These losses were meaningless when compared to the lost time with her children. In addition to Vanna, three of her children were still in high school, and they spent those crucial years without the full presence of their mother, who had always been an anchor in their lives. "All because the social worker snitched," said Rith, her middle son.

Criminalizing Motherhood in the Hyperghetto

Notwithstanding Rith's belief, Ra's predicament cannot be reduced to the actions of individual agents. The criminalization of motherhood in the hyperghetto is unrelenting and pervasive. Not only is the hyperghetto an "ethnoracial prison," as Loïc Wacquant asserts, but it is a profoundly gendered site of captivity.[4] Indeed, the extension of the prison interior into impoverished neighborhoods is made possible by the marriage of the social welfare and penal arms of the state, one carried out through and against the bodies of poor women of color, particularly Black women. Activist-scholar Beth E. Richie elucidates the gendered entrapment of poor and marginalized Black women and its responsibility for so much daily violence in the hyperghetto. She claims that these women are among the most susceptible in the United States to sexual assault, battery, and emotional abuse by men. Their vulnerability does not afford them the protections of the state and civil society; on the contrary, the most vulnerable among them are often criminalized and incarcerated.

In *Compelled to Crime: The Gendered Entrapment of Battered Black Women*, Richie tells of women detained in New York City's jail on Riker's Island. In stark and harrowing detail, she draws a direct line between the terror committed by men against poor women in the domestic sphere, crimes committed by these women in response to such violence, and the violence of the prison cell.[5] Her analysis suggests that social welfare programs often do more harm than good for such women because they are undergirded by a logic that a priori frames the lives of women of color as deviant and undeserving.

In *Arrested Justice: Black Women, Violence and America's Prison Nation*, Richie elaborates the ways in which abused Black women are more often cast as criminals than as victims.[6] Significantly, the "prison nation" includes key hyperghetto sites—public housing overrun by rogue police; schools where young women are punished for adolescent pregnancy and other "deviance"; and the welfare state, in which poverty is equated with bad motherhood. State and civil institutions enclose and capture women who are already trapped in dangerous interpersonal relationships, making it impossible for these institutions to regard, for example, a young Black woman who commits a desperate act after being raped and abused by male relatives as anything other than a criminal. Richie asserts that "Black women in low-income communities are perhaps in greater danger than ever."[7]

Richie's research suggests that gendered violence against Black women is not another way to analyze hyperghetto captivity but rather the *only* way to accurately understand its structure and function. The centering of the experiences of Black women in the hyperghetto calls for a ground-level analysis of the fusion of social welfare and penality, an analysis which inextricably links interpersonal and state violences. This more exacting analysis in turn raises several questions about the racial and gendered particularity of different populations of women who survive in the hyperghetto. Indeed, how might we understand the distinct position of Southeast Asian refugee women who are situated in relation to the demonization and criminalization of Black women?

Although Ra's experiences are similar to those of the women discussed in Richie's study, it would be myopic to suggest that Cambodian refugee women are compelled, criminalized, and confined in the hyperghetto in precisely the ways that Black women are. A relational analysis is in order, one that takes into account how the violence committed against some women is strengthened and extended through the discursive obfuscation or outright erasure of violence against others. Here I am calling attention to how the forms of refugee exceptionalism discussed throughout this book play out in distinctly gendered ways. Even as refugee women are confined to the hyperghetto, they are the subjects of a discursive rescue from this space and its attendant violences—a rescue that distinguishes them from their Black counterparts. To understand this removal requires one to confront the ideologies and discourses that have, for nearly five decades, pathologized, vilified, and criminalized Black women in urban America.

In 1965, responding to fomenting urban unrest in U.S. cities, Patrick D. Moynihan, then assistant secretary of labor, published *The Negro Family: The Case for National Action*. The "Moynihan Report," as it became known, has served as a foundational text in the unending debate over the roots of Black urban poverty and social marginalization. Moynihan claimed that the Black family was a "tangle of pathology" because Black women had been structurally and discursively favored over Black men in education and employment.[8] He insisted that the Black matriarch had taken control of the family, weakening the traditional patriarchal family structure. This familial rearrangement, according to Moynihan, could only beget crime, shiftlessness, and poverty for urban African Americans.

Moynihan's argument was not entirely original; the report was mostly a rehash of other scholarly arguments that reformulated, as social science, longstanding racist and sexist tropes about Black families. Perhaps its longevity has had less to do with its stated argument than with its deft reinscription of white supremacist and patriarchal logics in the guise of racial liberalism. Moynihan would have a long and distinguished career in the U.S. Senate, demonstrating that the liberal can indict structural racism and simultaneously render the subjects of that racism blameworthy.

Moynihan began his report by describing structural racism as the "virus in the American blood stream" and then acknowledging that Black oppression in the 1960s was rooted in the horrors of slavery and Jim Crow.[9] He and those he quoted repeatedly relied on the passive voice when discussing the peculiar institution of slavery. For example, he quoted Nathan Glazer on the emasculation of Black slaves: "His children could be sold, his marriage was not recognized, his wife could be violated or sold (there was something comic about calling the woman with whom the master permitted him to live a 'wife'), and he could also be subject, without redress, to frightful barbarities."[10] Similarly, Moynihan described Jim Crow's gendered effects as "keeping the Negro 'in his place' [which] can be translated as keeping the Negro male in his place: the female was not a threat to anyone."[11] In both instances, the report identified no specific agents who had driven (and continued to drive) white supremacy and patriarchy.

In contrast, Moynihan used the active voice in his discussion of Black matriarchs: "The matriarchal pattern of so many Negro families reinforces itself over the generations"[12] and "Negro females have established a strong position for themselves in white collar and professional employment, precisely the areas of the economy which are growing most rapidly, and to which the highest prestige is accorded."[13] Here the active voice clearly identified Black women as the agents behind the emasculation of Black men and the breakdown of the Black family in postwar urban America.

Moynihan made the racism, sexism, and economic exploitation that Black women experienced in the labor market irrelevant, including those putative white-collar jobs he lauded. He said nothing about the low-wage industrial, service, and domestic work in which so many Black women toiled, nor did he make anything of the fact that they continued to labor as uncompensated homemakers and caregivers. What is most stunning, however, is Moynihan's treatment of rape. He drew on Glazer's assertion that Black women could be "violated and sold" with impunity as a way to convey, without hesitation or qualification, that the systemic rape of Black women was a unique problem for *Black men*. He made no mention of the suffering endured by Black women or their resistance to sexual terror.

In 1972 Angela Davis issued a rebuttal to Moynihan, critiquing him not only for promulgating the myth of Black matriarchs whom he pointed to as complicit in the emasculation of Black men (and so complicit in their own violation under slavery) but also for failing to recognize their resistance to sexual violence—how "the countless children brutally fathered by whites were conceived in the thick of battle."[14] According to Davis, Moynihan's Black matriarch figure did the ideological work of rendering Black women's victimization and resistance impossible, reinforcing their object status—the status of the slave who as property was disqualified from female victimhood and agency. Again, according to Moynihan, "the female was not a threat to anyone."

Moynihan's disqualification comes into sharper focus when we consider the crude binary to which the matriarch is always bound. Black feminist thinkers have long maintained that the myth of the Black matriarch works so effectively because its only alternative is the "bad mother" whose negligence and abusive behavior are attributed to her assumed social and sexual deviance. The bad mother is a derivative of the "Jezebel" and more recently of the "welfare queen"—the woman whose sexuality and fertility must come under patriarchal social control. The matriarch and the bad mother are the two sides of one coin. Throughout the 1970s, as the post-insurrectionary ghetto gave way to the hyperghetto, the bad mother replaced the matriarch as the dominant figure in representations of the urban terrain.

Southeast Asian Refugee Matriarchs?

During their resettlement in the United States throughout the 1980s and 1990s, many Southeast Asian refugee families supposedly experienced shifting gender dynamics consistent with Moynihan's thesis. Resettlement was said to grant refugee women greater opportunities to become primary income earners, and those who did not secure employment were buoyed by a welfare state that either granted benefits directly in their names or, at the very least, listed both husbands and wives as heads of households. In contrast, refugee men were said to possess fewer opportunities once they arrived in the United States because the postindustrial economy had little need for their unskilled labor. According to sociologist Yen Le Espiritu, these dynamics played out across multiple Asian immigrant groups in the United States during the 1980s, but they were particularly pronounced among poorer Asians.[15] Aihwa Ong explains these shifting gender dynamics and how they took shape among low-income Cambodian refugees in the San Francisco Bay Area. She says that high rates of unemployment among Cambodian men led to their devalued status in the household, which in turn led to a breakdown in the traditional Cambodian family structure:

> The Cambodians' customary family roles and gender norms became, if not irrelevant, at least severely undermined, as men failed to support their families and wives became more assertive in seeking help. Relations between husband and wife, parents and children came to be dictated, to a significant degree, not by Cambodian customs of unchallenged male power, as they remembered them, but by the pressing daily concerns.[16]

Ong further notes that "the frustration these men felt contributed to cases of wife battering and women seeking refuge in shelters."[17] Many of these women found support from feminist social workers, who encouraged their clients to challenge or leave their husbands.

According to Ong, while the dynamic between social workers and refugee women was paternalistic, "based on racial difference and female clientelism,"[18] the refugee women used the social workers, extracting what material benefits they could out of the relationship even as they were privately critical of those in the helping professions.[19]

In sharp contrast to Moynihan's analysis, Ong does not believe that these shifting gender dynamics led to a subversion of the patriarchal order in refugee communities.[20] Certainly there is no evidence to suggest that the term "matriarch" was ever used to describe Cambodian and other Southeast Asian refugee women, even though these women vied to become heads of households and their husbands became increasingly disempowered, withdrawn, resentful, and abusive. Rather, it appears that they were subjected to a different form of racialization and gendering, one that figured them to be in need of rescue by Western liberal feminism. This is apparent in Ong's critique of social workers who, through their prodding and condescension, sought to Americanize refugee women. Indeed, in her assessment, the gender conflict between Cambodian men and women was emblematic of a new and distinctly American condition: "American values [shaped] the motivations and actions of women and men as their Cambodian family ethics faded and they gradually became American persons."[21]

The examples drawn from Ong's study certainly resonate with Ra's experiences. She, too, was subjected to the belief of those in the helping professions that the refugee was to be saved from what they perceived to be a backward and authoritarian Cambodian culture. However, I argue that Ra's experiences with patriarchal control and violence (both state and interpersonal) were neither new nor definitively "American" contradictions but rather extensions of an unbroken line of patriarchal power. Although each pivotal event that Southeast Asian refugee women experienced—Khmer Rouge captivity, camp detention, resettlement in the United States—presented unique conditions, one cannot easily discern the junctures in space or time at which they experienced the closing of one set of patriarchal relations and the opening of another. If anything, the experiences of women like Ra speak to a *longue durée* of gendered violence that reveals an underlying and undisturbed current of power cutting through these putative turning points.

The Americanization of gendered violence seems to hinge on oversimplified tropes of shiftless and irresponsible men. Recall that Ra's husband Heng was never jobless. He did his share of the homeworking, and he did workfare when the state mandated it. He was not given to the excessive drinking and gambling that kept many refugee men in the neighborhood from their domestic responsibilities. Indeed, the two main factors that Ong describes as destabilizing the traditional Cambodian family did not apply in Ra's situation—men's inability to generate income and their refusal to participate in the domestic sphere. Still, Ra felt no less trapped than the women Ong interviewed.

Ra's relationship with her husband emerged out of a ceremonial act of gendered violence. As discussed earlier, because she was never freed—her emancipatory moment never quite arrived—she did not end her marriage after her release from captivity in 1979. No sooner had the Khmer Rouge faded into the background than Ra came under the control of other lethal forces that required her to stay married to survive:

> When the Khmer Rouge had us in the jungle, I had to stay with Heng. I couldn't leave him because a woman can't be alone. If you are alone then you are nobody . . . you are not safe. You had to be part of a family. I didn't have my father or my brothers. I had a husband—that was my only family.

In the Thai refugee camp, marriage and motherhood were the keys to material survival and eventual resettlement. After nearly two decades in the Bronx, Ra finally saw an opportunity to end her marriage only to come under the control of a criminal justice/social welfare system that kept her physically bound to Heng before displacing her from the household without her children. I am compelled to ask: At what point did the violence of her forced marriage come to an end, inaugurating the supposedly new *American* moment?

Ra was subjected to an unbroken continuity of patriarchal power that continued to shape her experiences with gendered violence in the United States. The same power served as the basis on which various agents interpellated her, situating her as a distinct subject within the hyperghetto. I argue that as Ra encountered various state agents—police, judges, child welfare workers, social workers—she was consistently figured as the refugee whose troubles stemmed from her foreignness, not her Americanization. This leads me to question whether the social workers in Ong's study who sought to convert Cambodian women into American subjects were, paradoxically, invested in the refugees' perpetual foreignness.[22] That is, how did they recognize the long trajectory of gendered violence in the lives of refugee women and draw on it to engage in refugee exceptionalism? By refusing to allow the women to Americanize and become that "American dilemma" that encodes Black urban poverty, the social workers preserved their function as continually delivering the refugees to freedom. For this ongoing rescue to take effect, refugee exceptionalism demanded that Cambodian women remain foreign/deserving subjects as opposed to domestic/undeserving subjects worthy of punishment.

The racialized and gendered distinction between undeserving and deserving women in the hyperghetto is evident in the difference between the Black matriarchal trope and the supposed empowerment of refugee women at the expense of refugee men. Refugee women were not subject to the same binary; indeed, the "other side" of their empowerment was not the vilified bad mother but the war-touched migrant who had yet to be fully saved. If the refugee mother in the hyperghetto remained on welfare for long periods of time and exhibited high fertility, she was quickly exempted from welfare queen status.

This distinction was made clear in social science research conducted during the early 1980s on Southeast Asian refugee adaptation. For example, from 1982 to 1985 sociologist Rubén Rumbaut directed a study known as the Indochinese Health and Adaptation Research Project (IHARP), one of the first comprehensive evaluations of the economic and social conditions of Cambodian, Hmong, Laotian, and Vietnamese refugees who had resettled in impoverished Southern Californian urban centers. In one key IHARP study, "Fertility and Adaptation: Indochinese Refugees in the United States," Rumbaut and coauthor John Weeks offer an explanation for the high fertility among Southeast Asian refugee women on welfare. They provide several rationales, including the notion that refugees view childbearing as a means to secure and strengthen future networks of labor and capital. They also propose that high fertility is simply a matter of cultural retention, particularly among second-wave refugees with rural backgrounds, and argue that such practices fade away as refugees assimilate.[23]

In the three and a half decades since Southeast Asian refugees began arriving in large numbers, there has been little evidence to suggest that their reproductive choices have helped them escape working poverty and chronic unemployment. Meanwhile, high fertility rates have persisted, even among second-generation welfare recipients who maintain no connection to a rural Southeast Asian past. These young women were "acculturated" into U.S. capitalist democracy at the intersection of social welfare and punitive policies, and by the mid-to-late 1980s their political and personal choices were being shaped by them.[24]

Here I am less interested in proving the IHARP prognosis wrong than in highlighting, once again, the ideological, discursive, and structural work of refugee exceptionalism. My interest lies in understanding how adaptation research abstracts refugee women from the hyperghetto, even though these women are fully subjected to its economic and state violences. In this sense, the research conceals the trajectory of state violence extending from refugees' Southeast Asian homelands through the refugee camps and into the urban terrains of asylum-granting nations. At the same time, it disassociates refugee women from other women in the hyperghetto, considering them the deserving exception among women in urban poverty because of their circumstances of war, newcomer status, and cultural retention. This disassociation indirectly reinforces the undeserving status of poor Black women, whose high fertility rates are attributed to their supposed desire for more welfare benefits or to a "culture of poverty" that is said to be reproductive as opposed to productive.

The consequences of instantiating an undeserving group cannot be overstated. At stake here is not merely sociological misrepresentation and disrespect; rather, as Beth Richie reminds us, it is often a matter of life and death. Black women who fall into this category are routinely denied material resources as well as support and legal protection from the men who abuse them. They become particularly susceptible to abuses committed by law enforcement, and they are fast-tracked for prison. Refugee exceptionalism makes the hyperghetto much more lethal for Black women.

Herein lies the paradox for refugee women such as Ra. She may be regarded as the exception in the hyperghetto, but she is certainly not spared its realities.

Making Family in the Hyperghetto

In spring 2004, Ra and Vanna were officially reunited by the state after nearly two years, although during that interval they actually saw each other quite often, certainly more often than the law permitted. Vanna often sneaked into whatever apartment Ra was squatting in to spend time with her, occasionally spending the night. She never stopped his visits, even though she was aware of the risk that she would be sent to jail immediately if she were caught violating her order of protection.

The events leading up to their reunion began a year earlier, during spring 2003, when without warning, Ra briefly lost track of Vanna. She called the apartment where he lived with Heng and her other children, but he wasn't there. She learned from her other children, with whom she was allowed to communicate, that Vanna often stayed out past midnight and on some nights didn't come home at all. Heng did nothing to challenge or stop this behavior.

Ra, desperate to find Vanna one evening, finally called the police. Vanna returned before the police arrived, but Ra decided to file the report anyway, using it as the basis for a complaint with the very child welfare workers who had prohibited her from being with her son. Ra now had proof that Vanna was being neglected, and she was prepared to fight for him.

Perhaps cognizant of its potential culpability if anything were to happen to Vanna, the child welfare agency eventually decided to modify its case against Ra and restore her right to live with him; he was now ordered to split his time between his parents. Ra, however, was determined to fight for full custody despite the fact that she was homeless. She had been bouncing between the apartments of friends and adult children (Rann was now in her early twenties and living with her fiancé), and not having a stable place to live, even a temporary one, jeopardized her case. Ra needed an address, and the only way she could obtain one was to enter the city's family shelter system. In the spring of 2005, she and Vanna began their six-month shelter residency, and several months later she was awarded full custody. (According to Ra, Heng did not fight this decision.)

While living in the shelter, Ra and Vanna had little privacy. They were buzzed in and out of front doors, corridors, and common rooms, and had a nighttime curfew.

> I remember the first nights we were in the shelter Vanna would cry every night. He didn't know why we had to be there. Some nights I felt so bad for him, I took him out and we just walked somewhere. But the shelter had a curfew. So I had to find someplace for us to go and sleep. I called one of the other kids or my friends to see if we could stay there. The shelter felt like a prison.

Ra was again a mother to her son but only in this distinct state of confinement. "I didn't know what would happen to us next, but we were together." Life in the shelter crystallized the terms of the hyperghetto, clearly illustrating the union of the social welfare and penal systems. In the shelter, several indistinguishable state practices were carried out simultaneously, among them the criminalization of motherhood, the ostensible protection of women and children from domestic violence, and the provision of a social safety net for the homeless. The meshing of these functions represented the rule, not the exception, for the poorest and most vulnerable of mothers in early-twenty-first-century urban America—a rule that applied no less to the Cambodian refugee.

Discourses on refugee exceptionalism would proclaim that Ra and Vanna's residency in the shelter was anomalous—that Cambodian refugees, racialized and gendered as Asian immigrants, did not truly belong there. However, Ra's experiences with gendered violence across three decades and two continents suggest that quite the opposite was true: such spaces of captivity were all she had ever truly known.

Conclusion: "Unsettled"

Ra doesn't know how many times the van rolled over. She can only say that a lamppost along that stretch of the New Jersey Turnpike probably saved her life. It was shortly after midnight, and Ra, sitting two rows directly behind the driver, couldn't see that he had fallen asleep. The van careened left, but before it struck the median the driver woke up and swerved sharply in the opposite direction. The sudden change in direction at that velocity caused the van to flip over on its side. Only the lamppost prevented the van from rolling down a steep embankment.

That September evening in 2005 was much like all the other evenings that Ra and other Cambodian workers had been driven to the Bronx from New Jersey, where they had just ended a night shift at the cookie factory. Ever since the courts had removed her from her home—a decision that left her with no welfare benefits or any way to do homework—Ra relied almost exclusively on factory wages. For several months she had worked double shifts, hoping to save enough to move herself and Vanna into their own apartment.

The accident left Ra with a shattered knee and several deep head lacerations, and she spent one week in St. Joseph's hospital in Patterson, New Jersey. Her children tried to visit each day, but the commute proved too difficult, requiring a series of transfers on subways, regional trains, and buses that amounted to nearly three hours in each direction.

Ra never fully recovered. She walked with a limp and occasionally suffered from severe headaches and dizziness—post-concussion symptoms, according to her doctors. Because these ailments prevented her from returning to work, she was without welfare benefits, homeworking income, or factory wages. She had always scratched out a living by seizing the next opportunity, but now her constrained movements limited her options. Her friends asked her if she would consider moving back to Cambodia, but Ra had long ago given up on that idea.

A few months after the accident, a friend told Ra that social workers at a South Bronx nonprofit organization called Part of the Solution (POTS) had helped a mutual acquaintance find permanent housing. The friend suggested that Ra contact POTS for help, but Ra was reluctant to deal with social workers after her experiences with the one who reported her to the city's child welfare agency in 2002. The friend assured Ra that POTS would not betray her.

POTS staff members told Ra that her injuries qualified her for Supplemental Security Income (SSI) for people with disabilities, and they offered to assist with the application. If it was approved, they would help Ra find an apartment that she could afford on her monthly check. Within one year of her accident, Ra received her first SSI check. In another nine months, in May 2007, Ra and Vanna finally moved into their own apartment. Ra occupies it to this day.

Refugee Movements

Movement is this book's enduring motif. Ra's story concludes in the form of a violent car accident that, ironically, closed the most volatile period of her Bronx years. After the accident, Ra was no longer subject to recurring crises. This is not to say that she was finally resettled (in the way the state agencies described it) or that the hyperghetto's structural violences and poverty no longer affected her life. Rather, she now experienced a significant shift in her daily activities. For the first time in her Bronx unsettlement, Ra was granted an extended reprieve. From her time in Cambodia to her time in the Thai camps to her time in the Bronx, constant movement was always a necessity, never an option. Now, however, she was no longer compelled to stay one step ahead of slumlords, welfare bureaucrats, garment middlemen, or the criminal justice system.

Nevertheless, Ra's desire for movement persisted. She told me of her ongoing need to "go here, go there," as if something awaited her and time was running out. Throughout this book, I use the term "refugee temporality" to describe how Ra experienced the time and space of her resettlement in the hyperghetto as a critical pause that was not a transition. Refugee temporality is the refugee's knowledge that state-mediated resettlement is a false proposition; it is the disavowal of resolution, an unclosed refugee sojourn. This does not mean that Ra, her children, and other Cambodian refugees gave up on redemption. Instead, they now regarded it as deferred by extending what Saidiya Hartman and Stephen Best describe as the pause between the "no longer and the not yet":

> The political interval in which all captives find themselves—
> the interval between the no longer and the not yet, between
> the destruction of the old world and the awaited hour of deliv-
> erance. That interval is the hour of the captive's redemption.[1]

Best and Hartman write specifically about survivors of the U.S. plantation who, since slavery's abolition, have been burdened with questions of redress and redemption. They ask, "How does one compensate for centuries of violence that have as their consequence the impossibility of restoring a prior existence, of giving back what was taken, or repairing what was broken?"[2] For survivors, there is no compensation, no wiping the slate clean. There is only "fugitive justice," which is justice that must remain elusive to "index . . . the incommensurability between grief and grievance, pain and compensation."[3] Fugitive justice resists social and legal redemption, which, after all, only redoubles violence through a premature resolution. Fugitive justice is experienced fleetingly in the unclosed interval between past injury and an awaited redemption, "between the no longer and the not yet."

The challenge for the captive is to keep this interval open, to continually defer the question of final redemption.

How might this concept of fugitive justice apply to the Cambodian genocide survivor who has resettled in the U.S. hyperghetto? Throughout this book I represent and analyze Ra's constant movements in the form of housing displacements, navigation of the welfare state, homeworking, motherhood, and factory work. Through each of these interrelated movements her past remained unclosed and she refused to succumb to false propositions of crossing, transition, and settlement. I argue that these movements kept the interval of fugitive justice open. In what follows, I present one last rendering of Ra's movements by showing that she continued to move, even during moments of relative repose. Indeed, even as the daily exigencies of her life abated after 2007, she continued to refuse the terms of resettlement.

Never Stop

A year after Ra moved into her apartment, her home showed no trace of her past homeworking life save for her favorite sewing machine. The sewing machine table sat in the kitchen, repurposed as a counter for junk mail, the yellow pages, and a pile of jackets. It symbolized Ra's inner conflict: she had clearly moved on but had not quite broken with the past. Stacked boxes and bags in her living room suggested anticipation of the next removal, but the framed family portraits and the lush plants sagging along the windowsill all said that Ra was finally home, that she had entered a détente with the forces of displacement.

With her youngest granddaughter napping next to her on the sofa, Ra spoke of her fondness for her new apartment. The heat was consistent during the winter months, the hallways were tidy, and the only street noise came from the buses that rumbled down the Grand Concourse. Located on 175th Street, just north of Tremont Avenue, in that ambiguous zone between the South and the Northwest Bronx, the apartment was close enough to the main concentrations of the Cambodian community that Ra could easily see children and friends or drop in at the gathering points of her refugee community. At times, the chronic pain in her legs made these excursions difficult, but Ra insisted on going out almost daily. She seemed to rely on the criss-crossing, the back and forth:

> Going over there, coming back here—food, children. Always running around. Sometimes I go to school. But maybe my mind isn't on it. So then I run to the store to buy some food for the children. Then go back to the apartment to cook it for them. I need to go here, go there. Never stop.

Ra said that she was accustomed to this rapid pace. Before being separated from her children by the city's child welfare agency in 2002, her daily activities had been predictable and circumscribed: when she wasn't homeworking, she was grocery shopping, preparing meals, or negotiating with the welfare bureaucracy. In the spring of 2002, she was suddenly cut loose, cast into an unsettling still-ness. For more than four years, Ra bounced from one apartment to another, her nomadic life keeping matters open and unresolved. This was precisely how Ra wanted to experience life while she was separated from her children.

During that separation and until the van accident, Ra took up full-time factory work, and this, too, satiated her need for constant motion. During the first two decades of her life in the United States, Ra had rarely traveled outside of the Northwest Bronx. Now she began commuting an average of three and a half hours each day between the Bronx and New Jersey.

Ra worked at several factories, beginning with what she referred to as the "perfume factory," where an assortment of products, includ-ing cheap perfume, cough syrup, and sour candies, were packed and shipped. The work was easy, but paid very little. Next, she found work even farther away from the Bronx at the "pet factory," which packed and shipped pet supplies. This job paid slightly better, but the boss soon began cutting back on her hours. Ra then turned to the packag-ing warehouses of two large retailers: an office supply store and what she referred to as the "cookie factory," where she worked until the van accident in September 2005.

Factory work required long hours of standing, repetitive motion, and heavy lifting in warehouses that were frigid during the winter and sweltering during the summer and where powerful odors nause-ated some workers. According to Ra, a worker knew on her first day whether or not she would last.

Sometimes the perfume and pet supply factories paid the work-ers late or not at all. In 2000, when I was a community organizer in the Northwest Bronx, young Cambodian factory workers told me that they risked having their wages stolen. Factory owners hired a workforce largely consisting of undocumented Latino immigrants and refugee welfare recipients, knowing that they would be unlikely to file legal complaints for stolen wages for fear of being exposed as "illegals" or "welfare cheats."[4] Ra said that her wages had once been stolen by the perfume factory owner.

The factory owners worked with a Cambodian middleman to re-cruit refugee workers through his community networks. The middle-man also functioned as the companies' factotum; he drove the van, managed the payroll, and announced layoffs. Ra claimed that she was never denied work, even during slow periods. "I always had work. . . . It gets slow and the middleman never calls some people back. But they call me back every time. They know my work." In September 2005, however, her factory days came to a sudden and violent end in a mat-ter of seconds. The van accident proved yet again that life was nothing but constant movements—some more shattering than others.

After qualifying for SSI and moving into her new apartment, Ra could have rested. The back and forth she described was no lon-ger essential to her livelihood—it did not provide food and rent as the welfare and homeworking once had. And although Ra cared for her grandchildren, they could have been brought to her. Still, she kept moving—just as she had when the landlords kept her in ruin-ous housing conditions (Chapter 2) and the social workers insisted that it was all "temporary," or when the punitive welfare state kept her trapped (Chapter 3), or when the global economy forced her to convert her home into a sweatshop (Chapter 5), or when the state criminalized her for protecting her children (Chapter 6). In each in-stance, Ra kept moving, resisting the terms of a false resettlement, of a premature resolution to her long sojourn. In the stillness of her new apartment, those fictions imposed themselves with renewed rigor, and Ra responded by keeping up her hyperkinetic pace.

Return

Contributing to Ra's restlessness was the excitement of many of her peers about the possibility of visiting Cambodia. Indeed, by 2000—twenty years after the passage of the 1980 Refugee Act—many were preparing for their first visits, including her daughter Rann, the oldest, and her son Rom, the third child. Rann was the only one of Ra's children born in Cambodia. The rest were born either in refugee camps or in the Bronx. (Rom would be the first to make the trip to Cambodia in 2010; Rann went in 2012.) Ra felt ambivalent about returning and made no plans to go. The more her friends and children talked about their pending trips, however, the more she felt the unsettling stillness of her life.

The possibility of return came about as a result of several pivotal events that signaled the end of the Khmer Rouge nightmare and the opening of an era of supposed peace, reconciliation, and Cambodian global economic integration: the 1998 death of Pol Pot, President Bill Clinton's 2000 visit to Vietnam (Clinton was the first U.S. president to visit the region since the end of the U.S. war), the 2001 creation of the UN/Cambodian war crimes tribunal (known as the Khmer Rouge Tribunal), and the 2006 admission of Cambodia into the World Trade Organization (WTO). As Cathy J. Schlund-Vials reminds us, each of these events represented the official state sanctioning of what was worth remembering and what should be forgotten about the "zero years."[5] That is, each event quickly sutured wounds that had yet to heal—indeed, that may never heal—as a way to consecrate Cambodia's transition to peace and prosperity.

Ra was unmoved, believing that warfare and poverty still pervaded Cambodia:

> *There is no real peace in Cambodia. There is only peace if you say nothing, if you don't criticize whoever is in charge. If you say anything bad about the current government, if you protest, then you have no peace. They will hurt you. You still have to say "yes" to whoever is in charge.*

Ra pointed to the skirmishes between warring factions that continued to take the lives of innocent civilians. She knew that starvation was rampant in the rural areas where she grew up, and she questioned whether the Khmer Rouge tribunal could ever achieve reconciliation. She wanted to see her father and siblings in Battambang, but she feared going back.

Ra's fears heightened in March 2002, when President George W. Bush signed a Memorandum of Understanding with Cambodia that granted the United States the right to deport Cambodians who had been convicted of aggravated felonies. Many of those the United States sought to deport had never lived in Cambodia, having been born in the Thai refugee camps. Because the United States had had no repatriation agreement with Cambodia prior to the memorandum, thousands of Cambodians in the United States with felony records were not deportable and many of them languished indefinitely in immigration holding centers. Known as "lifers," they won a Supreme Court victory in the case of *Kimho Ma v. Reno* (2000) that ruled such indefinite detentions unconstitutional.[6]

The victory was short-lived. The Bush administration circumvented the 2000 ruling by negotiating an understanding with the Cambodian government in which, according to some reports, Cambodia agreed to Bush's terms because it feared that, otherwise, the United States, in retaliation, would withhold visas from Cambodians seeking U.S. entry.[7] It had little negotiating power because of recently signed trade agreements with the United States and pending membership in the WTO.

By mid-2002, the first wave of Cambodian deportees from the United States had landed in Phnom Penh. Virtually all of them were young men who had grown up in the United States and knew nothing of life in Cambodia (some of them hardly spoke Khmer), even though the U.S. state rationalized that it was deporting foreign criminals back to their country of origin.[8] News of the deportations sent shock waves through Cambodian refugee communities because many feared the beginning of mass removals. Here was refugee exceptionalism at its crescendo: more than twenty years after the passage of the Refugee Act, the U.S. state preferred to deport Cambodian refugees rather than link their alleged criminality to the poverty, racism, and urban abjection they were experiencing in America.

During one of our last interviews, Ra told me that her fear that one of her children could be deported was what drove her to strike Vanna with a belt—an action that ultimately led to her removal from her home by the city's child welfare agency.

I hit Vanna because I was afraid that if he kept getting in trouble he would be taken away forever. I was confused about the law back then. I didn't know that Vanna couldn't be deported because he was born here. I just heard about the other Cambodian children who were sent to prison and then deported. Not all of them were bad kids. Maybe they stole something or they fought with each other. They did stupid things. But then the government moves them back to Cambodia. So I was scared. I wanted Vanna to stop doing stupid things. So that's why I hit him that day.

She recalled a seventeen-year-old Cambodian boy named Kosal who had pled guilty to a crime he hadn't committed in order to receive a "youthful offender" adjudication that exempted him from deportation. (In New York State, a youthful offender finding is technically not a conviction, thus rendering the matter of deportation irrelevant.) Although he was innocent—with ample evidence to prove it—Kosal refused to go to trial for fear that a guilty verdict would earn him a one-way ticket to Cambodia. Instead, he accepted a plea bargain that required him to serve eighteen months in a juvenile prison. Ra was close to Kosal's family, and she felt both enraged and terrified by his circumstances. She feared that this could be Vanna's fate, so out of desperation she tried to rein him in.

I knew Kosal's case well because his parents had asked me to help prove his innocence. Kosal was accused of robbing one of his neighbors at gunpoint. In my conversations with nearby tenants, I discovered that the robbery had never taken place. The neighbor had lost a fight to Kosal and his friends and retaliated by making false accusations to the police. Regretting his actions, the neighbor tried to recant his statement, but the prosecutor intimidated him, suggesting that making false statements was a serious crime. Soon thereafter, the neighbor disappeared, but the case moved forward based on his original statement.

I sat next to Kosal's parents during their son's sentencing. As we waited for the proceedings to begin, Kosal's father asked me to step outside the courtroom with him. He thanked me for trying to help his son and then asked me for one last thing. "Can you ask the judge if we can trade places? . . . Can I stay in jail, so my son can go home today?" His expression told me that my job was not to explain to him the impossibilities but only to pose his question to those in power, and so I did.

Home

Kosal was sent upstate to serve time, and Ra was sent away from her Bronx apartment and her children for punishing Vanna. Both displacements were spurred by the specter of deportation. For both Kosal and Ra, the notion of returning to Cambodia would always hold complex meanings.

In the winter of 2005, several months before the van accident, Ra's ambivalence about returning home ended. On a bitterly cold January night, she received a call that led her to disown her country. "They told me my brother was gone, killed by a landmine." Her youngest brother, who lived in Battambang—the one she had raised from infancy, the one she had not seen since they were separated in the wake of the 1978 Vietnamese invasion—had been killed by one of the cruelest remnants of the war. Ra had been very close to him. After their mother's death from illness shortly before the Khmer Rouge took over their village, she became his primary caregiver: "He became like my son."

An untold number of active landmines litter the northwestern region bordering Thailand, having been laid by both the Vietnamese-backed Cambodian regime and Khmer Rouge fighters. Since 1979, they have accounted for over 64,000 deaths, with nearly 900 casualties in 2005, Ra's brother among them.[9] In our interviews, Ra emphasized the ongoing warfare in Cambodia, and her brother's death in 2005 proved this painfully. "Landmine, bullet, or starve. You still die."

With the news of her brother's death, Ra felt a profound shift. Whatever hopes she had of an eventual return, of coming to terms with her past, were vanquished in that moment:

> You know, I decided to hate my country, when they told me that my baby brother died. I just returned home from the pet factory. My sister called to tell me he stepped on a landmine. That was it. From that moment—that's when I decided to hate Cambodia.

Ra told me that she cried harder that night than in all her years of living in the Bronx. It was so intense that it took her someplace else. When she returned, the sun was up and it was seven in the morning. Ra put on her coat and walked out the door. She cut through the streets and neighborhood playgrounds, retracing her steps from hours earlier. Her eyes were so swollen that she could hardly see. It was a wonder she made it anywhere at all. Finally, she reached the northeast corner of Devoe Park, where she came on a small group huddled in the cold. Ra quietly took her place among the refugees waiting for the van that would take them to their morning shift.

Generations

Nine months after learning of her youngest brother's death, Ra was involved in the van accident that prevented her from ever again working in the factories. After recovering and moving into her own apartment in 2007, her main occupation was caring for her grandchildren, Rann's two daughters and Rorth's two sons. Ra claimed that this was the best way for her to support her daughters, who both worked long hours for a major hotel chain. Indeed, Rann and Rorth told me that without their mother's help, they could not work full-time. "Without this job, [my family] would definitely be struggling," Rorth said. Always driven by the goal of ensuring her children's safety, Ra saw her work as far from over, although now it took the form of child care. Although her children were doing well compared to many other 1.5-generation Cambodians—at the time of writing, five of her seven children were working full-time and two had bachelor's degrees—the specter of chronic unemployment and welfare dependency loomed over them.

Rorth started working for the hotel shortly after she finished high school. She began at minimum wage—"checking coats, standing on my feet and smiling for ten hours straight." She then moved up to the housekeeping department before being promoted to an events-planning position. She told me that she had no illusions that, if she lost this job, she could move to a new company for the same pay and benefits. "Losing this means starting all over again—probably at minimum [wage]." She had been an above-average high school student and could have excelled at a four-year college. But when she graduated in 2002, her family was in crisis: Ra had just been displaced from their apartment, Vanna was going astray, and the family was struggling to hold on to what remained of their welfare benefits: "My family needed my help. I had to find work . . . there was just no question about it." Rann, who was already working at the hotel, helped Rorth find that entry-level job.

I asked Rorth if she regretted not attending college. "Yeah, of course. Sometimes I feel a lot of regret." But she was quick to add that some of her college-graduate friends weren't faring much better:

> I have this tight group of girlfriends from way back . . . we're all still really close. When we were in high school we all had the same vision: Let's go to college and then all become schoolteachers. Two of them did it. They now teach elementary. But you know these schoolteachers don't get paid that much. At least not enough to live in New York City. They have to take part time jobs working at JCPenney. It's not easy for them either. So I can't really say how different my life would be if I went to college.

Rom agreed with his sister. Only he and his older brother Rasmey—the second and third oldest of Ra's children—had graduated from college. I wondered if male privilege had led the daughters down a different path, so I asked Rorth if she felt that it had been expected that Ra's daughters would work and her sons would pursue higher education. Rorth denied any explicit suggestion of this sort: "Nobody was told to go, and nobody was told not to go [to college]." Recognizing that patriarchy works in indirect and subtle ways, she said that since adolescence she had felt accountable for her family's economic wellbeing and felt certain that gender conditioning played a part in that. She acknowledged that by the time she graduated the family's circumstances had deteriorated. When Rasmey and Rom graduated from high school—in 1998 and 2000—the family had not yet entered its most turbulent economic time. Back then, the homeworking orders were steady and welfare reform was only beginning. Although Ra was still serving out her probation, she continued to anchor the family. Just two years later, matters had worsened. Rorth could not be sure whether or not she would have gone to college had she graduated before or after 2002—a period she described as "absolutely the worst time in my family's life."

Rom also felt uncertain about whether male privilege played any role in the educational disparity between him and his sisters. However, he was sure that his bachelor's degree—earned over ten years in several community and city colleges—had not been essential to landing his current job as a clerk in the New York Department of Motor Vehicles. This was a position he had earned by scoring well on a civil service exam. "The exam was enough for me to get the job. I didn't need the college degree," but he pursued it for as long as he did "out of pride. If I ever have a son or daughter, I want to them to know I went to college."

I cannot say if Rasmey felt the same way about his college degree (Rasmey and Vanna are the only children I did not interview).[10] However, Ra's five oldest children—the ones who were born either in Cambodia or in the refugee camps of Thailand or the Philippines—generally agreed that their work lives were now defined by long hours at relatively low-paying jobs that enabled them to make ends meet on a month-to-month basis. All of them continued to live in the Northwest Bronx, and none of them claimed to have reached anything resembling economic success or security. They seemed to fit the profile of overworked service economy employees who draw steady paychecks but are only one layoff or health crisis away from poverty.

Among Ra's children, Rith might be regarded as an outlier, the one who took a different path. He had decided against going to college and taking the first steady paycheck offered to him. Choosing to become a hairstylist, he worked his way through an intensive cosmetology program between 2009 and 2012 and apprenticed at a salon in downtown Manhattan. In 2014, he began to take on his own clients. As his siblings had, Rith worked long hours for paltry or erratic pay early in his career. However, he saw himself in an occupation that could bring him long-term economic security and possibly success. According to Rith, the promise of economic mobility—combined with his belief that he was doing something creative—set him apart from his siblings.

All five of the children who were born outside of the United States had adopted their mother's penchant for movement, for anticipating the dangers that lay ahead. Like her, they had refused to settle for the false notion that they were somehow better off in the United States, that they had found refuge. In the past, this refusal had taken the form of community activism, with Rom, Rorth, and Rith taking leadership roles with YLP. More than a decade later, however, their rejection of the myth translated into working long hours to avoid the depths of urban poverty. The three regretted that they no longer had the time for community activism. "I feel really guilty about it sometimes," said Rorth, but added that she occasionally helped out with events at the local Cambodian Buddhist temple.

Similar to Rorth, Rann spoke of how frustrated she was that her time was not her own, that she worked only to be able to work another day. Rann seemed to chafe at my question: "Don't you feel that life in the United States is easier compared to life in Cambodia?" Rann visited Cambodia for the first time in 2012, staying with Ra's father and sister in Battambang. "Cambodia is definitely poorer," she said, although she thought that the way Cambodians moved through time and space, especially in the countryside, marked the more significant difference. "When I visited, everything was open and you just *lived*." She told me that her family grew their own food and took time each day to rest and have conversations. Despite her awareness that Cambodia is one of the poorest countries in Asia, Rann asserted that she had never felt healthier than during her month there. "There was nowhere to go . . . *there was no way up*," she said, referring to her extended family's inability to change their social, economic, and political situation.

Rann had felt healthy because progressive time was irrelevant in the Cambodian countryside; her extended family expressed neither the need nor the desire to move on to something better.

This ultimately proved to be the point of incommensurability between Rann and her family. "I don't think I could ever live like that long-term," she said, but she also wondered if she was fooling herself about her allegiance to progressive time and whether the two contexts weren't similar. "You can say the same thing about the Bronx—*there's no way up* . . . you keep working, and you think everything will get better, but you know [it won't]."

Rann's critique of progress in the United States rested on her belief that, as her family's time in the Bronx wore on, the economic and social conditions faced by the second (and now third) generations of Bronx Cambodians were worsening. The travails of Ra's two youngest children—the only ones born in the United States—proved this point. Sonya, Ra's second-youngest, had been the first to be born in the Bronx and the first to drop out of high school. "It was 2004, when I was sixteen years old . . . I wasn't getting anything from school . . . school wasn't a good place. It wasn't safe there." According to Sonya, her high school treated students like criminals, and so "they acted like criminals." Here Sonya invoked what some have termed the "school to prison pipeline," in which many public schools in the hyperghetto now serve as preparatory sites for a life under correctional control.

After dropping out, Sonya drew scrutiny from law enforcement. She recalled a 2005 incident in which she had been caught up in a drug sweep on Valentine Avenue and held in jail for two days before the charges against her were dropped. A year later, she was detained following another sweep and interrogated about her gang affiliations:

> I told them I wasn't in a gang. I didn't know what the cop was talking about. But then they pulled out this gang book, a big binder with a lot of people's pictures in it. They showed me I was in it. They said I was "VCG"—the Valentine Cambodian Gang. How is that possible? I didn't have any record. So why was I in the gang book? That's when I knew I had to get out of there. I had to leave the Bronx.

Sonya moved from one friend's apartment to another; the farther away from the Northwest Bronx she moved, the better, she told me. She eventually wound up in Brooklyn, where she now lived. She earned her GED in 2010, but it did little to help her secure steady work. Chronically unemployed, she applied for welfare as a single adult without children and was immediately placed in workfare before being accepted into a new training program that claimed to help recipients find work in the low-wage retail sector. Even there, however, she could not obtain full-time work. Sonya removed herself from welfare—"too much of a hassle"—and eventually found work with a cleaning service. "Cleaning houses is the most steady work I've had in the past few years," she said. Rann and Rorth helped her stay afloat until 2014, when they found her a job as a housekeeper in their hotel.

Vanna, Ra's youngest child, had lived with Ra since the two of them had moved into her apartment in 2007. I did not officially interview him for this project and therefore cannot speak in detail about his adult life. However, his siblings all agreed that Vanna probably had the most difficult adolescence among the seven of them. Only ten when Ra was removed from their home, he was the one most affected by his parents' divorce and the only one who lived with Ra in the homeless shelter. Like Sonya, Vanna never finished high school but earned a GED. He had worked odd jobs over the years, but never became economically independent. According to Rorth, he enrolled in classes at a local community college in 2014—a move that surprised the family. Still, they worried about him because he had fallen into a group of second-generation Bronx Cambodians whose life chances seemed to have diminished in recent years. Rith explained:

> This is going to sound crazy, so I'll just say it. I think the young people are dying more quickly now. They're dying in really random ways: rare diseases, suspicious accidents— things that don't make sense. It's not just about the violence we saw when we were young. It's something else. Like they don't want to live, so they die more easily.

Rorth had her own theory: "I think the conditions are just a lot harder now. It's harder economically, so families can't hold it together." She added something that highlighted the specific condition of the refugees:

> I think the young Cambodians who are dying are just going with it. They go with what *they* say. They believe it. Their parents didn't believe it. And those of us who are a little older were taught not to believe it. But this younger generation only knows the Bronx, so they believe it more. That's why they die more easily.

I asked Rorth to elaborate on who "they" were and what exactly the youngest generation of Bronx Cambodians believed that the older generation did not. "They" were not the government per se but a range of forces that once tried to sell her family on the idea that "everything was going to be okay when we got here." The first generation knew better than to buy into this notion. They remained skeptical and never let their guard down. According to Rorth, the older children, including those with only the faintest memory of the refugee camp, seemed to follow their parents' lead, but the youngest—the ones born in the United States who were supposed to be the full beneficiaries of their parents' sacrifices—seemed less capable of defending themselves. Rorth attributed this to the effect on the latest generation of both deepening structural inequalities and the false promises of liberalism. Taken together, these ideas suggest that the youngest Cambodians had been robbed of the ability to move as their parents once had, that they had been disconnected from refugee temporality.

Refugee temporality is not another way of stating that the refugee is haunted by the past—through trauma or survivor guilt. Instead, it is the distinct way in which refugees know that the power of their past captivities remains in the present—in the supposed land of salvation that promised them safety and freedom. However, for the youngest Bronx Cambodians, there were only present-day captivities in the hyperghetto—intensive policing, the meshing of the punitive and social welfare arms of the state, the school-to-prison pipeline, mass incarceration, and deportation. If, as Rorth suggested, the youngest generation seemed to "just go with it," perhaps it was because they had not yet developed their own alternative temporality, one that generated their own resistance, that enabled them to emerge as a counterhegemonic problem for those in power, not a false solution.

Problem Refugees

In 1909, W. E. B. Du Bois famously wrote in *The Souls of Black Folk*, "How does it feel to be a problem?"[11] He was critiquing the willful mislabeling by white people of the problem they were observing, while claiming to sympathize with the suffering of African Americans. According to Du Bois, it was not that African Americans had yet to find their rightful place in the United States nearly forty-five years after the abolition of slavery; it was that white supremacy had refused to allow such a place to exist. The problem, in other words, was that a society structured by white racism continued to rely—indeed, thrive—on the modalities of Black exploitation, captivity, punishment, and exclusion endemic to the U.S. plantation. Du Bois accurately predicted that this problem would pervade the twentieth century. As the century progressed, it took hold in urban settings and acquired different names: the "American dilemma," the "crisis of the Negro family," and the "underclass." With each rhetorical turn, the Black subject continued to be cast as an unresolved problem while white supremacy remained invisible. Since the beginning of the twenty-first century, the dominant discourse on poverty, unemployment, and criminalization has seemed to begin and end with the notion that impoverished African Americans have failed to take personal responsibility in an otherwise colorblind society.

This construction of the intractable Black problem in urban America depends, in part, on white supremacy's simultaneous positioning of other nonwhites, particularly Asian Americans, in relation to African Americans. Recognizing the continued relevance of Du Bois's question, contemporary scholars and activists who analyze the racial location of Asian Americans have posed a related question: "How does it feel to be a *solution*?"[12] In this, they are calling attention to the figuring of Asian Americans as those who, in contrast to poor African Americans, achieved socioeconomic success despite past racial injustices. According to this model-minority thesis, Asian Americans seized the new opportunities afforded to all nonwhites during the era of supposed racial liberalism that followed the passage of the Civil Rights Act in 1964 and the Immigration Act in 1965. In many ways, talk of model minorities was not so much about celebrating Asian American virtues as it was about delegitimizing Black claims for redress, simultaneously obscuring the profound economic stratification and heterogeneity of Asian Americans.

Since the mid-1990s, the high poverty and unemployment rates of Cambodians and other Southeast Asian refugee groups, particularly Laotians and Hmong, have served as a rebuttal to the model-minority thesis. For example, according to the 2010 Census, approximately one-third of Cambodians in the United States had no more than a high school education, which suggests that working poverty will continue to define the lives of the second and third generations.[13]

As I argue throughout, even though Cambodian refugees contradict the model-minority thesis, they nevertheless have a role in the underclass narrative as contradistinctive "good refugees" who posit the difference between the deserving and undeserving poor. The good refugees are the deserving poor who were first saved by the U.S. war in Southeast Asia, then by its humanitarian refugee resettlement program, and finally by the opportunities in the free market. Bronx Cambodians have been subjected to what I call *refugee exceptionalism*—a set of ideologies and discourses that render their persistent underachievement as an always temporary phenomenon distinct from the intractable problem of Black urban poverty. Refugee exceptionalism sees impoverished Cambodians as suspended in a perpetual state of arrival, with their refugee poverty disassociated from that of the "true inhabitants" of the hyperghetto. Casting this dichotomy in terms of liberal warfare, we might say that refugee exceptionalism insists on the unending rescue of the Cambodian refugee from urban abjection as a way to justify unending warfare against an undeserving underclass. The Cambodians have never truly been saved but only used in the continuing war against the urban poor.

Over the past three decades, few if any other refugee groups have served the war in urban America quite as the Cambodians and other Southeast Asian refugees have. Since the passage of the 1980 Refugee Act, the United States has engaged in two invasions and occupations of Iraq (1991 and 2003) and one invasion of Afghanistan (2001). These wars, particularly the two fought after 9/11, produced scores of refugees. Although tens of thousands of Iraqis would eventually be resettled in the United States, none were deemed deserving of the same level of compassion shown to their Southeast Asian counterparts.

In a post–Cold War era in which liberal empire and warfare take the form of endless wars on terrorism and drugs, the refugees produced by these conflicts are immediately cast as threats, not victims. Today's refugees are construed as an entirely unique racial problem that reflects the public's anxieties over national security and is managed by practices such as racial profiling, surveillance, and detention rather than humanitarian resettlement. Two immediate examples stand out. As of the writing of this conclusion, approximately 3.2 million Syrian refugees displaced by their country's civil war—a war partially rooted in instability created by the U.S. interventions in Iraq and Afghanistan—are languishing in refugee camps in neighboring countries, particularly Turkey and Jordan. According to the Office of the United Nations High Commissioner for Refugees, the Syrian crisis is the "biggest humanitarian emergency of our era."[14] As of summer 2014, however, the United States had resettled fewer than 200 Syrian refugees since the civil war began in 2011, although U.S. officials had said that ten times as many Syrians would be resettled by now. Officials claim that intensive background checks and other security vetting required by the Department of Homeland Security are impeding the resettlement process.[15]

At the same time, tens of thousands of Central Americans, many of them unaccompanied minors, are fleeing violence in Latin America and making their way to the U.S. border. In countries like Honduras, which has the highest murder rate in the world, the violence and instability that drive the exodus is linked to U.S. interventions, specifically America's drug war and its support for the current Honduran regime, which took power in a 2009 coup. On reaching the United States, asylum seekers have been met by angry U.S. citizens demanding that the federal government either refuse to grant them entry or deport them immediately. Although President Barack Obama has called on Americans to show compassion, particularly for the unaccompanied children seeking refuge, his administration's policies seem to favor the demands of anti-immigration protestors. Many Hondurans are now being immediately sent back to the war zones they fled, denied the opportunity to seek asylum in the United States.[16] In response to the influx of migrant children, the Obama administration reinstated the detaining of undocumented mothers and children in jails (reversing his 2009 decision to end the policy of family detentions begun in the previous administration).[17]

We now live in an era in which the refugee is no longer needed to carry out the ideological and discursive work that Cambodian and other Southeast Asians were enlisted for thirty-five years ago. The ostensible compassion that the U.S. state demonstrated toward Southeast Asian refugees—the compassion that was said to be behind passage of the 1980 Refugee Act—was always a reflection of the state's ongoing imperial ambitions in Southeast Asia as well as its need to discipline and punish the underclass in postinsurrectionist urban America. Those ambitions and needs are less relevant today than they were three decades ago—specifically in the hyperghetto, where the state's unending war against the poorest of the urban poor has been a complete success. Today, terms such as "compassion fatigue" merely index the shifting political interests and needs of the state.

Other scholars will have to delve into the complex reasons for the American public's refusal to see Syrian and Honduran asylum seekers as worthy of compassion. I raise the issue only to speculate that we have seen the last of the good refugee. No new refugee wave will be arriving in the hyperghetto in the near future; no new group waits to be enlisted in the work of refugee exceptionalism, which is to stand in contrast to the underclass.

The absence of ethnic succession among refugees in the hyperghetto may help to explain why the youngest generation of Bronx Cambodians continues to be the hyperghetto's collateral damage. As Rorth said, they are particularly vulnerable because, although subjected to the poverty, economic exploitation, and punitive state regulation that afflicted their parents, they are less capable of moving themselves out of harm's way. Rorth, however, remained hopeful, believing that there would still be time for the youth in her community to develop their own movements—both literally and figuratively.

Rorth also believed that young refugee movements would have to draw on both the resilience of the first generation and the political and cultural struggles of African Americans and Puerto Ricans, the long-term captives of the Bronx hyperghetto. Indeed, if an alternative temporality is to emerge among the younger generation, it should be grounded in the knowledge that Bronx Cambodians have never been, as refugee exceptionalism claims, merely visitors to the hyperghetto. The persistence of their poverty over three decades is evidence of their continued captivity. More significant, the forces of liberal empire and war that drove their families out of Cambodia are inscribed in the liberal war carried out in the Bronx. As community organizer Chhaya Chhoum reminds us, the Bronx Cambodians "have never left the camps." How might this knowledge serve as the condition of possibility for lasting alliances among Cambodians, African Americans, Puerto Ricans, and others held captive in the hyperghetto? How might it help them emerge as a different kind of problem for the keepers of the hyperghetto: the problem of collective resistance?

Organizations like Mekong NYC, which Chhaya cofounded, are building such alliances. Mekong is part of a multiracial coalition of Northwest Bronx groups working to address issues such as skyrocketing rents, cuts in funding of community health clinics, and the privatization of public space. According to Chhaya, it represents the new milieu of Southeast Asian grassroots groups throughout the country that have made multiracial organizing a strategic priority. In Rhode Island, the Providence Youth and Student Movement (PrYSM)—which is rooted in the Cambodian refugee community—has become the lynchpin of the city's multiracial youth organizing. One of its core values is "Ghetto roots," which, according to PrYSM's mission statement, means "organizing on the streets, in homes, and in the heart of the communities . . . affirming solidarity with the most oppressed and most in need."[18] PrYSM was active in a recent campaign to pass state legislation to stop racial profiling, which would serve the interests of all youth of color in the state.

Another youth group, Freedom Inc. in Madison, Wisconsin, works with both Hmong and African American youth to address a range of economic, health, and educational inequalities afflicting both communities. It emphasizes the need to challenge patriarchy and heteronormativity through projects that support queer and gender-nonconforming Hmong and African American high-school students.

Freedom Inc.'s slogan is "Our Community Is Our Campaign,"[19] which underscores the organization's belief that winning specific political battles is secondary to addressing the community's need to heal from traumas past and present.

Organizations such as PrYSM and Freedom Inc. represent the next phase of refugee movement in the hyperghetto. They prove that resistance is taking shape among the children and grandchildren of refugees, articulated by and through members of other oppressed groups. At the same time, they are rooted in the particular histories and conditions of Southeast Asian refugees because their activism draws on and extends the resiliency of the first generation. The strong intergenerational focus of the work of all three groups—Mekong NYC, PrYSM, and Freedom Inc.—keeps the first generation close at hand to remind the third generation that matters of justice remain unsettled, that redemption is elusive.

If Ra Pronh has anything to teach this new movement about fugitive justice, it is that the refugee is never saved or freed. Ra didn't wait for her deliverance. Instead, she survived the Khmer Rouge genocide, the civil war, the refugee camps, and nearly thirty years of Bronx unsettlement by continuing to move and never accepting the terms of resettlement. In this way, she conceived of her arrival in the United States in the 1980s not as salvation but as a transfer from one site of captivity to the next. She was transferred to what in the camps was referred to as "country number three":

> That's what they called the United States. The camp worker asked me, "Where you want to go?" Then he said, "You ready to go to country number three—USA?" I said okay—country number three.

Notes

Introduction

1. Throughout, I use "Cambodian" instead of "Cambodian American." This word choice is driven by the simple fact that the community in the Bronx with whom I worked rarely if ever used the latter to describe themselves. They referred to themselves as either "Cambodian" or "Khmer."

2. For statistics and historical data on the Cambodian genocide, I draw on the Cambodian Genocide Program (CGP) at Yale University, which is under the direction of historian Ben Kiernan; available at http://www.yale.edu/cgp.

3. Ben Kiernan, *The Pol Pot Regime: Race, Power, and Genocide in Cambodia under the Khmer Rouge, 1975–79*, 3rd ed. (New Haven, CT: Yale University Press, 2008), x.

4. Tens of thousands of Cambodians remained captives of the Khmer Rouge long after Vietnamese forces took Phnom Penh and installed the People's Republic of Kampuchea (PRK). The status of these captives after the Vietnamese invasion of December 25, 1978, was ambiguous: some were hostages held entirely against their will; others felt they had no choice but to stay with their Khmer-Rouge–controlled groups for survival.

5. Sucheng Chan, *Survivors: Cambodian Refugees in the United States* (Urbana: University of Illinois Press, 2004), 79–81. Historian Sucheng Chan's *Survivors* provides a comprehensive accounting of the number of Cambodians resettled in the United States between 1975 and 1994, and presents a clear breakdown of Cambodians who were resettled as refugees, immigrants, or parolees.

6. The total number of refugees who resettled in the Bronx during the 1980s is contested. According to some community service providers such as Sister Jean Marshall, founder and director of the St. Rita's Refugee Center, there were as many as 10,000 Cambodians in the Bronx at one point during the 1980s. Photojournalist Leah Melnick, who worked closely with Bronx Cambodians during the 1980s, concurs. See Melnick, "Cambodians in Western Massachusetts and the Bronx, New York," *Migration World* 18, no. 2 (1990): 4. By the end of the decade, the Bronx Cambodian population was in sharp decline, with more than half the population having left for other northeastern cities. Still, the 1990 Census grossly undercounted it (1,603). When I began working in the Northwest Bronx during the mid-1990s, the consensus among service providers (in particular those who worked for St. Rita's Center and the Montefiore Family Health Center) was that the population stood at approximately 4,000. They based their estimate on the number of Cambodian households they served and the average number per household.

7. Chan, *Survivors*, 81–85.

8. Yen Le Espiritu, "Toward a Critical Refugee Study: The Vietnamese Refugee Subject in US Scholarship," *Journal of Vietnamese Studies* 1, no. 1–2 (2006): 410–11.

9. Yen Le Espiritu, *Body Counts: Vietnam War and Militarized Refuge(es)* (Berkeley: University of California Press, 2014), 91, 104.

10. See *CAAAV: Organizing Asian Communities*, available at http://www.caaav.org. The team that developed CAAAV's first sets of programs in the Northwest Bronx was led by staff organizer Thoai Nguyen and included members Jane Sung E. Bai, Ngô Thanh Nhàn, and Lynn Pono.

11. The first group of Cambodians to be resettled in New York City were placed in Brooklyn between 1981 and 1982 as part of what was known as the Khmer Guided Placement Project or the Khmer Cluster Project. As Sucheng Chan notes, the goal of the project was to place Cambodian refugees across a dozen chosen localities where they would have the best opportunities to achieve economic self-sufficiency. According to Chan, "The only unsuccessful site was New York City" because many decided to leave after being victims of robberies and other crimes. See Chan, *Survivors*, 101. The few that stayed in Brooklyn account for the borough's small Cambodian enclave.

12. For a comprehensive overview of the ethnic economy concept, see Ivan Light, "The Ethnic Economy," in *The Handbook of Economic Sociology*, ed. Neil J. Smelser and Richard Swedberg (Princeton, NJ: Princeton University Press, 2005), 650–77. To understand how this concept has been misapplied to Southeast Asian refugees, particularly Cambodians living in urban poverty, see Eric Tang, "Collateral Damage: Southeast Asian Poverty in the United States," *Social Text* 18, no. 1 (2000): 61–64.

13. In 2000, YLP conducted a survey of over 100 refugee families. In addition to finding that 65 percent continued to receive a monthly welfare check and 80 percent received at least one form of public assistance, it discovered that

93 percent were never provided interpretation services at the welfare centers and 86 percent of the youth had on more than one occasion missed school to translate for their parents.

14. Chan, *Survivors*, 151–61.

15. U.S. Census Bureau. *2000 Census* (Washington, DC: U.S. Department of Commerce, 2003), available at www.census.gov/html. I am grateful to Chunhui Ren for gathering this data.

16. For an overview of the economic diversity among Vietnamese Americans, see Boat People SOS, *2010 Vietnamese American Needs Assessment: Report on Findings* (Falls Church, VA: Boat People SOS, 2011).

17. On Cambodians in New England, particularly in Lowell, Massachusetts, see Peter Kiang, "When Know-Nothings Speak English Only: Analyzing Irish and Cambodian Struggles for Community Development and Educational Equity," in *The State of Asian America: Activism and Resistance in the 1990s*, ed. Karin Aguilar–San Juan and M. Annette Jaimes (Boston: South End Press, 1994), 125–45; on Cambodian and Vietnamese resettlement in Philadelphia, see Ellen Somekawa, "On the Edge: Southeast Asians in Philadelphia and the Struggle for Space," in *Reviewing Asian America: Locating Diversity*, ed. Wendy L. Ng (Pullman: Washington State University Press, 1995), 33–47.

18. Loïc J. D. Wacquant, "Deadly Symbiosis: When Ghetto and Prison Meet and Mesh," *Punishment and Society* 3, no. 1 (2001): 95–133. In this article Wacquant provides his fullest elaboration of the hyperghetto concept.

19. Loïc J. D. Wacquant, "From Slavery to Mass Incarceration," *New Left Review* 13 (January–February 2002): 48, 55. Here Wacquant traces the origins of the hyperghetto to the Black urban insurrections of the late 1960s.

20. Loïc J. D. Wacquant, "The Wedding of Workfare and Prisonfare in the 21st Century," *Journal of Urban Poverty* 16, no. 2 (2012): 242.

21. Ibid., 241. Here Wacquant writes that "the sudden growth and glorification of punishment partakes of a broader reengineering of the state that also entails the replacement of the right to welfare by the obligation of workfare (i.e., forced participation in subpar employment as a condition of public support). The downsizing of public aid and the upsizing of the prison are the two sides of the same coin."

22. Michelle Alexander, *The New Jim Crow: Mass Incarceration in the Age of Colorblindness* (New York: New Press, 2010), 1–19.

23. Ibid., 9.

24. Wacquant, "Deadly Symbiosis," 98–103.

25. Hortense J. Spillers, "Mama's Baby, Papa's Maybe: An American Grammar Book," *Diacritics* 17, no. 2 (1987): 1–20.

26. Steven Gregory, *Black Corona: Race and the Politics of Place in an Urban Community* (Princeton, NJ: Princeton University Press, 1999), 9–10. Similarly João Costa Vargas demonstrates the complex and heterogeneous forms of survival and resistance in the hyperghettos of postinsurrectionary Los Angeles. Moving beyond the popular culture tropes of "South Central LA," Costa Vargas

reveals that residents in some of the most vulnerable areas of the city create political and cultural meanings out of their struggles. See Costa Vargas, *Catching Hell in the City of Angels: Life and Meanings of Blackness in South Central Los Angeles* (Minneapolis: University of Minnesota Press, 2006).

27. We might conceive of this as the convergence of two genealogies of "unsettlement." Here I am reminded of Stefano Harney and Fred Moten's invocation of that unending, unsettled condition that originated in the slave hold; I argue that this condition extends into the era of the hyperghetto. Harney and Moten write: "Never being on the right side of the Atlantic is an unsettled feeling, the feeling of a thing that unsettles with others. It's a feeling, if you ride with it, that produces a certain distance from the settled, from those who determine themselves in space and time, who locate themselves in a determined history." Their notion of a "thing that unsettles with others" points us to an analysis of Ra's presence in the hyperghetto beyond the discourse of refugee exceptionalism. See Harney and Moten, *The Undercommons: Fugitive Planning and Black Study* (Brooklyn, NY: Minor Compositions, 2013), 97.

28. Aihwa Ong, *Buddha Is Hiding: Refugees, Citizenship, the New America* (Berkeley: University of California Press, 2003). Ong's ethnography is arguably the most comprehensive ethnographic account of Cambodian refugees in urban America. Here she argues that Cambodian refugees have been racialized as a new underclass. I engage with this argument in Chapter 3.

29. Michael B. Katz, "The Urban 'Underclass' as a Metaphor of Social Transformation," in *The Underclass Debate: Views from History*, ed. Michael B. Katz (Princeton, NJ: Princeton University Press, 1993), 8.

30. Stephen Best and Saidiya Hartman, "Fugitive Justice," *Representations* 92, no. 1 (2005): 3.

31. In October 2014, I conducted follow-up interviews with Ra and her children. These interviews form the basis of the book's conclusion.

32. I had the privilege of conversing with Richard Mollica on two occasions in April 2008 while I was visiting assistant professor in the history department at Harvard University.

33. Richard F. Mollica, *Healing Invisible Wounds: Paths to Hope and Recovery in a Violent World* (Nashville, TN: Vanderbilt University Press, 2008), 133.

34. Sandra Harding, "Rethinking Standpoint Epistemology: What Is 'Strong Objectivity'?" in *Feminist Epistemologies*, ed. Linda Alcoff and Elizabeth Potter (New York: Routledge, 1993), 56.

35. Ibid.

36. Robin D. G. Kelley, *Yo Mama's Dysfunktional! Fighting the Culture Wars in Urban America* (Boston: Beacon, 1998), 2.

37. John Langston Gwaltney, *Drylongso: A Self-Portrait of Black America* (New York: Random House, 1980), xxii.

38. James Clifford, "Introduction: Partial Truths," in *Writing Culture: The Poetics and Politics of Ethnography*, ed. James Clifford and George E. Marcus (Berkeley: University of California Press, 1986), 7.

39. John Brown Childs, *Transcommunality: From the Politics of Conversion to the Ethics of Respect* (Philadelphia: Temple University Press, 2003), 63. My emphasis.

40. Ibid., 23.

41. Ibid., 22.

42. Bindi V. Shah, *Laotian Daughters: Working toward Community, Belonging, and Environmental Justice* (Philadelphia: Temple University Press, 2011).

43. Peter Kiang, "Crouching Activists, Hidden Scholars: Reflections on Research and Development with Students and Communities in Asian American Studies," in *Engaging Contradictions: Theory, Politics, and Methods of Activist Scholarship*, ed. Charles R. Hale (Berkeley: University of California Press, 2008), 299–318; Shirley Suet-Ling Tang, "Community Centered Research as Knowledge/Capacity-Building in Immigrant and Refugee Communities," in *Engaging Contradictions: Theory, Politics, and Methods of Activist Scholarship*, ed. Charles R. Hale (Berkeley: University of California Press, 2008), 237–64.

44. Barbara Tomlinson and George Lipsitz, "American Studies as Accompaniment," *American Quarterly* 65, no. 1 (2013): 11.

Chapter 1

1. Created in 1950 by the United Nations General Assembly, the United Nations High Commissioner for Refugees (UNHCR) is mandated to co-coordinate with partnering nation-states the protection and possible resettlement or repatriation of refugees—displaced subjects who cross into another nation seeking asylum. In addition to setting up and administering refugee camps, UNHCR screens refugees for nation-states that are open to resettling them.

2. For a compelling account of the arbitrary and at times contradictory actions leading to Thailand's brief "open-door" policy, see Fiona Terry, *Condemned to Repeat? The Paradox of Humanitarian Action* (Ithaca, NY: Cornell University Press, 2002), 114–19.

3. William Shawcross, *Sideshow: Kissinger, Nixon and the Destruction of Cambodia* (New York: Simon and Schuster, 1979). This book is the first comprehensive account of Operation Menu, the U.S. covert bombing of Cambodia under the Nixon presidency. In the fall of 2000, President Bill Clinton, before his visit to Vietnam (the first by a U.S. president since Nixon), released previously classified data on the 1964–1975 bombings of Indochina. The data revealed that the bombing of Cambodia began as early as 1965 under President Lyndon B. Johnson.

4. See Owen Taylor and Ben Kiernan, "Bombs over Cambodia: New Information Reveals That Cambodia Was Bombed Far More Heavily than Previously Believed," *The Walrus*, October 2006, 62–69, available at http://thewalrus.ca/2006-10-history/, accessed January 8, 2013.

5. According to historian Ben Kiernan, the number of bombing casualties mounted that year and Pol Pot's most radical claims gained traction

throughout the countryside. See Kiernan, *How Pol Pot Came to Power: Colonialism, Nationalism, and Communism in Cambodia, 1930-1975*, 2nd ed. (New Haven, CT: Yale University Press, 2004), 349–50.

6. Here I am quoting Schanberg from his interview in Gregory Oliver, "Remembering the Killing Fields," *Oxonian Globalist*, November 20, 2010, available at http://toglobalist.org/2010/11/remembering-the-killing-fields/, accessed January 20, 2013.

7. Kiernan, *How Pol Pot Came to Power*, 357. See also David P. Chandler, *Brother Number One: A Political Biography of Pol Pot* (Boulder, CO: Westview, 1992), 120–29.

8. Ben Kiernan, *The Pol Pot Regime: Race, Power, and Genocide in Cambodia under the Khmer Rouge, 1975-79*, 3rd ed. (New Haven, CT: Yale University Press, 2008). Kiernan argues against the notion that the Cambodian genocide was an "autogenocide" and proposes that the Pol Pot regime's decision to liquidate a certain sector of the population was driven by an ethnoracial logic.

9. Sydney H. Schanberg, *The Death and Life of Dith Pran* (New York: Penguin, 1985).

10. These estimates are drawn from the Yale Cambodian Genocide Program, available at http://www.yale.edu/cgp/.

11. The full-scale Vietnamese invasion and occupation of Cambodia that began on December 25, 1978, extended from an ongoing border war that had steadily escalated over the previous two years. In November 1977, approximately 50,000 Vietnamese troops penetrated deep into Cambodian territory in response to a series of Khmer Rouge provocations. Hanoi withdrew them a few months later, in January 1978. According to the Ministry of Foreign Affairs of the Socialist Republic of Vietnam, the invasion of December 1978 was a key turning point of the unresolved border war. On top of this, Hanoi claimed that it was motivated by a desire bring an end to Khmer Rouge crimes against the Cambodian population. I am grateful to Ngô Thanh Nhàn for providing me with a copy of a booklet that includes translated statements of Hanoi's official positions on Pol Pot and its decision to intervene in the Cambodian crisis. The booklet was compiled and edited by the "Association of Patriotic Vietnamese in the US" in February 1979. For a survey of Vietnamese statements on the border war and its rationale for invading Cambodia, see Karl D. Jackson, "Cambodia 1978: War, Pillage, and Purge in Democratic Kampuchea," *Asian Survey*, no. 1 (January 1979): 72–84.

12. Stephen Morris, *Why Vietnam Invaded Cambodia: Political Culture and the Causes of War* (Stanford, CA: Stanford University Press, 1999), 88–116. Here Morris elaborates on the complex regional events leading up to the December 1978 invasion.

13. For a comprehensive account of President Jimmy Carter's post-1978 support of the Khmer Rouge, see Kenton Clymer, *The United States and Cambodia, 1969-2000* (New York: Routledge, 2004), 113–39. Clymer builds on earlier accounts, including Elizabeth Becker, *When the War Was Over: The*

Voices of Cambodia's Revolution and Its People (New York: Simon and Schuster, 1986).

14. See John Pilger, "The Long Secret Alliance: Uncle Sam and Pol Pot," *Covert Action Quarterly*, no. 4 (1997): 5–9, available at http://www.worldcat.org/title/the-long-secret-alliance-uncle-sam-and-pol-pot/oclc/202617498&referer=brief_results, accessed October 18, 2014; Jack Calhoun, "On the Side of Pol Pot: U.S. Supports Khmer Rouge," *Covert Action Quarterly* 34 (Summer 1990): 37–40. Calhoun notes, "Former Deputy Director of the CIA, Ray Cline, visited a Khmer Rouge camp inside Cambodia in November 1980. When asked about the visit, the Thai Foreign Ministry denied that Cline had illegally crossed into Cambodian territory. However, privately, the Thai government admitted that the trip had occurred."

15. Carter is quoted in Clymer, *United States and Cambodia*, 134.

16. By 1982, with the U.S. refugee resettlement program fully under way, the United States began to hide its Khmer Rouge support behind the Coalition Government of Democratic Kampuchea (CGDK). The CGDK was a coalition of exiled anti-Vietnamese factions made up of the Khmer Rouge; Prince Norodom Sihanouk's National United Front for Peaceful, Cooperative, Independent and Neutral Cambodia (FUNCIPEC); and the Khmer People's National Liberation Front (KPNLF), which was organized by former Cambodian prime minister Son Sann. FUNCIPEC and KPNLF were the coalition's self-proclaimed anticommunist members, which allowed the Reagan administration and the United Nations to recognize CGDK as the official Cambodian government in exile. However, CGDK was nothing without the Khmer Rouge, which possessed the coalition's only real military force. The Reagan administration found this inconvenient and insisted that any aid given to CGDK (estimated at $12–15 million annually) would be nonlethal and go directly to FUNCIPEC and KPNLF forces—what U.S. officials referred to as the Non-Communist Resistance (NCR). None of it was to be shared with the Khmer Rouge. Of course, this was unenforceable. Kenton Clymer points to one account claiming that, between November 1983 and March 1985, 85 percent of American food relief along the Thai-Cambodian border went to the Khmer Rouge army. Additionally, there was no way to prevent nonlethal aid from being traded for arms that would fall into Khmer Rouge hands. Again, Clymer notes that members of the U.S. State Department understood such aid to be entirely "fungible." It could be swapped easily with Thai or Singaporean military forces for weapons or used to free up other funds so that weapons could be directly purchased from any number of sellers. See Clymer, *United States and Cambodia*, 184. All told, support for CGDK bolstered the Khmer Rouge, keeping its cadres well fed and well armed for nearly a decade. Meanwhile, the United States cited noncommunist resistance to symbolically separate itself from the Khmer Rouge—allowing U.S. officials to publicly repudiate the murderous regime without seeming hypocritical. This sublimation also helped the United States manage its refugee settlement policy's most glaring contradictions. By taking a hard public stance against the Khmer Rouge, the

Reagan administration defended its moral imperative to resettle genocide survivors. The administration also merged the victims of the Khmer Rouge with other Cold War asylum seekers whose persecution under Vietnamese, Cuban, and Soviet communisms was more clearly aligned with UN refugee criteria.

17. A full reading of the 1951 Convention Relating to the Status of Refugees is available on the UNHCR website at http://www.unhcr.org/pages/49da0e466 .html, accessed March 15, 2013.

18. For an account of how U.S. refugee policy, drawing upon the UNHCR definition, has been unevenly applied and based largely on the logic of exclusion as opposed to humanitarianism, see Norman L. Zucker and Naomi Flink Zucker, *The Guarded Gate: The Reality of American Refugee Policy* (San Diego: Harcourt Brace Jovanovich, 1987). For a deft analysis of how U.S. refugee policies of exclusion have been driven by the legacy of anti-Black, and specifically anti-Haitian, racism and U.S. neoimperialism, see A. Naomi Paik, "Carceral Quarantine at Guantánamo: Legacies of US Imprisonment of Haitian Refugees, 1991–1994," *Radical History Review*, no. 115 (2013): 142–68.

19. For an analysis of the 1967 protocol, see Sara E. Davies, "Redundant or Essential? How Politics Shaped the Outcome of the 1967 Protocol," *International Journal of Refugee Law* 19, no. 4 (2007): 703–28.

20. Sucheng Chan, *Survivors: Cambodian Refugees in the United States* (Urbana: University of Illinois Press, 2004), 63–64.

21. For an analysis of how members of Congress and the courts interpreted the 1980s Refugee Act, see Karen K. Jorgensen, "The Role of the U.S. Congress and Courts in the Application of the Refugee Act of 1980," in *Refugee Law and Policy: International and U.S. Responses*, ed. Ved P. Nanda (New York: Greenwood, 1989), 129–50.

22. Walter F. Mondale, speech delivered to the UN Conference on Indochinese Refugees at the Palais des Nations, Geneva, July 21, 1979.

23. Ibid.

24. Catherine J. Schlund-Vials, *War, Genocide, and Justice: Cambodian American Memory Work* (Minneapolis: University of Minnesota Press, 2012), 13.

25. Gil Loescher and John A. Scanlan, *Calculated Kindness: Refugees and America's Half-Open Door, 1945 to the Present* (New York: Free Press, 1986), 147–69.

26. For a history of the construction and ultimate failure of Sa Kaeo, see William Shawcross, *The Quality of Mercy: Cambodia, Holocaust and the Modern Conscience*, rev. ed. (New York: Simon and Schuster, 1985), 169–90.

27. On Rosalynn Carter's visit to Sa Kaeo, see "Cambodia: A Devastating Trip," *Time*, November 19, 1979, available at http://content.time.com/time/ magazine/article/0,9171,948784,00.html, accessed March 23, 2013. The UNHCR constructed new and improved sites such as Khao-I-Dang, but overcrowding and lawlessness continued to define camp life. Violent crime was pervasive, with detainees at the mercy of Thai soldiers and criminal organizations that

controlled the borderlands. Some refugees encountered their Khmer Rouge tormentors who had entered the UNHCR camps.

28. This quotation is taken from the *U.S. News and World Report* article by D. Whitman, "Trouble for America's 'Model' Minority," which is referenced in Bill Ong Hing, "Detention to Deportation: Rethinking the Removal of Cambodian Refugees," *UC Davis Law Review* 38 (2005): 891, available at http://works.bepress.com/billhing/2, accessed August 21, 2013.

29. See, for example, "Dole Asks for U.S. Relief of Cambodian Refugees," press release, June 12, 1978, Robert J. Dole Archive and Special Collections, available at http://dolearchivecollections.ku.edu/collections/press_releases/780612ask.pdf, accessed September 22, 2013.

30. Hannah Arendt, *Origins of Totalitarianism* (New York: World, 1951), 377.

31. Giorgio Agamben, *Homo Sacer: Sovereign Power and Bare Life* (Stanford, CA: Stanford University Press, 1998), 15–70.

32. Ibid.

33. Agamben first expounded on this "original fiction" in a 1995 article, "We Refugees," trans. Michael Rocke, *Symposium* 49, no. 2 (1995): 117.

34. Michael Dillon and Julian Reid, *The Liberal Way of War: Killing to Make Life Live* (New York: Routledge, 2009), 7.

35. Ibid.

36. Mimi Thi Nguyen, *The Gift of Freedom: War, Debt and Other Refugee Passages* (Durham, NC: Duke University Press, 2012), 20.

37. Ibid., 14. Here Nguyen, echoing Agamben, suggests that the Vietnamese refugees are the subjects simultaneously of the gift of freedom and of the "racial death" that evinces the "divisions between those who possess full freedom and those who are the constitutive outside."

38. As Sucheng Chan points out, this two-step process often led to clashes between the State Department and the INS. The former desired to see as many Cambodians qualify for resettlement as part of its broader foreign policy strategy of discrediting the Vietnamese-backed regime in Phnom Penh. The latter brought a traditional border patrol mentality to the work, scrutinizing applicants to ensure that they met refugee criteria. See Chan, *Survivors*, 70.

39. Walter Benjamin, "Theses on the Philosophy of History," in *Illuminations*, ed. Hannah Arendt (New York: Schocken, 1968), 262.

Chapter 2

1. Southern California, particularly Long Beach, was the first Cambodian enclave in the United States. Prior to the Khmer Rouge takeover of Cambodia, the Lon Nol government sent some elite students to study engineering and agriculture at California State University, Long Beach. When the Khmer Rouge took control in 1975, these students became exiles and quickly organized to sponsor relatives who were attempting to flee Cambodia. Afterwards, Long Beach became the main U.S. Cambodian resettlement city, and today it is home

to the largest Cambodian population outside of Southeast Asia. It should come as no surprise that Ra was greeted by Cambodian volunteers at Los Angeles International Airport. Many of these volunteers had been living in California for over a decade. See Susan Needham and Karen I. Quintiliani, *Cambodians in Long Beach* (Charleston, SC: Arcadia, 2008), 9–16.

2. Building upon Wacquant's reconceptualization of the traditional ghetto territory, I also wish to call attention to the fact that hyperghettos, as sites of captivity, are not necessarily geographically contiguous territories within a city (or even a section of a city). In other words, a given inner city can be home to multiple hyperghetto pockets (some only a few square blocks) broken up by commercial districts, large thoroughfares, or even expressways (such as the Cross Bronx Expressway). The Northwest Bronx is certainly home to multiple hyperghetto clusters—what law enforcement terms "hot spots"—that surround the Fordham Road commercial district.

3. Some portions of my interview with Blanca Ramirez were previously published in Eric Tang, "How the Refugees Stopped the Bronx from Burning," *Race and Class* 54, no. 4 (2013): 57–59.

4. The NWBCC's work is chronicled by Jill Jonnes in *South Bronx Rising: The Rise, Fall, and Resurrection of an American City*, 2nd ed. (New York: Fordham University Press, 2002).

5. Some portions of my description on the history of the Bronx arsons and the influence of RAND and researcher Anthony Downs were previously published in "How the Refugees Stopped the Bronx from Burning," 53–54.

6. Deborah Wallace and Rodrick Wallace, *A Plague on Your Houses: How New York Was Burned Down and National Public Health Crumbled* (London: Verso, 1998), xvi, 56.

7. Jonnes, *South Bronx Rising*, 366–67.

8. Ibid., 258–59.

9. Joe Flood, *The Fires: How a Computer Formula Burned Down New York City—and Determined the Future of American Cities* (New York: Riverhead, 2010), 1–24.

10. Lee Dembart, "Carter Takes 'Sobering' Trip to the South Bronx," *New York Times*, October 6, 1977.

11. The eight cities that were categorized as "Major Disorders" were Buffalo, Cambridge (Maryland), Cincinnati, Detroit, Milwaukee, Minneapolis, Newark, and Tampa.

12. National Advisory Commission on Civil Disorders, *Report of the National Advisory Commission on Civil Disorders*, with Introduction by Tom Wicker (New York: Dutton, 1968).

13. For a discussion on President Lyndon B. Johnson's reaction to the Kerner Commission recommendations, see Linda Lupo, *Flak-Catchers: One Hundred Years of Riot Commission Politics in America* (Lanham, MD: Lexington, 2011), 147.

14. Ibid., "Future of Cities," chap. 16.

15. Flood, *Fires*, 241.

16. For a history of RAND's emergence, see Alex Abella, *Soldiers of Reason: The RAND Corporation and the Rise of the American Empire* (New York: Harcourt, 2008).

17. On the singular role that RAND played in developing counterinsurgency research, strategies, and tactics in Southeast Asia during the 1960s and 1970s, see Mai Elliott, *RAND in Southeast Asia: A History of the Vietnam War Era* (Santa Monica, CA: RAND Corporation, 2010). In 1971 RAND became a household name when one of its researchers, Daniel Ellsberg, leaked a set of classified documents to the *New York Times* that came to be known as the Pentagon Papers. These documents exposed the extent to which the Johnson administration was willing to extend the war—and indeed expand it into neighboring Cambodia and Laos—even after it was deemed "unwinnable."

18. See Anthony Downs, "Alternative Futures for the American Ghetto," *Daedalus: The Conscience of the City* 97, no. 4 (1968): 1331–78.

19. Flood, *Fires*, 241.

20. I elaborate on this point in my article "How the Refugees Stopped the Bronx from Burning."

21. Wayne King, "Houston Housing Authority Accused of Racial Steering," *New York Times*, March 19, 1985, available at http://www.nytimes.com/1985/03/19/us/houston-housing-authority-accused-of-racial-steering.html, accessed February 4, 2013.

22. Eric Tang, "A Gulf Unites Us: The Vietnamese Americans of Black New Orleans East," *American Quarterly* 63, no. 1 (2011): 117–49.

23. Tram Nguyen, "Unsettled Refugees," *Colorlines*, September 15, 2001, available at http://colorlines.com/archives/2001/09/unsettled_refugees.html, accessed May 19, 2013.

24. Dan Reed, "Laotians Greeted by Violence in Contra Costa: Hard Times, Cultural Differences and Racism Blamed," *San Francisco Chronicle*, September 8, 1992.

25. Tang, "A Gulf Unites Us," 126–30.

26. Eric Tang, "Collateral Damage: Southeast Asian Poverty in the United States," *Social Text* 18, no. 1 (2000): 55–79.

27. Aihwa Ong, *Buddha Is Hiding: Refugees, Citizenship, the New America* (Berkeley: University of California Press, 2003), 78.

28. Ibid., 86.

29. Ibid.

30. Ibid.

31. Here the theory of "racial triangulation" proves instructive. This theory argues that Asian Americans and immigrants (and to this I would add other "new immigrants") are held at a distinct racial coordinate that not only distinguishes them from African Americans but actually serves to locate the latter as the underclass. Inversely, African Americans locate Asians as the perpetually foreign. In other words, Asian, African Americans, and white people

situate one another in a power-laden racial field, each occupying a coordinate that mutually reinforces the other. Therefore, one racial group cannot simply "slide" into the position of another. We might say that white racial dominance is always based on a triangular structure as opposed to a spectrum. In this spectrum, Asians are said to be bookended by white people and African Americans and to slide to one end or the other depending on a given context. See Claire Jean Kim, "The Racial Triangulation of Asian Americans," *Politics and Society* 27, no. 1 (1999): 105–38.

32. See Jared Sexton, "People-of-Color-Blindness: Notes on the Afterlife of Slavery," *Social Text* 28, no. 2 (2010): 31–56, for a generative analysis of how the racial location of those genealogically linked to racial slavery cannot be occupied by other oppressed racial groups, including (or particularly) the refugee—even when the refugee appears to be subjected to identical forms of power. Sexton cautions against the conflation of colonial and slave genealogies, noting that the basis of the latter is the natal alienation of the slave.

33. Mimi Thi Nguyen, *The Gift of Freedom: War, Debt, and Other Refugee Passages* (Durham, NC: Duke University Press, 2012), 10.

34. Shiori Ui analyzes the communal networks in Cambodian refugee apartments and their importance, especially for refugee women. See Ui, "Unlikely Heroes: The Evolution of Female Leadership in a Cambodian Ethnic Enclave," in *Ethnography Unbound: Power and Resistance in the Modern Metropolis*, ed. Michael Burawoy (Berkeley: University of California Press, 1991), 161–77.

35. I attribute this to the presence of genocide survivors in one of New York City's poorest neighborhoods, which lent itself to the human-interest stories, neighborhood profiles, and long-form journalism that the *Times* was known for.

36. Noirmitsu Onishi, "University Heights: New Culture; New Stresses," *New York Times*, October 23, 1994, available at http://www.nytimes.com/1994/10/23/nyregion/neighborhood-report-university-heights-new-culture-new-stresses.html, accessed April 19, 2014.

37. Edward Wong, "Children of the Killing Fields," *New York Times*, March 26, 2000, available at http://www.nytimes.com/2000/03/26/nyregion/children-of-the-killing-fields.html, accessed April 26, 2014.

38. Sam Dolnick, "After Camps, New Horizons," *New York Times*, March 17, 2012, available at http://lens.blogs.nytimes.com/2012/03/17/after-camps-new, accessed April 26, 2014.

Chapter 3

1. As I discuss in the Introduction, YLP was a program of CAAAV: Organizing Asian Communities, a citywide organization that worked in several Asian immigrant enclaves. The designations "YLP" and "CAAAV" were often used interchangeably throughout my years working in the Northwest Bronx.

At times this conflation was appropriate because CAAAV staff and members who belonged to other relatively autonomous program areas—specifically, Chinatown tenant organizing and labor organizing with Filipina domestic workers—actively supported the community-organizing work in the Bronx and vice versa. Suffice it to say that we took seriously the importance of belonging to a panethnic organization. Still, notwithstanding our organizational synergy, I use "YLP" to describe the work carried out in the Bronx to call attention to the specific organizing conditions and challenges faced by Southeast Asian refugees. I do so, too, to distinguish YLP organizing decisions and practices (and my reflections on the ones I was directly involved in) from those of other CAAAV program areas. Indeed, my thoughts on community organizing, neoliberalism, and multiculturalism refer exclusively to the welfare organizing I was directly involved in during the late 1990s and early 2000s; they certainly cannot account for CAAAV's political orientations and practices as a whole.

2. For an analysis of New York City welfare fair hearings, see Robert E. Scott, "The Welfare Hearing Process: The Law and Administrative Regulations Examined," *William and Mary Law Review* 11, no. 2 (1969): 291–370.

3. For an overview of U.S. community-organizing orthodoxies, see Saul David Alinsky, *Rules for Radicals: A Practical Primer for Realistic Radicals* (New York: Random House, 1971).

4. Loïc J. D. Wacquant, *Punishing the Poor: The Neoliberal Government of Social Insecurity* (Durham, NC: Duke University Press, 2009), 76–109.

5. This dilemma was captured in the documentary *Eating Welfare*.

6. See Personal Responsibility and Work Opportunity Reconciliation Act, Pub. L. No. 104-193, 110 Stat. 2105 (1996). The provision regarding the denial of food stamps and SSI to non-citizens was eventually amended by Congress in 1997 and 1998 (Pub. L. 105-18, Pub. L. 105-33, Pub. L. 105-185).

7. For an analysis of the return to "state's rights," see Kenneth J. Neubeck and Noel A. Cazenave, *Welfare Racism: Playing the Race Card against America's Poor* (New York: Routledge, 2001), 179–214.

8. For an analysis of the impact that devolution had on recipients, see Joe Soss, Sanford F. Schram, Thomas P. Vartanian, and Erin O'Brien, "Setting the Terms of Relief: Explaining State Policy Choices in the Devolution Revolution," *American Journal of Political Science* 45, no. 2 (2001): 378–95.

9. For a comprehensive overview of welfare reform's implementation in New York City under Rudolph Giuliani, see Demetra S. Nightingale, Nancy M. Pindus, Fredrica D. Kramer, John Trutko, Kelly S. Mikelson, and Michael Egner, *Work and Welfare Reform in New York City during the Giuliani Administration: A Study of Program Implementation* (Washington, DC: Urban Institute Labor and Social Policy Center, 2002).

10. For an incisive analysis of the shortcomings and contradictions of some forms of "youth organizing," particularly those that conform to neoliberal logics, see Soo Ah Kwon, *Uncivil Youth: Race, Activism, and Affirmative Governmentality* (Durham, NC: Duke University Press, 2013), 52.

11. Felicia Ann Kornbluh, *The Battle for Welfare Rights: Politics and Poverty in Modern America* (Philadelphia: University of Pennsylvania Press, 2007), 14–38.

12. For an analysis of the right to a guaranteed income and how this is distinct from "welfare rights," see Theresa Funiciello, *The Tyranny of Kindness: Dismantling the Welfare System to End Poverty in America* (New York: Atlantic Monthly Press, 1993), 257–64.

13. Grassroots Organizing for Welfare Leadership (GROWL) was initiated in 1999 under the leadership of the Center for Third World Organizing. Its original membership included forty organizations from around the country advocating for welfare rights in the aftermath of federal welfare reform. For a full listing of organizations, see Center for Third World Organizing, *Hear Our Voices: Welfare Reform Exposed* (Oakland, CA: Center for Third World Organizing, 2001).

14. Jill S. Quadagno, *The Color of Welfare: How Racism Undermined the War on Poverty* (New York: Oxford University Press, 1994), 117–52.

15. It goes without saying that modern nation-states, imperialist nation-states in particular, have historically conquered markets and removed profit impediments. Under neoliberalism, however, the state is not the main architect of these policies. Corporations and international institutions such as the World Bank and the International Monetary Fund drive what historian and cultural critic Lisa Duggan describes as the "policies [that] reinvented practices of economic, political and cultural imperialism for a supposedly postimperial world." See Duggan, *The Twilight of Equality: Neoliberalism, Cultural Politics, and the Attack on Democracy* (Boston: Beacon, 2003), xiii. Similarly, anthropologist David Harvey points out that these architects of neoliberalism fashion themselves not as state policy makers or ideologues but as technocrats who believe they are serving the common good by "bringing all human action into the domain of the market." See Harvey, *A Brief History of Neoliberalism* (Oxford: Oxford University Press, 2005), 3.

16. Lisa Lowe, *Immigrant Acts: On Asian American Cultural Politics* (Durham, NC: Duke University Press, 1996), 86.

17. For a deft analysis of the welfare state's replication of the patriarchal order of the domestic sphere and domestic violences, see Priya Kandaswamy, "'You Trade in *a* Man for *the* Man': Domestic Violence and the U.S. Welfare State," *American Quarterly* 62, no. 2 (2010): 253–77.

18. Loïc J. D. Wacquant, "The Wedding of Workfare and Prisonfare Revisited," *Social Justice* 38, no. 1–2 (2011): 210.

19. Ibid.

20. Wacquant, *Punishing the Poor*, 14–15.

Chapter 4

1. Human Resources Administration website, available at http://www.nyc.gov/html/hra/html/serv_welfarework.html, accessed October 28, 2013.

2. For an analysis of how workfare programs such as New York City's WEP are used punitively to remove people from welfare, see Theresa Funiciello, "The Work of Women (and the Mistakes of Workfare Organizing)," *Third Force*, no. 5 (1997): 22–25.

3. Vivian S. Toy, "Tough Workfare Rules Used as Way to Cut Welfare Rolls," *New York Times*, April 15, 1988, available at http://www.nytimes.com/ 1998/04/15/nyregion/tough-workfare-rules-used-as-way-to-cut-welfare-rolls .html, accessed November 1, 2013.

4. This quote is taken from an interview with Kun Thea conducted in the spring of 2000, in which she spoke through an interpreter. I conducted a follow-up interview with her ten years later on April 17, 2010.

5. On how poor women on welfare secure supplemental income through multiple informal channels, see Kathryn Edin, "Surviving the Welfare System: How AFDC Recipients Make Ends Meet in Chicago," *Social Problems* 38, no. 4 (1991): 462–74.

6. Alan Finder, "Evidence Is Scant That Workfare Leads to Full-Time Jobs," *New York Times*, April 12, 1998, available at http://www.nytimes .com/1998/04/12/nyregion/evidence-is-scant-that-workfare-leads-to-full-time -jobs.html, accessed November 7, 2013.

7. Steven Greenhouse, "Wages for Workfare," *New York Times*, July 7, 1997, available at http://www.nytimes.com/1997/07/07/nyregion/wages-of-workfare .html, accessed November 7, 2013.

8. Loïc J. D. Wacquant, "The Wedding of Workfare and Prisonfare in the 21st Century," *Journal of Poverty* 16, no. 2 (2012): 236–49.

9. According to the Department of Justice, Title VI of the 1964 Civil Rights Act "prohibits discrimination on the basis of race, color, and national origin in programs and activities receiving federal financial assistance." This information is provided on the United States Department of Justice website, available at http://www.justice.gov/crt/about/cor/coord/titlevi.php.

10. From 1999 to 2004, YLP was also part of a loose citywide coalition of welfare rights organizations. Its proposal to remove as many refugees from WEP as possible through complaints over national-origins discrimination (based on unequal language access) was questioned by a few of our allies in the coalition who were invested in broader WEP reforms that they believed would impact all participants as opposed to what they saw as YLP's "loophole" tactic that seemed to benefit only a few.

11. Paulo Freire, *Pedagogy of the Oppressed* (New York: Herder and Herder, 1970).

12. Ira Shor and Paulo Freire, *A Pedagogy for Liberation: Dialogues on Transforming Education* (New York: Greenwood, 1987), 153.

13. Catherine J. Schlund-Vials, *War, Genocide, and Justice: Cambodian American Memory Work* (Minneapolis: University of Minnesota Press, 2012), 25.

14. Ibid., 17.

Chapter 5

1. There is as yet no comprehensive published study of contemporary Asian "new-immigrant" garment homeworkers in New York City. Many European immigrants worked in the industry during the late nineteenth and early twentieth centuries. See Daniel Soyer, ed., *A Coat of Many Colors: Immigration, Globalism, and Reform in the New York City Garment Industry* (New York: Fordham University Press, 2005). For an analysis of homeworking among new-immigrant Latinas, see M. Patricia Fernandez-Kelly and Anna M. Garcia, "Informalization at the Core: Hispanic Women, Homework, and the Advanced Capitalist State," in *The Informal Economy: Studies in Advanced and Less Developed Countries*, ed. Alejandro Portes, Manuel Castells, and Lauren Benton (Baltimore: Johns Hopkins University Press, 1989), 247–64.

2. *Eating Welfare*, produced by the Youth Leadership Project, CAAAV: Organizing Asian Communities (New York: CAAAV Organizing Asian Communities, 2000), DVD.

3. Rorth Chy, in *Eating Welfare*.

4. Ibid.

5. Ibid.

6. Ibid.

7. Robin D. G. Kelley, *Race Rebels: Culture, Politics, and the Black Working Class* (New York: Free Press, 1994), 8.

8. Ibid.

9. Among the many books and articles that argue this point, three stand out to me, shaping my analysis of Ra's homeworking life: Chela Sandoval, *Methodology of the Oppressed* (Minneapolis: University of Minnesota Press, 2000); Chandra Talpade Mohanty, *Feminism without Borders: Decolonizing Theory, Practicing Solidarity* (Durham, NC: Duke University Press, 2003); M. Jacqui Alexander, *Pedagogies of Crossing: Meditations on Feminism, Sexual Politics, Memory, and the Sacred* (Durham, NC: Duke University Press, 2005).

10. For an analysis of the solidarities made possible by homeworking "time," see Miriam A. Glucksmann, "'What a Difference a Day Makes': A Theoretical and Historical Exploration of Temporality and Gender," *Sociology* 32, no. 2 (1998): 239–58.

11. Immanuel Maurice Wallerstein, *World-Systems Analysis: An Introduction* (Durham, NC: Duke University Press, 2004).

12. Saskia Sassen, *The Global City: New York, London, Tokyo* (Princeton, NJ: Princeton University Press, 1991).

13. Ibid., 282.

14. Saskia Sassen, *Territory, Authority, Rights: From Medieval to Global Assemblages* (Princeton, NJ: Princeton University Press, 2006), 317.

15. In addition to *The Global City* and *Territory, Authority, Rights*, Sassen's body of work includes *The Mobility of Capital and Labor: A Study in*

International Investment and Labor Flow (New York: Cambridge University Press, 1988), *Globalization and Its Discontents* (New York: New Press, 1998), and *Cities in a World Economy*, 2nd ed. (New York: Sage, 2011). Sassen's emphasis on the potential resistances of the low-wage worker in the service economy is summarized in "The Other Workers in the Advanced Corporate Economy," *S&F Online*, no. 8.1 (2009): 1–4, available at http://sfonline.barnard.edu/work/sassen_01.htm, accessed June 18, 2013.

16. Sassen, *Territory, Authority, Rights*, 317. My emphasis.

17. National Advisory Commission on Civil Disorders, *Report of the National Advisory Commission on Civil Disorders*, with Introduction by Tom Wicker (New York: Dutton, 1968).

18. As discussed in the film by Carvin Eisen *July '64* (San Francisco: California Newsreel, 2006).

19. Dan Georgakas and Marvin Surkin, *Detroit, I Do Mind Dying: A Study in Urban Revolution* (Cambridge, MA: South End Press, 1998), 23–83.

20. Grace Lee Boggs, *Living for Change: An Autobiography* (Minneapolis: University of Minnesota Press, 1998), 117–43.

21. This marks a significant difference in my conceptualization of the hyperghetto and that of Loïc Wacquant. Wacquant would be quite skeptical of my claim that these forms of liberal warfare—police violence, incarceration, drug wars—are profitable and "necessary." He is unconvinced that prisoners and those trapped in the hyperghetto remain sources of extraction; see Loïc Wacquant, "Prisoner Reentry as Myth and Ceremony," *Dialectical Anthropology* 34, no. 4 (2010): 605–20. According to Wacquant, the structural and functional parallels between ghetto and hyperghetto break down precisely at the function of extraction; see Wacquant, "Deadly Symbiosis: When Ghetto and Prison Meet and Mesh," *Punishment and Society* 3, no. 1 (2001): 95–133. In Wacquant's assessment, the city's ongoing structural integration of the hyperghetto is a "liminal and perverse articulation . . . a limiting case" (author's personal correspondence with Wacquant).

22. Clyde Adrian Woods, "Do You Know What It Means to Miss New Orleans? Katrina, Trap Economics, and the Rebirth of the Blues," *American Quarterly* 57, no. 4 (2005): 1009. My emphasis.

23. Clyde Adrian Woods, "'Sittin' on Top of the World': The Challenges of Blues and Hip Hop Geography," in *Black Geographies and the Politics of Place*, ed. Katherine McKittrick (Cambridge, MA: South End Press, 2007), 55.

24. Ruth Wilson Gilmore, *Golden Gulag: Prisons, Surplus, Crisis, and Opposition in Globalizing California* (Berkeley: University of California Press, 2007), 128–78.

25. On the influence of the war on drugs on biomedical research, see Carl L. Hart, *High Price: A Neuroscientist's Journey of Self-Discovery That Challenges Everything You Know about Drugs and Society* (New York: Harper, 2013).

26. Woods, "Sittin' on Top of the World," 57.

27. Woods, "Do You Know What It Means to Miss New Orleans?" 1005.

28. Woods, "Sittin' on Top of the World," 57.

29. On the radical transformation of Times Square, see Samuel R. Delany, *Times Square Red, Times Square Blue* (New York: New York University Press, 1999).

30. Woods, "Sittin' on Top of the World," 59.

31. Ibid., 60.

Chapter 6

1. For an account of Khmer Rouge forced marriages, see Peg LeVine, *Love and Dread in Cambodia: Weddings, Births, and Ritual Harm under the Khmer Rouge* (Singapore: National University of Singapore Press, 2010). For an ethnographic account of the long-term impact of these forced marriages under *ankgar*, see Annuska Derks, *Khmer Women on the Move: Exploring Work and Life in Urban Cambodia* (Honolulu: University of Hawai'i Press, 2008).

2. See the study by Theresa de Langis, Judith Strasser, Thida Kim, and Sopheap Taing, *Like Ghost Changes Body: A Study on the Impact of Forced Marriage under the Khmer Rouge Regime* (Phnom Penh, Cambodia: Transcultural Psychosocial Organisation, 2014), 76–79.

3. See Eithne Luibhéid, *Entry Denied: Controlling Sexuality at the Border* (Minneapolis: University of Minnesota Press, 2002). I would like to thank Cathy Hannabach for bringing to my attention several articles that address how asylum seekers whose sexual and gender identities fall outside (or are assumed to fall outside) heteronormative ideals have been barred from entry into the United States, which prevents them from submitting asylum applications. For example, see Siobhan B. Somerville, "Notes toward a Queer History of Naturalization," *American Quarterly* 57, no. 3 (2005): 659–75.

4. Loïc J. D. Wacquant, *Punishing the Poor: The Neoliberal Government of Social Insecurity* (Durham, NC: Duke University Press, 2009), 195–207.

5. Beth E. Richie, *Compelled to Crime: The Gender Entrapment of Battered Black Women* (New York: Routledge, 1996), 69–99.

6. Beth E. Richie, *Arrested Justice: Black Women, Violence, and America's Prison Nation* (New York: New York University Press, 2012), 99–124.

7. Ibid., 4.

8. Daniel P. Moynihan, *The Negro Family: The Case for National Action* (Washington, DC: U.S. Department of Labor, Office of Planning and Research, 1965), 29.

9. Ibid., 15.

10. Ibid.

11. Ibid., 16.

12. Ibid., 31.

13. Ibid., 32.

14. Angela Y. Davis, "Reflections on the Black Woman's Role in the Community of Slaves," *Massachusetts Review* 13, no. 1–2 (1972): 97.

15. Yen Le Espiritu, "Gender and Labor in Asian Immigrant Families," *American Behavioral Scientist* 42, no. 4 (1999): 628.

16. Aihwa Ong, *Buddha Is Hiding: Refugees, Citizenship, the New America* (Berkeley: University of California Press, 2003), 148.

17. Ibid., 149.

18. Ibid., 158.

19. Ibid.

20. Nazli Kibria makes a similar point in her study of Vietnamese refugee families. She says that, although Vietnamese refugee women experienced new freedoms and opportunities once resettled, they did not necessarily subvert traditional (patriarchal) family structure, norms, and traditions. See Kibria, *Family Tightrope: Changing Lives of Vietnamese Americans* (Princeton, NJ: Princeton University Press, 1995).

21. Ibid., 160.

22. Ong, *Buddha Is Hiding*, 147.

23. Rubén G. Rumbaut and John R. Weeks, "Fertility and Adaptation: Indochinese Refugees in the United States," *International Migration Review* 20, no. 2 (1986): 428–66.

24. See Shiori Ui, "Unlikely Heroes: The Evolution of Female Leadership in a Cambodian Ethnic Enclave," in *Ethnography Unbound: Power and Resistance in the Modern Metropolis*, ed. Michael Burawoy (Berkeley: University of California Press, 1991), 162. I agree with Ui's assessment of Cambodian refugee women's political and personal choices in Stockton's impoverished Cambodian refugee community of the mid-to-late 1980s. Ui says, "Women's leadership emerged, rather, as a result of unique structural conditions in Stockton's ethnic enclaves—conditions that were shaped primarily by the state."

Conclusion

1. Stephen Best and Saidiya Hartman, "Fugitive Justice," *Representations* 92, no. 1 (2005): 3.

2. Ibid., 2.

3. Ibid., 3.

4. For a brief discussion of young Bronx Cambodian factory workers, see Eric Tang, "Collateral Damage: Southeast Asian Poverty in the United States," *Social Text* 18, no. 1 (2000): 74–75.

5. Catherine J. Schlund-Vials, *War, Genocide, and Justice: Cambodian American Memory Work* (Minneapolis: University of Minnesota Press, 2012), 13–14. Here Schlund-Vials elaborates on what she terms the "Cambodian syndrome."

6. Bill Ong Hing, "Detention to Deportation: Rethinking the Removal of Cambodian Refugees," *UC Davis Law Review* 38 (2005): 891–971, available at http://works.bepress.com/billhing/2, accessed August 12, 2014.

7. Gaby Coppola, "Dearly Deported," *College Hill Independent*, September, 16, 2003, 1.

8. See Soo Ah Kwon, "Deporting Cambodian Refugees: Youth Activism, State Reform, and Imperial Statecraft," *positions* 20, no. 3 (2012): 737–62.

9. These numbers are provided by the HALO Trust, an international, nongovernmental organization whose mission is landmine clearance. See HALO Trust, *Getting Mines Out of the Ground for Good*, available at http://www.halotrust.org/where-we-work/Cambodia, accessed September 9, 2014.

10. Rasmey and Vanna are pseudonyms because I did not officially interview these two family members. However, I did discuss the project with both of them (on separate occasions) and benefited from the insights they each had to offer about their mother and their family's struggles with poverty and the criminal justice system.

11. W. E. B. Du Bois, *The Souls of Black Folk* (repr., New York: Penguin Classics, 1996), 3–4.

12. Vijay Prashad, *The Karma of Brown Folk* (Minneapolis: University of Minnesota Press, 2000), 6.

13. Khatharya Um, *A Dream Denied: Educational Experiences of Southeast Asian American Youth: Issues and Recommendations* (Washington, DC: Southeast Asia Resource Action Center, 2003), 1–21.

14. Office of the United Nations High Commissioner for Refugees (UNHCR), "Syria Emergency: On the Road: One Family's Exhausting Journey from Kobani to Northern Iraq," available at http://www.unhcr.org/emergency/5051e8cd6-545106adc.html, accessed November 10, 2014.

15. Lauren Gambino and Raya Jalabi, "Syria's Civil War Has Forced 3M Refugees to Flee the Country—Why Is the US Accepting So Few?" *theguardian*, October 7, 2014, available at http://www.theguardian.com/world/2014/oct/06/syria-refugees-syria-civil-war-guide, accessed November 15, 2014.

16. Human Rights Watch, *"You Don't Have Rights Here": US Border Screenings and Returns of Central Americans to Risk of Serious Harm* (New York: Human Rights Watch, 2014), available at http://www.hrw.org/reports/2014/10/16/you-don-t-have-rights-here-0, accessed November 15, 2014.

17. Shannon Speed, "The U.S. Is Jailing Immigrant Women and Children under Appalling Conditions," *Global Post*, October 10, 2014, available at http://www.globalpost.com/dispatches/globalpost-blogs/commentary/us-jailing-immigrant-women-and-their-children-under-appalling-con, accessed November 15, 2014.

18. Providence Youth and Student Movement, "Who We Are," available at http://www.prysm.us/who-we-are/, accessed November 17, 2014.

19. Freedom Inc., "About Us," available at http://freedom-inc.org/index.php?page=about-us, accessed November 17, 2014.

Bibliography

Abella, Alex. *Soldiers of Reason: The RAND Corporation and the Rise of the American Empire*. New York: Harcourt, 2008.

Agamben, Giorgio. *Homo Sacer: Sovereign Power and Bare Life*. Stanford, CA: Stanford University Press, 1998.

———. "We Refugees." Translated by Michael Rocke. *Symposium* 49, no. 2 (1995): 114–19.

Alexander, Michelle. *The New Jim Crow: Mass Incarceration in the Age of Colorblindness*. New York: New Press, 2010.

Alexander, M. Jacqui. *Pedagogies of Crossing: Meditations on Feminism, Sexual Politics, Memory, and the Sacred*. Durham, NC: Duke University Press, 2005.

Alinsky, Saul David. *Rules for Radicals: A Practical Primer for Realistic Radicals*. New York: Random House, 1971.

Amott, Teresa. "Black Women and AFDC: Making Entitlement Out of Necessity." In *Women, the State, and Welfare*, edited by Linda Gordon, 280–94. Madison: University of Wisconsin Press, 1990.

Arendt, Hannah. *Origins of Totalitarianism*. New York: World, 1951.

Bailis, Lawrence Neil. *Bread or Justice: Grassroots Organizing in the Welfare Rights Movement*. Lexington, MA: Lexington, 1974.

Becker, Elizabeth. *When the War Was Over: The Voices of Cambodia's Revolution and Its People*. New York: Simon and Schuster, 1986.

Benjamin, Walter. *Illuminations*. Edited by Hannah Arendt. New York: Schocken, 1968.

Best, Stephen, and Saidiya Hartman. "Fugitive Justice." *Representations* 92, no. 1 (2005): 1–15.

Boat People SOS. *2010 Vietnamese American Needs Assessment: Report on Findings*. Falls Church, VA: Boat People SOS, 2011.

Boggs, Grace Lee. *Living for Change: An Autobiography*. Minneapolis: University of Minnesota Press, 1998.

Calhoun, Jack. "On the Side of Pol Pot: U.S. Supports Khmer Rouge." *Covert Action Quarterly* 34 (Summer 1990): 37–40.

"Cambodia: A Devastating Trip." *Time*, November 19, 1979. Available at http://content.time.com/time/magazine/article/0,9171,948784,00.html, accessed April 23, 2014.

Center for Third World Organizing. *Hear Our Voices: Welfare Reform Exposed*. Oakland, CA: Center for Third World Organizing, 2001.

Chan, Sucheng. *Survivors: Cambodian Refugees in the United States*. Urbana: University of Illinois Press, 2004.

Chan, Sucheng, and Audrey U. Kim. *Not Just Victims: Conversations with Cambodian Community Leaders in the United States*. Urbana: University of Illinois Press, 2003.

Chandler, David P. *Brother Number One: A Political Biography of Pol Pot*. Boulder, CO: Westview, 1992.

———. *A History of Cambodia*. Boulder, CO: Westview, 1983.

———. *The Tragedy of Cambodian History: Politics, War, and Revolution since 1945*. 2nd ed. New Haven, CT: Yale University Press, 1993.

Childs, John Brown. *Transcommunality: From the Politics of Conversion to the Ethics of Respect*. Philadelphia: Temple University Press, 2003.

Clifford, James, George E. Marcus, and Kim Fortun. "Introduction: Partial Truths." In *Writing Culture: The Poetics and Politics of Ethnography*, edited by James Clifford and George E. Marcus. Berkeley: University of California Press, 1986.

Clymer, Kenton J. *The United States and Cambodia: 1969–2000: A Troubled Relationship*. New York: Routledge, 2004.

Coppola, Gaby. "Dearly Deported." *College Hill Independent*, September, 16, 2003, 1.

Costa Vargas, João Helion. *Catching Hell in the City of Angels: Life and Meanings of Blackness in South Central Los Angeles*. Minneapolis: University of Minnesota Press, 2006.

Criddle, JoAn D. *To Destroy You Is No Loss: The Odyssey of a Cambodian Family*. 2nd ed. Auke Bay, AK: East/West Bridge, 1998.

Davies, Sara E. "Redundant or Essential? How Politics Shaped the Outcome of the 1967 Protocol." *International Journal of Refugee Law* 19, no. 4 (2007): 703–28.

Davis, Angela Y. "Reflections on the Black Woman's Role in the Community of Slaves." *Massachusetts Review* 13, no. 1–2 (1972): 81–100.

Davis, Mike. *City of Quartz: Excavating the Future in Los Angeles.* New York: Verso, 1990.

Deac, Wilfred P. *Road to the Killing Fields: The Cambodian War of 1970–1975.* College Station: Texas A&M University Press, 1997.

DeGenova, Nicholas, and Ana Yolanda Ramos-Zayas. *Latino Crossings: Mexicans, Puerto Ricans, and the Politics of Race and Citizenship.* New York: Routledge, 2003.

Delany, Samuel R. *Times Square Red, Times Square Blue.* New York: New York University Press, 1999.

Dembart, Lee. "Carter Takes 'Sobering' Trip to the South Bronx." *New York Times,* October 6, 1977.

Derks, Annuska. *Khmer Women on the Move: Exploring Work and Life in Urban Cambodia.* Honolulu: University of Hawai'i Press, 2008.

Dillon, Michael, and Julian Reid. *The Liberal Way of War: Killing to Make Life Live.* New York: Routledge, 2009.

"Dole Asks for U.S. Relief of Cambodian Refugees." Press release, June 12, 1978. Robert J. Dole Archive and Special Collections. Available at http:// dolearchivecollections.ku.edu/collections/press_releases/780612ask.pdf, accessed April 4, 2014.

Dolnick, Sam. "After Camps, New Horizons." *New York Times,* March 17, 2012. Available at http://lens.blogs.nytimes.com/2012/03/17/after-camps-new, accessed April 26, 2014.

Downs, Anthony. "Alternative Futures for the American Ghetto." *Daedalus: The Conscience of the City* 97, no. 4 (1968): 1331–78.

Du Bois, W. E. B. *The Souls of Black Folk.* Reprint. New York: Penguin Classics, 1996.

Duggan, Lisa. *The Twilight of Equality: Neoliberalism, Cultural Politics, and the Attack on Democracy.* Boston: Beacon, 2003.

Edin, Kathryn. "Surviving the Welfare System: How AFDC Recipients Make Ends Meet in Chicago." *Social Problems* 38, no. 4 (1991): 462–74.

Elliott, Mai. *RAND in Southeast Asia: A History of the Vietnam War Era.* Santa Monica, CA: RAND Corporation, 2010.

Espiritu, Yen Le. *Body Counts: Vietnam War and Militarized Refuge(es).* Berkeley: University of California Press, 2014.

———. "Gender and Labor in Asian Immigrant Families." *American Behavioral Scientist* 42, no. 4 (1999): 628–47.

———. "Toward a Critical Refugee Study: The Vietnamese Refugee Subject in US Scholarship." *Journal of Vietnamese Studies* 1, no. 1–2 (2006): 410–33.

Fernandez-Kelly, M. Patricia, and Anna M. Garcia. "Informalization at the Core: Hispanic Women, Homework, and the Advanced Capitalist State." In *The Informal Economy: Studies in Advanced and Less Developed Countries,* edited by Alejandro Portes, Manuel Castells, and Lauren Benton, 247–64. Baltimore: Johns Hopkins University Press, 1989.

Finder, Alan. "Evidence Is Scant That Workfare Leads to Full-Time Jobs." *New York Times*, April 12, 1998. Available at http://www.nytimes .com/1998/04/12/nyregion/evidence-is-scant-that-workfare-leads-to-full -time-jobs.html, accessed November 7, 2013.

Flood, Joe. *The Fires: How a Computer Formula Burned Down New York City—and Determined the Future of American Cities*. New York: Riverhead, 2010.

Freire, Paulo. *Pedagogy of the Oppressed*. New York: Herder and Herder, 1970.

Fujiwara, Lynn. *Mothers without Citizenship: Asian Immigrant Families and the Consequences of Welfare Reform*. Minneapolis: University of Minnesota Press, 2008.

Funiciello, Theresa. *Tyranny of Kindness: Dismantling the Welfare System to End Poverty in America*. New York: Atlantic Monthly Press, 1993.

———. "The Work of Women (and the Mistakes of Workfare Organizing)." *Third Force*, no. 5 (1997): 22–25.

Gambino, Lauren, and Raya Jalabi. "Syria's Civil War Has Forced 3M Refugees to Flee the Country—Why Is the US Accepting So Few?" *theguardian*, October 7, 2014. Available at http://www.theguardian.com/world/2014/ oct/06/syria-refugees-syria-civil-war-guide, accessed November 15, 2014.

Georgakas, Dan, and Marvin Surkin. *Detroit, I Do Mind Dying: A Study in Urban Revolution*. Cambridge, MA: South End Press, 1998.

Gilmore, Ruth Wilson. *Golden Gulag: Prisons, Surplus, Crisis, and Opposition in Globalizing California*. Berkeley: University of California Press, 2007.

Glucksmann, Miriam A. "'What a Difference a Day Makes': A Theoretical and Historical Exploration of Temporality and Gender." *Sociology* 32, no. 2 (1998): 239–58.

Greenhouse, Steven. "Wages for Workfare." *New York Times*, July 7, 1997. Available at http://www.nytimes.com/1997/07/07/nyregion/wages-of-work fare.html, accessed November 7, 2013.

Gregory, Steven. *Black Corona: Race and the Politics of Place in an Urban Community*. Princeton, NJ: Princeton University Press, 1999.

Gwaltney, John Langston. *Drylongso: A Self-Portrait of Black America*. New York: Random House, 1980.

Hale, Charles R. *Engaging Contradictions: Theory, Politics, and Methods of Activist Scholarship*. Berkeley: University of California Press, 2008.

Hall, Stuart. "When Was the Postcolonial? Thinking at the Limit." In *The Post-colonial Question: Common Skies, Divided Horizons*, edited by Iain Chambers and Lidia Curti, 242–60. New York: Routledge, 1996.

Harding, Sandra. "Rethinking Standpoint Epistemology: What Is 'Strong Objectivity'?" In *Feminist Epistemologies*, edited by Linda Alcoff and Elizabeth Potter, 49–82. New York: Routledge, 1993.

Harney, Stefano, and Fred Moten. *The Undercommons: Fugitive Planning and Black Study*. Brooklyn, NY: Minor Compositions, 2013.

Hart, Carl L. *High Price: A Neuroscientist's Journey of Self-Discovery That Challenges Everything You Know about Drugs and Society.* New York: Harper, 2013.

Harvey, David. *A Brief History of Neoliberalism.* Oxford: Oxford University Press, 2005.

Hing, Bill Ong. "Detention to Deportation: Rethinking the Removal of Cambodian Refugees." *UC Davis Law Review* 38 (2005): 891–971. Available at http://works.bepress.com/billhing/2, accessed August 21, 2013.

Human Rights Watch. *"You Don't Have Rights Here": US Border Screenings and Returns of Central Americans to Risk of Serious Harm.* New York: Human Rights Watch, 2014. Available at http://www.hrw.org/sites/default/files/reports/us1014_web_0.pdf, accessed November 15, 2014.

Jonnes, Jill. *South Bronx Rising: The Rise, Fall, and Resurrection of an American City.* 2nd ed. New York: Fordham University Press, 2002.

Jorgensen, Karen K. "The Role of the U.S. Congress and Courts in the Application of the Refugee Act of 1980." In *Refugee Law and Policy: International and U.S. Responses,* edited by Ved P. Nanda, 129–50. New York: Greenwood, 1989.

July '64. Directed by Carvin Eisen. San Francisco: California Newsreel, 2006. DVD.

Kandaswamy, Priya. "'You Trade in *a* Man for *the* Man': Domestic Violence and the U.S. Welfare State." *American Quarterly* 62, no. 2 (2010): 253–77.

Katz, Michael B. "The Urban 'Underclass' as a Metaphor of Social Transformation." In *The Underclass Debate: Views from History,* edited by Michael B. Katz, 3–23. Princeton, NJ: Princeton University Press, 1993.

Kelley, Robin D. G. *Race Rebels: Culture, Politics, and the Black Working Class.* New York: Free Press, 1994.

———. *Yo Mama's Dysfunktional! Fighting the Culture Wars in Urban America.* Boston: Beacon, 1998.

Kiang, Peter. "Crouching Activists, Hidden Scholars: Reflections on Research and Development with Students and Communities in Asian American Studies." In *Engaging Contradictions: Theory, Politics, and Methods of Activist Scholarship,* edited by Charles R. Hale, 299–318. Berkeley: University of California Press, 2008.

———. "When Know-Nothings Speak English Only: Analyzing Irish and Cambodian Struggles for Community Development and Educational Equity." In *The State of Asian America: Activism and Resistance in the 1990s,* edited by Karin Aguilar–San Juan and M. Annette Jaimes, 125–45. Boston: South End Press, 1994.

Kibria, Nazli. *Family Tightrope: Changing Lives of Vietnamese Americans.* Princeton, NJ: Princeton University Press, 1995.

Kiernan, Ben. *Cambodia: The Eastern Zone Massacres: A Report on Social Conditions and Human Rights Violations in the Eastern Zone of Democratic*

Kampuchea under the Rule of Pol Pot's (Khmer Rouge) Communist Party of Kampuchea. New York: Columbia University's Center for the Study of Human Rights, 1986.

———. *How Pol Pot Came to Power: Colonialism, Nationalism, and Communism in Cambodia, 1930–1975*. 2nd ed. New Haven, CT: Yale University Press, 2004.

———. *The Pol Pot Regime: Race, Power, and Genocide in Cambodia under the Khmer Rouge, 1975–79*. 3rd ed. New Haven, CT: Yale University Press, 2008.

Kim, Claire Jean. "The Racial Triangulation of Asian Americans." *Politics and Society* 27, no. 1 (1999): 105–38.

King, Wayne. "Houston Housing Authority Accused of Racial Steering." *New York Times*, March 19, 1985. Available at http://www.nytimes .com/1985/03/19/us/houston-housing-authority-accused-of-racial-steering .html, accessed February 4, 2013.

Kornbluh, Felicia Ann. *The Battle for Welfare Rights: Politics and Poverty in Modern America*. Philadelphia: University of Pennsylvania Press, 2007.

Kwon, Soo Ah. "Deporting Cambodian Refugees: Youth Activism, State Reform, and Imperial Statecraft." *positions* 20, no. 3 (2012): 737–62.

———. *Uncivil Youth: Race, Activism, and Affirmative Governmentality*. Durham, NC: Duke University Press, 2013.

Le, Ngoan. "Policy for a Community 'At-Risk.'" In *The State of Asian Pacific America: A Public Policy Report: Policy Issues to the Year 2020*. Los Angeles: LEAP Asian Pacific American Public Policy Institute and UCLA Asian American Studies Center, 1993.

LeVine, Peg. *Love and Dread in Cambodia: Weddings, Births, and Ritual Harm under the Khmer Rouge*. Singapore: National University of Singapore Press, 2010.

Lewis, Oscar. *The Children of Sánchez: Autobiography of a Mexican Family*. New York: Random House, 1961.

Light, Ivan. "The Ethnic Economy." In *The Handbook of Economic Sociology*, edited by Neil J. Smelser and Richard Swedberg, 650–77. Princeton, NJ: Princeton University Press, 2005.

Lipsitz, George. *La Vida: A Puerto Rican Family in the Culture of Poverty—San Juan and New York*. New York: Random House, 1966.

———. *A Life in the Struggle: Ivory Perry and the Culture of Opposition*. Philadelphia: Temple University Press, 1995.

Loescher, Gil, and John A. Scanlan. *Calculated Kindness: Refugees and America's Half-Open Door, 1945 to the Present*. New York: Free Press, 1986.

Louie, Miriam Ching Yoon. *Sweatshop Warriors: Immigrant Women Workers Take on the Global Factory*. Cambridge, MA: South End Press, 2001.

Lowe, Lisa. *Immigrant Acts: On Asian American Cultural Politics*. Durham, NC: Duke University Press, 1996.

Luibhéid, Eithne. *Entry Denied: Controlling Sexuality at the Border*. Minneapolis: University of Minnesota Press, 2002.

Lupo, Lindsey. *Flak-Catchers: One Hundred Years of Riot Commission Politics in America.* Lanham, MD: Lexington, 2010.

Madison, D. Soyini. *Critical Ethnography: Methods, Ethics, and Performance.* 2nd ed. London: Sage, 2011.

Melnick, Leah. "Cambodians in Western Massachusetts and the Bronx, New York." *Migration World* 18, no. 2 (1990): 4–9.

Mohanty, Chandra Talpade. *Feminism without Borders: Decolonizing Theory, Practicing Solidarity.* Durham, NC: Duke University Press, 2003.

Mollica, Richard F. *Healing Invisible Wounds: Paths to Hope and Recovery in a Violent World.* Nashville, TN: Vanderbilt University Press, 2008.

Mondale, Walter. Speech delivered to the UN Conference on Indochinese Refugees, Palais des Nations, Geneva, July 21, 1979.

Mortland, Carol M., and Judy Ledgerwood. "Secondary Migration among Southeast Asian Refugees in the United States." *Urban Anthropology and Studies of Cultural Systems and World Economic Development* 16, no. 3–4 (1987): 291–326.

Moynihan, Daniel P. *The Negro Family: The Case for National Action.* Washington, DC: U.S. Department of Labor, Office of Planning and Research, 1965.

National Advisory Commission on Civil Disorders. *Report of the National Advisory Commission on Civil Disorders.* Introduction by Tom Wicker. New York: Dutton, 1968.

Needham, Susan, and Karen I. Quintiliani. *Cambodians in Long Beach.* Charleston, SC: Arcadia, 2008.

Neubeck, Kenneth J., and Noel A. Cazenave. *Welfare Racism: Playing the Race Card against America's Poor.* New York: Routledge, 2001.

Ngor, Haing. *Haing Ngor: A Cambodian Odyssey.* New York: Macmillan, 1987.

Ngor, Haing, and Roger Warner. *Survival in the Killing Fields.* New York: Carroll and Graf, 1987.

Nguyen, Mimi Thi. *The Gift of Freedom: War, Debt, and Other Refugee Passages.* Durham, NC: Duke University Press, 2012.

Nguyen, Tram. "Unsettled Refugees." *Colorlines,* September 15, 2001. Available at http://colorlines.com/archives/2001/09/unsettled_refugees.html, accessed May 19, 2013.

Nightingale, Demetra S., Nancy M. Pindus, Fredrica D. Kramer, John Trutko, Kelly S. Mikelson, and Michael Egner. *Work and Welfare Reform in New York City during the Giuliani Administration: A Study of Program Implementation.* Washington, DC: Urban Institute Labor and Social Policy Center, 2002.

Oliver, Gregory. "Remembering the Killing Fields." *Oxonian Globalist,* November 20, 2010. Available at http://toglobalist.org/2010/11/remembering-the-killing-fields/, accessed January 20, 2013.

Ong, Aihwa. *Buddha Is Hiding: Refugees, Citizenship, the New America.* Berkeley: University of California Press, 2003.

———. *Spirits of Resistance and Capitalist Discipline: Factory Women in Malaysia*. Albany: State University of New York Press, 2010.

Ong, Paul M., and Evelyn Blumenberg. "Welfare and Work among Southeast Asians." In *The State of Asian Pacific America: Reframing the Immigration Debate*. Los Angeles: LEAP Asian Pacific American Public Policy Institute and UCLA Asian American Studies Center, 1994.

Onishi, Noirmitsu. "University Heights: New Culture; New Stresses." *New York Times*, October 23, 1994. Available at http://www.nytimes.com/1994/10/23/nyregion/neighborhood-report-university-heights-new-culture-new-stresses.html, accessed April 19, 2014.

Owen, Taylor, and Ben Kiernan. "Bombs over Cambodia: New Information Reveals That Cambodia Was Bombed Far More Heavily than Previously Believed." *The Walrus*, October 2006, 62–69. Available at http://thewalrus.ca/2006-10-history/, accessed January 8, 2013.

Paik, A. Naomi. "Carceral Quarantine at Guantánamo: Legacies of US Imprisonment of Haitian Refugees, 1991–1994." *Radical History Review*, 2013, no. 115 (2013): 142–68.

Pilger, John. "The Long Secret Alliance: Uncle Sam and Pol Pot." *Covert Action Quarterly* 62, no. 4 (1997): 5–9. Available at http://www.worldcat.org/title/the-long-secret-alliance-uncle-sam-and-pol-pot/oclc/202617498&referer=brief_results, accessed October 18, 2014.

PoKempner, Dinah. *Political Control, Human Rights, and the UN Mission in Cambodia*. New York: Asia Watch, a Division of Human Rights Watch, 1992.

Prashad, Vijay. *The Karma of Brown Folk*. Minneapolis: University of Minnesota Press, 2000.

Pyles, Loretta. *Progressive Community Organizing: A Critical Approach for a Globalizing World*. New York: Routledge, 2009.

Quadagno, Jill S. *The Color of Welfare: How Racism Undermined the War on Poverty*. New York: Oxford University Press, 1994.

Reed, Dan. "Laotians Greeted by Violence in Contra Costa: Hard Times, Cultural Differences and Racism Blamed." *San Francisco Chronicle*, September 8, 1992.

Richie, Beth E. *Arrested Justice: Black Women, Violence, and America's Prison Nation*. New York: New York University Press, 2012.

———. *Compelled to Crime: The Gender Entrapment of Battered Black Women*. New York: Routledge, 1996.

Robinson, Courtland W. *Terms of Refuge: The Indochinese Exodus and the International Response*. New York: Zed Books, 1998.

Ross, Andrew. *Low Pay, High Profile: The Global Push for Fair Labor*. New York: New Press, 2004.

Rumbaut, Rubén G., and Kenji Ima. *The Adaptation of Southeast Asian Refugee Youth: A Comparative Study*. San Diego: San Diego State University, Department of Sociology, 1987.

Rumbaut, Rubén G., and John R. Weeks. "Fertility and Adaptation: Indochinese Refugees in the United States." *International Migration Review* 20, no. 2 (1986): 428–66.

———. "Mental Health and the Refugee Experience: A Comparative Study." In *Southeast Asian Mental Health: Treatment, Prevention, Services, Training, and Research*, edited by Tom Owan and Bruce Bliatout, 433–86. Rockville, MD: National Institute of Mental Health, Public Health Service, Alcohol, Drug Abuse, and Mental Health Administration, in Collaboration with Office of Refugee Resettlement, Social Security Administration, 1985.

———. "Portraits, Patterns, and Predictors of the Refugee Adaptation Process." In *Southeast Asian Refugees in the United States*, edited by David W. Haines, 138–82. Totowa, NJ: Rowman and Littlefield, 1988.

Sandoval, Chela. *Methodology of the Oppressed*. Minneapolis: University of Minnesota Press, 2000.

Sassen, Saskia. *Cities in a World Economy*. 2nd ed. New York: Sage, 2011.

———. *The Global City: New York, London, Tokyo*. Princeton, NJ: Princeton University Press, 1991.

———. *Globalization and Its Discontents*. New York: New Press, 1998.

———. *The Mobility of Capital and Labor: A Study in International Investment and Labor Flow*. New York: Cambridge University Press, 1988.

———. "The Other Workers in the Advanced Corporate Economy." *S&F Online*, no. 8.1 (2009): 1–4. Available at http://sfonline.barnard.edu/work/sassen_01.htm, accessed June 18, 2013.

———. *Territory, Authority, Rights: From Medieval to Global Assemblages*. Princeton, NJ: Princeton University Press, 2006.

Schanberg, Sydney H. *The Death and Life of Dith Pran*. New York: Penguin, 1985.

Schlund-Vials, Catherine J. *War, Genocide, and Justice: Cambodian American Memory Work*. Minneapolis: University of Minnesota Press, 2012.

Scott, Robert E. "The Welfare Hearing Process: The Law and Administrative Regulations Examined." *William and Mary Law Review* 11, no. 2 (1969): 291–370.

Sexton, Jared. "People-of-Color-Blindness: Notes on the Afterlife of Slavery." *Social Text* 28, no. 2 (2010): 31–56.

Shah, Bindi V. *Laotian Daughters: Working toward Community, Belonging, and Environmental Justice*. Philadelphia: Temple University Press, 2011.

Shawcross, William. *The Quality of Mercy: Cambodia, Holocaust and the Modern Conscience*. Rev. ed. New York: Simon and Schuster, 1985.

———. *Sideshow: Kissinger, Nixon and the Destruction of Cambodia*. New York: Simon and Schuster, 1979.

Shor, Ira, and Paulo Freire. *A Pedagogy for Liberation: Dialogues on Transforming Education*. New York: Greenwood, 1987.

Somekawa, Ellen. "On the Edge: Southeast Asians in Philadelphia and the Struggle for Space." In *Reviewing Asian America: Locating Diversity*, edited by Wendy L. Ng, 33–47. Pullman: Washington State University Press, 1995.

Somerville, Siobhan B. "Notes toward a Queer History of Naturalization." *American Quarterly* 57, no. 3 (2005): 659–75.

Soss, Joe, Sanford F. Schram, Thomas P. Vartanian, and Erin O'Brien. "Setting the Terms of Relief: Explaining State Policy Choices in the Devolution Revolution." *American Journal of Political Science* 45, no. 2 (2001): 378–95.

Soyer, Daniel, ed. *A Coat of Many Colors: Immigration, Globalism, and Reform in the New York City Garment Industry.* New York: Fordham University Press, 2005.

Speed, Shannon. "The U.S. Is Jailing Immigrant Women and Children under Appalling Conditions." *Global Post*, October 10, 2014. Available at http://www.globalpost.com/dispatches/globalpost-blogs/commentary/us-jailing-immigrant-women-and-their-children-under-appalling-con, accessed November 15, 2014.

Spillers, Hortense J. "Mama's Baby, Papa's Maybe: An American Grammar Book." *Diacritics* 17, no. 2 (1987): 1–20.

Tang, Eric. "Collateral Damage: Southeast Asian Poverty in the United States." *Social Text* 18, no. 1 (2000): 55–79.

———. "A Gulf Unites Us." *American Quarterly* 63, no. 1 (2011): 117–49.

———. "How the Refugees Stopped the Bronx from Burning." *Race and Class* 54, no. 4 (2013): 48–66.

Tang, Shirley Suet-Ling. "Community Centered Research as Knowledge/Capacity-Building in Immigrant and Refugee Communities." In *Engaging Contradictions: Theory, Politics, and Methods of Activist Scholarship*, edited by Charles R. Hale, 237–64. Berkeley: University of California Press, 2008.

Terry, Fiona. *Condemned to Repeat? The Paradox of Humanitarian Action.* Ithaca, NY: Cornell University Press, 2013.

Tomlinson, Barbara, and George Lipsitz. "American Studies as Accompaniment." *American Quarterly* 65, no. 1 (2013): 1–30.

Toy, Vivian S. "Tough Workfare Rules Used as Way to Cut Welfare Rolls." *New York Times*, April 15, 1988. Available at http://www.nytimes.com/1998/04/15/nyregion/tough-workfare-rules-used-as-way-to-cut-welfare-rolls.html, accessed November 1, 2013.

Ui, Shiori. "Unlikely Heroes: The Evolution of Female Leadership in a Cambodian Ethnic Enclave." In *Ethnography Unbound: Power and Resistance in the Modern Metropolis*, edited by Michael Burawoy, 161–77. Berkeley: University of California Press, 1991.

Um, Khatharya. *A Dream Denied: Educational Experiences of Southeast Asian American Youth: Issues and Recommendations.* Washington, DC: Southeast Asia Resource Action Center, 2003.

Ung, Loung. *First They Killed My Father: A Daughter of Cambodia Remembers.* New York: Harper Perennial, 2006.

Vickery, Michael. *Cambodia, 1975–1982*. Boston: South End Press, 1984.

———. "Refugee Politics: The Khmer Camp System in Thailand." In *The Cambodian Agony*, edited by David A. Ablin and Marlowe Hood, 293–331. Armonk, NY: Sharpe, 1987.

Wacquant, Loïc J. D. "Deadly Symbiosis: When Ghetto and Prison Meet and Mesh." *Punishment and Society* 3, no. 1 (2001): 95–133.

———. "From Slavery to Mass Incarceration." *New Left Review* 13 (January–February 2002): 41–60.

———. "Prisoner Reentry as Myth and Ceremony." *Dialectical Anthropology* 34, no. 4 (2010): 605–20.

———. *Punishing the Poor: The Neoliberal Government of Social Insecurity*. Durham, NC: Duke University Press, 2009.

———. "The Wedding of Workfare and Prisonfare in the 21st Century." *Journal of Poverty* 16, no. 2 (2012): 236–49.

———. "The Wedding of Workfare and Prisonfare Revisited." *Social Justice* 38, no. 1–2 (2011): 203–11.

Wallace, Deborah, and Rodrick Wallace. *A Plague on Your Houses: How New York Was Burned Down and National Public Health Crumbled*. London: Verso, 1998.

Wallerstein, Immanuel Maurice. *World-Systems Analysis: An Introduction*. Durham, NC: Duke University Press, 2004.

Welaratna, Usha. *Beyond the Killing Fields: Voices of Nine Cambodian Survivors in America*. Stanford, CA: Stanford University Press, 1994.

Wong, Edward. "Children of the Killing Fields." *New York Times*, March 26, 2000. Available at http://www.nytimes.com/2000/03/26/nyregion/children-of-the-killing-fields.html, accessed April 26, 2014.

Woods, Clyde Adrian. "Do You Know What It Means to Miss New Orleans? Katrina, Trap Economics, and the Rebirth of the Blues." *American Quarterly* 57, no. 4 (2005): 1005–18.

———. "'Sittin' on Top of the World': The Challenges of Blues and Hip Hop Geography." In *Black Geographies and the Politics of Place*, edited by Katherine McKittrick, 46–81. Cambridge, MA: South End Press, 2007.

Yathay, Pin, and John Man. *Stay Alive, My Son*. New York: Free Press, 1987.

Youth Leadership Project, CAAAV: Organizing Asian Communities. *Eating Welfare*. Directed by the Youth Leadership Project. Bronx: CAAAV Organizing Asian Communities, 2000. DVD.

Zucker, Norman L., and Naomi Flink Zucker. *The Guarded Gate: The Reality of American Refugee Policy*. San Diego: Harcourt Brace Jovanovich, 1987.

Index

9/11, 106–107, 176

activism, 18, 93, 146, 170, 174, 176, 179
activist scholarship, 26–27
Afghanistan, 65, 175–176
Africa, 118. *See also individual countries*
African Americans, 15, 133, 174,
    191n31; criminalization of, 11–12; in
    hyperghetto, 13, 56, 58–59, 62–65,
    71–72, 129, 178; targeted by police, 8.
    See also Black communities
Agamben, Giorgio, 41–42, 189n33,
    189n37
Aid to Families with Dependent Children
    (AFDC), 82
Alexander, Michelle, 11
American Council of Voluntary Associa-
    tions (ACVA), 52, 55
Americanization, 137, 151–153
ankgar, 138–139, 145
Arendt, Hannah, 41
arson, 1, 15, 56–57, 59–60, 190n5
Asian Americans, 6, 9, 62, 191n31;
    model-minority discourse and, 13,
    174–175

Asian Pacific Environmental Network, 26
Association of Southeast Asian Nations
    (ASEAN), 36
asylum, 3, 13, 74, 154, 177, 187n16; legal
    process of, 28–29, 37–38, 185n1, 198n3;
    Ra's experience of, 44–49, 52, 54–55,
    94, 97, 141. *See also* Refugee Act
Austria, 39

Bainbridge welfare center, 109–111
base people, 33, 138–139
Begin Employment Gain Independence
    Now (BEGIN), 102–105
Benjamin, Walter, 50
Best, Stephen, 18, 159
Black communities, 23, 84, 101, 122,
    174–175; criminalization of, 93, 131–
    133, 146, 188n18; in hyperghetto, 17,
    54, 68; pathologization of, 14, 64–65,
    78, 81, 137, 147–149, 153–155; rela-
    tions with Cambodian refugees, 8, 56,
    62–63, 70–72; in urban insurrections,
    10–12, 57–60, 129–131, 183n19. *See
    also* African Americans
blackening, 65

Black Freedom movement, 130
Black Power movement, 84, 130
blues epistemology, 133–134
Bona, 121–122
Brooklyn, 6, 172, 182n11
Buddhism, 139, 170
Bunroeum, 121–122
Bush, George W., 164

CAAAV: Organizing Asian Communities, 6–7, 192n1. See also *Eating Welfare*; Southeast Asian Youth Leadership Project
Calhoun, Jack, 187n14
California, 153
Cambodia: Battambang, 2, 33, 67, 164, 166, 170; Phnom Penh, 2, 4, 32–33, 35, 164, 181n4, 189n38
Cambodian civil war, 31, 179
Cambodian genocide, 9, 28–32, 35, 38, 112, 186n8; survivors of, 2–4, 38, 40, 112, 160, 179, 187n16, 192n35. See also Khmer Rouge party; killing fields; Pol Pot
Cambodian Genocide Program (CGP), 181n2
Cambodian syndrome, 39–40
capitalism, 16, 100, 126–129, 139; asylum and, 37; critiques of, 86–87, 133; hyperghetto and, 116, 123, 131; racialized gender and, 84; refugee's position in, 6, 95, 154; welfare and, 80, 85, 93. See also globalization; neoliberalism
captivity, 95–96, 103–104, 133, 156, 159–160; in hyperghetto, 10–12, 17, 43, 54–55, 65, 70–74, 76, 93–94, 146–147, 174, 178, 190n2; under Khmer Rouge, 2–3, 24, 35, 68, 73, 140, 152, 181n4; refugee captivity, 5–6, 14–15, 18, 21, 44–51, 80, 100, 123, 136–137, 173, 179
Caribbean, 188. See also *individual countries*
Carter, Jimmy, 36, 38–40, 44, 57, 186n13
Carter, Rosalynn, 40
Catholic Charities, 52, 63

Center for Third World Organizing, 194n13
Central America, 65, 176. See also *individual countries*
Central Intelligence Agency (CIA), 36, 187n14
Cham communities, 32
Chan, Sucheng, 9, 18, 38, 181n5, 182n11, 189n38
Chhaya Chhoum, 16, 83–84, 88–89, 95–96, 106–108, 111–113, 115, 178
Childs, John Brown, 26
China, 56, 64, 117–118, 127; support for Khmer Rouge, 31, 35–36, 38
Chinatown, 88, 115–116, 126, 128–129, 144, 192n1
Chinese Americans, 13, 23, 64–65
Civil Rights Act, 58, 102, 175
Civil Rights movement, 10, 82, 84, 100, 130, 133
Cline, Ray, 187n14
Clinton, Bill, 78, 163, 185n3
Clymer, Kenton, 186n13, 187n16
Coalition Government of Democratic Kampuchea (CGDK), 187n16
Cold War, 37, 176, 187n16
colonialism, 13–15, 17, 21, 118, 192n32. See also imperialism
colorblind rhetoric, 12, 133, 174
Committee Against Anti-Asian Violence. See CAAAV: Organizing Asian Communities
Communist Party of Kampuchea (CPK), 31, 138. See also Khmer Rouge party
community organizing, 6, 18, 19, 20, 27, 71, 178; housing issues and, 15, 55–56, 60–63; welfare issues and, 16–17, 79–81, 83–96, 99–115, 118, 162, 192n1
Costa Vargas, João, 183n26
criminalization, 159; of activism, 110; of Cambodian refugees, 8, 164–166, 171, 181n5, 200n10; of genocide, 37; of hyperghetto residents, 5, 43, 54, 57, 64, 174; of mothers, 4, 17, 137, 142–150, 152, 156, 162, 169; of welfare recipi-

ents, 11, 78, 114. *See also* detention; police; prisons
critical refugee studies, 5
Cuba, 187n16
culture of poverty thesis, 64, 85, 154

Davis, Angela, 149
Democratic Kampuchea (DK) regime, 2, 32–36, 44, 138. *See also* Cambodian genocide; Khmer Rouge party; Pol Pot; zero years
deportation, 73, 164–166, 173, 176
detention, 151, 164, 177
Detroit, 58, 130, 190n11
Dillon, Michael, 42
disability, 7, 158
discrimination, 6, 85–86, 102, 109, 195nn9–10
Dith Pran, 31–32
domestic violence, 91, 144, 146, 156, 165
Douglass, Frederick, 111
Downs, Anthony, 59, 190n5
drug trade, 8, 69, 136, 144, 171
drug war, 131–132, 176, 197n21
Du Bois, W. E. B., 174
Duggan, Lisa, 194n15

Eating Welfare, 119–120, 123–124, 193n5
Ellsberg, Daniel, 191n17
Espiritu, Yen Le, 5, 150
Ethiopia, 65
ethnic economies, 7, 9, 115–116, 118, 126–127, 131

factory work, 24, 91–92, 94, 96–98, 100, 103, 124, 157–158, 160–162
feminism, 17, 84, 124, 149–151
Flood, Joe, 59
food stamps, 7, 77–78, 82, 99, 193n6
Foucault, Michel, 71
Freedom Inc., 178–179
free trade zones, 17, 118
Freire, Paulo, 108, 111, 179
fugitive justice, 159–160
Fujiwara, Lynn, 18

garment industry, 121–122, 126, 196n1; home-based work, 7, 24, 97, 114–118, 136, 143
gender, 26, 136–138, 168–169; in garment industry, 120–121, 124; hyperghetto and, 17, 146–147; methodology and, 23–25; refugees and, 5, 13–14, 150–156, 198n3; welfare and, 78, 84–87, 91–92, 147–149. *See also* patriarchy
gendered violence, 17, 105, 135–156. *See also* domestic violence; sexual violence
gender-nonconforming people, 178
Germany, 39, 57
Gilmore, Ruth Wilson, 132
Giuliani, Rudolph, 82, 96, 102
Glazer, Nathan, 148–149
global cities, 127–128, 131, 134
globalization, 17, 115–116, 127–129, 131–132, 134. *See also* free trade zones; International Monetary Fund; neoliberalism; World Bank; World Trade Organization
Grassroots Organizing for Welfare Leadership (GROWL), 84–85, 106, 194n13
Gregory, Steven, 12
Gwaltney, John Langston, 23

HALO Trust, 200n9
Hannabach, Cathy, 198n3
Harding, Sandra, 22–23
Hartman, Saidiya, 18, 159
Harvey, David, 194n15
hate crimes, 6
hegemony, 32, 36, 39, 42, 64, 174
Heng, 2–4; in the Bronx, 117, 137, 142–145, 152, 155–156; under Khmer Rouge, 29, 34–35, 44–46, 73, 138–141; resettlement, 48–49, 52
Heng Samrin, 35, 38
heteronormativity, 141, 178, 198n3
Hitler, Adolf, 39
Hmong communities, 9, 64, 153, 175, 178
homeless shelters, 4, 20, 136, 172

homophobia, 86
Honduras, 176–177
Hong Kong, 64
Housing Preservation and Development (HPD), 55, 61
humanitarianism, 13, 36, 46, 73, 141, 175–176, 188n18
human rights, 29, 36, 41–42, 44, 49, 57
Hurricane Katrina, 133
hyperghetto, 23, 43, 78, 80, 137, 146–156, 171, 177–179; characteristics of, 9–12, 18, 93–94, 131–133, 183n26, 184n27, 190n2, 197n21; history of, 57–60, 183nn18–19; refugees in, 12–17, 19, 21–22, 54–56, 63–66, 70–74, 126–131, 158–160, 173, 175; role in globalization, 115–118, 123

Immigration and Naturalization Service (INS), 48, 189n38
imperialism, 86, 176, 194n15; Cambodian civil war and, 2, 13, 139; resistance to, 118, 177; role of refugees in, 14–15, 21, 30–31, 42. *See also* colonialism
income support centers, 96
Indian Americans, 13
Indochina, 35, 185n3. *See also individual countries and regimes*
Indochinese Health and Adaptation Research Project (IHARP), 153–154
Indochinese Mental Health Program, 83
infrapolitics, 122–123
internally displaced people, 28
International Monetary Fund, 194n15
Iraq, 175–176
Islam, 32

Jim Crow laws, 11–12, 148
job centers, 96
Johnson, Lyndon B., 30, 58, 130, 185n3, 190n13, 191n17
Joint Voluntary Agency (JVA), 48
Jonnes, Jill, 57
Jordan, 176
Judaism, 39

Katz, Michael, 14
Kelley, Robin D. G., 23, 122
Kennedy, John F., 53
Kerner Commission, 58, 190n13
Khao-I-Dang refugee camp, 3–4, 29, 36, 46–47, 52, 55, 67, 97, 141, 188n27
Khmer Guided Placement Project, 182n11
Khmer Krom, 97
Khmer People's National Liberation Front (KPNLF), 187n16
Khmer Rouge party, 38, 94, 151, 163–164, 166, 187n14, 188n27; history of, 15, 30–36, 181n4, 186n11; Kun Thea's experience with, 97, 104; Ra's experience with, 2–4, 17, 22, 24–25, 28–29, 33–36, 44–50, 73, 79, 136–141, 145, 152, 179; U.S. support for, 39–40, 44, 187n16. *See also* Cambodian civil war; Cambodian genocide; Communist Party of Kampuchea; Democratic Kampuchea regime; Pol Pot
Khmer Rouge Tribunal, 163–164
Kiang, Peter, 26
Kibria, Nazli, 18, 199n20
Kiernan, Ben, 32, 181n2, 185n5, 186n8
killing fields, 2, 32, 72, 112
Kimho Ma v. Reno, 164
King, Martin Luther, Jr., 58, 84
Kissinger, Henry, 30
Korean Americans, 13
Koreatown, 115, 126
Kosal, 165–166
Kun Thea, 16, 96–98, 100–101, 103–105, 113, 195n4

landmines, 29, 34, 45, 47, 166–167, 200n9
language, 6, 53, 61, 66, 68, 144, 195n4; methodology and, 7, 20, 23–24; resettlement process and, 53; welfare system and, 78, 81, 83–87, 91, 101–105, 109–110, 183n13, 195n10
Laos, 3, 26, 30, 38, 40, 63–65, 153, 175, 191n17
Latin America, 118, 176. *See also individual countries*

Latinos, 8, 56, 62, 65, 70, 102, 162. *See also* Puerto Ricans

liberalism: liberal feminism, 17, 151; liberal warfare, 13, 15, 30, 41–44, 49, 54, 59, 63–65, 70, 73, 116, 127, 131, 133, 175–176, 178, 197n21; racial liberalism, 12, 148, 175; role of refugee in, 5, 14–15, 43–44, 72–73, 173. *See also* neoliberalism

Linh, 92–93

Lipsitz, George, 27

Long Beach, California, 10, 189n1

Lon Nol, 30–31, 33, 189n1

Los Angeles, 52–53, 57, 128, 183n26, 189n1

Lowe, Lisa, 87

Lowell, Massachusetts, 10, 70

Marshall, Jean, 72, 182n6

Marxism, 32

matriarchy, 17, 137, 148–151, 153

Medicaid, 7, 99

Mekong NYC, 111, 113, 178–179

Melnick, Leah, 182n6

methodology, 108; activist scholarship, 26–27; of book, 18–27

middlemen, 116–117, 121, 159, 162

model-minority discourse, 13, 64–65

Mollica, Richard, 22, 184n32

Mondale, Walter, 39–40, 43

motherhood, 16, 83, 92, 160, 167, 170, 200n10; criminalization of, 135–156; forced motherhood, 24; welfare and, 96–97, 114–115, 118, 147–150; youth organizing and, 87–88, 95

Mount Dangrek massacre, 29, 39

Moynihan, Daniel P.: Moynihan Report, 137, 147–151. *See also* culture of poverty thesis

multiculturalism, 86–88, 105, 110, 192n1

National Guard, 58

National United Front for Peaceful, Cooperative, Independent and Neutral Cambodia (FUNCIPEC), 187n16

National Welfare Rights Organization (NWRO), 84–85

neoliberalism, 27, 95, 99–101, 113, 123, 128, 132, 194n15; welfare under, 16, 80–88, 93, 104–105, 110, 115, 192n1. *See also* free trade zones; globalization; International Monetary Fund; liberalism; planned shrinkage; World Bank; World Trade Organization

neoplantation, 17, 116, 131–134

New Deal, 82, 100

New Jersey, 7–8, 58, 97, 157, 161

New Orleans, 63

new people, 33, 139

New York City child welfare agency, 4, 17, 136, 144, 155, 158, 161, 165

New York City Human Resource Administration (HRA), 78, 103

New York Times, 31, 71, 191n17

Ngô, Thanh Nhàn, 186n11

Nguyen, Mimi Thi, 42–43, 65, 189n37

Nixon, Richard, 30, 185n3

Non-Communist Resistant (NCR), 187n16

Norodom Sihanouk, 30–31, 187n16

Northwest Bronx Community and Clergy Coalition (NWBCC), 55, 190n4

Obama, Barack, 176–177

Office of Refugee Resettlement (ORR), 38, 55, 67, 81, 91

Ong, Aihwa, 64–65, 150–153, 184n28

Operation Menu, 30, 185n3

Part of the Solution (POTS), 158

patriarchy, 24–25, 88, 133, 135–156, 168–169, 199n20; challenges to, 121, 178. *See also* gendered violence

People's Republic of Kampuchea (PRK), 2, 28, 35–36, 38, 140, 181n4

Personal Responsibility and Work Opportunity Reconciliation Act (PRWORA), 16, 78, 80–82, 85, 95–97, 99, 106, 114, 193n6

Philadelphia, 10, 57, 63, 70

Philippines, 3, 52, 169, 192n1
Phnom Penh, 4, 32–33, 35, 164, 181n4, 189n38
planned shrinkage, 11, 59–60, 65
police, 75, 93, 109–110, 135–136, 144–146, 153, 155, 165; police violence, 10–11, 57–58, 130–131, 197n21. *See also* criminalization
Pol Pot, 2, 15, 21–36, 104, 163, 185n5, 186n11, 196n8
polyamory, 141
power, 5, 19, 79, 87–91, 94–96, 105, 107–113, 115, 122, 128–129, 166; knowledge/power regimes, 71; liberal warfare and, 65; methodology and, 23–26; patriarchal power, 24–25, 137, 150–152; race and, 191n31, 192n32; refugee temporality and, 21, 49–51, 74, 173; sovereign power, 41–42
prisons, 142–145, 165–166; under Khmer Rouge, 34, 45, 138; role in hyperghetto, 11, 80, 93–94, 132, 146–147, 155–156, 183n21, 197n21; school to prison pipeline, 171, 173. *See also* detention
Pronh Ra, 151–153, 179, 189n1; in the Bronx, 1, 4–6, 15–16, 27, 53–54, 66–70, 73–74, 76–80, 87–93, 97, 114–126, 128–129, 131, 135–137, 142–147, 155–172; interviews with, 18–25, 184n31; under Khmer Rouge, 2–3, 17, 28–29, 33–35, 44–50, 55, 75, 94, 137–141; resettlement, 52–53
Providence, Rhode Island, 10, 70, 178
Providence Youth and Student Movement (PrYSM), 178–179
Puerto Ricans, 13, 60, 63, 68, 71–72, 83, 178

race, 7, 26, 118, 151, 156, 174–176, 178; antidiscrimination law and, 195n9; in asylum claims, 37; in Cambodian genocide, 32, 139, 186n8; comparative racialization, 192n32; hate crimes and, 6, 23; in hyperghetto, 11–12, 43, 57–60, 64–65, 100, 130–134, 146–147, 153; intersectionality and, 84; motherhood and, 136, 147–150; neoliberalism and, 86–87, 93, 130; refugee figure and, 5, 13–14, 62–64, 184n28, 189n37; welfare and, 78, 84–86, 105. *See also* white supremacy
racial liberalism, 12, 148, 175
racial triangulation, 191n31
racism, 6, 23, 85, 87, 174; hyperghetto and, 58, 78, 130–132, 146–147; in Moynihan Report, 147–150; refugees and, 43, 61, 64, 79, 94, 164. *See also* white supremacy; xenophobia
Ramirez, Blanca, 7, 15, 55–56, 60–62, 66–67, 69–70
RAND Institute, 59, 190n5
Rann, 3–4, 48–49, 170–171; in the Bronx, 135–137, 142, 155, 163, 167–168, 172; under Khmer Rouge, 29, 45, 140
Rasmey, 3, 121, 141, 168–169, 200n10
Reagan, Ronald, 38, 187n16
refugee, definition of: critical refugee studies definition, 5; UNHCR definition, 28–29, 37–38; U.S. definition, 38–41
Refugee Act, 3, 15, 30, 38–41, 43, 55, 64, 163–164, 175, 177
refugee camps, 3–4, 7–8, 17, 20–22, 40–41, 44–47, 56, 67, 74, 83, 94–96, 104, 127, 136, 141, 159, 163–164, 169, 176, 178–179; asylum applications in, 28–29, 179, 185n1; criminal organizations in, 75, 188n27; power in, 15, 49, 68, 72–76, 79, 92–93, 112–113, 126, 151–152, 154. *See also* Khao-I-Dang refugee camp; Sa Kaeo refugee camp
refugee exceptionalism, 14–15, 17, 19, 21, 63–66, 70–71, 74, 78, 81, 127, 129, 133, 153–156, 164, 175, 177–178
refugee processing centers, 3
refugee temporality, 18, 21, 30, 44–50, 74, 80, 123–124, 126, 133, 159, 173
Reid, Julian, 42
religion, 32, 52, 86, 119, 138. *See also* Buddhism; Islam; Judaism

Ren, Chunhui, 183n15
Richie, Beth E., 146–147, 154
Richmond, California, 63
Rith, 1, 3–4, 6, 19–20, 24–25, 70, 122, 145–146, 169–170, 172
Rochester, New York, 57, 130
Rom, 3, 6, 19, 141, 163, 168–170
Rorth, 3, 6, 19, 47, 117–120, 123, 134, 141, 167–170, 172–173, 177
Rumbaut, Rubén, 153

Sa Kaeo refugee camp, 29, 36, 40, 46
Saloth Sar. See Pol Pot
Samorn, 135–136, 141–142
Sassen, Saskia, 127–130, 196n15
Schanberg, Sydney, 31
Schlund-Vials, Cathy, 39–40, 112, 163, 199n5
Schmidt, Carl, 41
Scott, James C., 122
sexism, 78, 85–87, 94, 148–149
Sexton, Jared, 192n32
sexuality, 24–25, 86–87, 141, 198n3. See also heteronormativity; polyamory
sexual violence, 24–25, 135, 138–142, 146–147, 149; forced marriage, 2, 17, 24, 34–35, 137–141, 143, 145, 152
Shah, Bindi V., 26
Singapore, 187n16
slavery, 100, 131–133, 148–149, 159, 174, 184n27, 192n32; afterlife of, 11–12, 15, 54, 115–116. See also neoplantation
socialism, 2, 31–32; Khmer Rouge socialism, 2, 31–32; Maoist agrarian socialism, 31
Social Security, 7
Son Sann, 187n16
Sonya, 3, 122, 145, 171–172
Southeast Asia, 41–43, 79, 137, 175, 189n1; U.S. imperialism in, 5, 13–14, 55, 57, 177. See also individual countries
Southeast Asian Youth Leadership Project (YLP), 6–8, 19–20, 77, 83–95, 99–103, 105–111, 114–115, 118, 121, 170, 182n13, 192n1, 195n10
sovereignty, 29, 41–42

Soviet Union, 35, 187n16
Spillers, Hortense, 12
Starr, Roger, 60
Stockton, California, 199n24
St. Rita's Refugee Center, 72, 182n6
Supplemental Security Income (SSI), 82, 158
sweatshops, 115, 126–129, 134; home-based sweatshops, 24, 116–123, 162
Syria, 176–177

Taiwan, 64
Tang, Shirley, 26
Temporary Aid to Needy Families (TANF), 82, 97
Thailand, 34, 39, 55, 79, 97, 166, 187n14, 187n16; refugee camps in, 2–3, 15, 17, 28–29, 36, 40, 44–47, 52, 67, 72–75, 94, 140–141, 152, 159, 164, 169, 188n27. See also Khao-I-Dang refugee camp; Sa Kaeo refugee camp
Third World, 17, 37, 71, 116, 118, 124, 126, 129, 133
Tomlinson, Barbara, 27
Trevy, 92–93

Ui, Shiori, 192n34, 199n24
Um, Khatharya, 112
UN Conference on Indochinese Refugees, 39–40, 43
UN Convention Relating to the Status of Refugees, 37, 188n17
UN Covenant on Human Rights, 57
underclass, 14–15, 55, 64–66, 73, 78, 85, 129, 174–175, 177, 184n28, 191n31
UN General Assembly, 36, 57, 185n1
United Kingdom, 36, 38
United Nations, 3, 73, 94, 187n16; General Assembly, 36, 57; refugee policy, 37–39, 185n1, 187n16. See also Khao-I-Dang refugee camp; Khmer Rouge Tribunal; refugee camps; Sa Kaeo refugee camp
United Nations High Commissioner for Refugees (UNHCR), 28–29, 36, 45, 47, 141, 176, 185n1, 188n18, 188n27

UN Protocol on the Status of Refugees, 37–38

urban insurrections, 10, 15, 23, 54, 56–59, 73, 118, 129–131, 149, 177, 183n19, 183n26

U.S.-Cambodian Memorandum of Understanding, 164

U.S. State Department, 48, 52, 187n16, 189n38

Vanna, 3–4, 119, 143–145, 155–158, 165–166, 168–169, 172, 200n10

Vietnam, 34, 91, 97, 103–104, 144, 187n16, 189n38; Clinton's visit to, 163, 185n3; invasion of Cambodia, 2–3, 28, 31–32, 34–36, 38, 44, 48, 140, 166, 181n4, 186n11; U.S. attacks on, 13, 30, 42–43, 59

Vietnamese refugees, 5, 6, 9, 40, 43, 63–65, 116, 153, 189n37, 199n20

Wacquant, Loïc, 10–12, 80, 93–94, 100, 146, 183nn18–19, 183n21, 190n2, 197n21

Wallerstein, Immanuel, 126

Weeks, John, 153

welfare, 4, 18, 25, 73, 119–129, 134, 141, 149, 157–159, 161–162; criminalization and, 11, 93–94, 143, 146–147, 152, 156, 173; refugees and, 9, 19–20, 64–65, 67–68, 153–154, 168, 182n13; welfare activism, 6–7, 77, 80–81, 83–85, 87–92, 94–95, 114, 192n1, 194n13, 195n10; welfare reform, 16, 78, 80, 81–83, 114, 169; welfare state, 22, 24, 58, 86, 115, 150; workfare, 11, 16, 82, 85, 88, 91, 93–115, 118, 124, 137, 152, 172, 183n21. *See also* Aid to Families with Dependent Children; food stamps; Medicaid; Personal Responsibility and Work Opportunity Reconciliation Act; Supplemental Security Income; Temporary Aid to Needy Families

whiteness, 23, 40, 43, 49, 57, 65, 130, 149, 191n31; white flight, 128

white supremacy, 11–13, 15, 39, 129, 133, 148, 174, 191n31

Woods, Clyde, 17, 131–134

Work Experience Program (WEP), 96–103

World Bank, 194n15

World Trade Organization (WTO), 106–107, 163–164

World War II, 30, 41, 57, 59

xenophobia, 86

zero years, 2, 7, 32–33, 35, 163. *See also* Cambodian genocide

Eric Tang is Assistant Professor of African and African Diaspora Studies and a faculty member in the Center for Asian American Studies at The University of Texas at Austin.